heartbreak
&triumph

D1100949

LIVERPOOL LIBRARIES

heartbreak &triumph

The Shawn Michaels Story

by shawn michaels

with Aaron Feigenbaum

POCKET BOOKS
New York   London   Toronto   Sydney

POCKET BOOKS, a division of Simon & Schuster, Ltd.
1st Floor, 222 Gray's Inn Road, London WC1X 8HB

Copyright © 2006 by World Wrestling Entertainment, Inc. All Rights Reserved.

World Wrestling Entertainment, the names of all World Wrestling Entertainment televised and live programming, talent names, images, likenesses, slogans and wrestling moves, and all World Wrestling Entertainment logos and trademarks are the exclusive property of World Wrestling Entertainment, Inc. Nothing in this book may be reproduced in any manner without the express written consent of World Wrestling Entertainment, Inc.

This book is a publication of Pocket Books, a division of Simon & Schuster, Ltd., under exclusive license from World Wrestling Entertainment, Inc.

All rights reserved, including the right to reproduce this book or portions thereof in any form whatsoever. For information address Pocket Books, 1st Floor, 222 Gray's Inn Road, London WC1X 8HB

Photos on pages 10–50, 65–98, 252, 290–301 Courtesy of Shawn Michaels. Photos on pages 62, 100, 108, 124, 129 Courtesy of *Pro Wrestling Illustrated* Photographs.

All other photos Copyright © 2006 World Wrestling Entertainment, Inc. All Rights Reserved.

A CIP catalogue record for this book is available from the British Library

  ISBN-13: 978-1-4165-2645-2

This Pocket Books paperback edition November 2006

10   9   8

POCKET and colophon are registered trademarks of Simon & Schuster, Ltd.

Designed by Trisia Tomanelli

Visit us on the World Wide Web
http://www.simonandschuster.co.uk
http://www.wwe.com

Printed and bound in Great Britain

To Jesus Christ, the lord of my life.

Thank you, my king, for loving me and saving me.

All that I am, and all that I hope to become, is meaningless apart from you.

To Rebecca, my Proverbs 31 virtuous wife.

No one person has impacted my life more than you, my love. God chose you for me before he laid the foundations of the earth. I've loved you from the moment I first laid eyes on you. I promise to lead, provide, and protect you all the days of my life.

I am honored to be your "Tender Warrior."

And to Cameron. The moment I held you, my life was forever changed.

The innocence of your words have done more than anyone's to inspire me to become a man of Godly character. I've known no greater joy than the day I became your father.

And to Cheyenne, my "Sugar Britches."

"It's a girl!" My eyes filled with tears and my heart was stolen forever. You now lead Daddy around by the finger—a sign of things to come, I'm told. As you grow to find the Lord's plan and purpose for your life, know in your heart that all you will ever have to do is reach up and Daddy's hand will be there.

To the three of you, my family. You are my life.

You are my reason for being: all I have, all I have ever hoped to have, all I have ever wanted, and all I will ever need. To have you is to have everything.

The words "I love you" will never truly describe your worth to me.

Thank you for loving me as I am, and thank you for making me whole.

Amazing Grace, how sweet it is that saved a wretch like me.

I once was lost, but now I'm found,

Was blind but now . . . now I see. . . .

heartbreak &triumph

prologue

November 9, 1997
Montreal, Quebec, Canada

The day you win the World Wrestling Federation

Championship should be among the happiest days of your life.

It's a reward for all the hard work you've put into your job and

recognition that you are one of if not *the* best at what you do.

A little over a year and a half ago, I won it for the first

time. After all the public celebrating was done, I had a few

moments alone in my hotel room. I sat on my bed and stared

at the championship belt. I had never felt so good in all

my life.

Ten months later, I won my second championship. This

time I did it in front of more than sixty thousand people in my hometown of San Antonio, Texas. When I started out in this business, I dreamed that some-day I would come home and have people recognize me when I walked through the local mall. It's safe to say that this had more than fulfilled that dream.

Tonight, I was going to win the championship for a third time. Only this time, I knew there would be no celebrating, no happy or peaceful moments, and no dreams fulfilled. There might be some angry words, a fight, or maybe even a riot might break out. Whatever was going to happen, I knew it wasn't going to be good.

Something big was about to go down in Montreal, and I was going to be at the center of it. Vince McMahon wanted Bret Hart to drop the World Wrestling Federation Championship to me. Bret, a native of Calgary, Alberta, Canada, didn't want to. Bret Hart believed he was a hero in his country and that if he lost a wrestling match in Canada, the country's collective psyche might shatter—I am being totally serious here. He also didn't like me, or more accurately, he hated me. I didn't care for him either.

Normally, these issues would not have caused any trouble. Vince was the boss, and whatever he said happened. Vince had a problem though. Bret was leaving to wrestle for our archrival, World Championship Wrestling (WCW), and had a creative control clause in his contract that basically allowed him to do what he wanted in his last thirty days. If Bret didn't want to lose the title, Bret wasn't going to lose the title—or so he thought.

The night before, Vince, myself, my friend and fellow Superstar, Triple H (Paul Levesque), and Jerry Brisco—one of Vince's close associates—met to con-firm that we were going to swerve Bret out of the championship. He had left us no choice.

There is a time-honored tradition in this business that when you leave one wrestling company to go to another, you "do the favor"—lose—on the way out. It's a sign of respect and gratitude for those who have put you on top in the first place. Bret was leaving, but he was refusing to lose. For all we knew, he might take our championship belt down to WCW and make a mockery of it and us. We couldn't afford to take the chance.

It may not seem like much to an outsider, but in the wrestling world, what we were going to do was the equivalent of a mafia hit. And I was going to be Jack Ruby. It may have been Vince's decision to swerve Bret out of the title, but I was going to be the one pulling the trigger. I had to figure out how it was going to happen, and I was going to be the one in the ring that everyone would see do it. Vince was going to try to do everything he could to put the focus and responsibility for the swerve on himself, but both he and I knew that I would catch most of the heat.

I already had an awful reputation within the industry because guys had been spreading rumors and lies about me for years. There was, and is, a wrestling subculture that lives off of gossip. They print newsletters—dirt sheets, as they are commonly referred to—post stories on Internet sites, and record telephone hotlines. I was not very popular in this subculture and had been targeted by them for years.

Soon after I began to be vilified in this world, I made the decision that I wasn't going to respond to the lies and half-truths. I wasn't going to play my detractor's game of "he said, he said." I'd been brought up to believe that if you had a problem with someone, you told them to their face, and that's what I did. This didn't win me many friends, but I had realized long ago that friends were a rare commodity in this business.

I knew most of my peers, and the small percentage of fans, who read the gossip were never going to like me. I didn't care. My philosophy was, "You may not like me, but I am going to be so good at what I do, you are going to have to respect me." So I poured everything I had into my craft and rose to the top of my profession.

I succeeded because I could wrestle. No one ever had any plans to go with Shawn Michaels. I was a small guy with a hateable gimmick. Ric Flair was cool. Hulk Hogan made you feel good. Steve Austin gave you the chance to be a rebel. Me, The Boy Toy? The Heartbreak Kid? What redeemable qualities did I have? Who really wanted to be me?

When I was just beginning my rise through the ranks, Tully Blanchard told me that the key to making it in this business is simple: you make them yell the loudest for the longest. And that's what I tried to do every time I stepped into the ring. It didn't matter if I was wrestling a champion or some no-name jobber—a wrestler hired to lose. I gave it everything I could.

Through my work, I ended up earning the respect of my peers. They may have been saying bad things about me behind my back, but they wanted to wrestle me. They knew I would bring out their best. I didn't care about doing something in the ring that would make me look "weak." I figured if I had a great match, I would get over anyway.

The fans could tell how much effort I was putting into my craft, and they rallied behind me. I became their darling, the one they wanted to see at the top. When I beat Bret Hart for my first World Wrestling Federation Championship at *WrestleMania XII,* they celebrated with me.

Soon, however, things changed. My world came crashing down. Everyone and everything seemed to turn against me. The gossip and the lies increased. I tried to block them out, but I couldn't. The world was changing too. I was a white-meat babyface, the kind of good guy that was popular in the seventies and eighties but was fast becoming hated in the rebellious nineties. Despite my successes in the ring, many fans turned against me.

I was devastated and responded by lashing out at just about everyone. I pushed buttons and became a real lightning rod. If someone started spreading rumors that I was refusing to put people over, I'd walk into the locker room and start shouting, "I'm not doing any jobs!" When I was hurt, it was often reported that I was faking the injury. So when I'd come back from my injury, I'd do something in the ring that no one else in my condition could possibly have done.

I'll be the first to admit that I was no saint, before, and after, my first title run. I could be obnoxious, cocky, and rude, but I never did anything malicious. I never spread rumors about other people. And, I always owned up to my shortcomings. If I did something wrong, I accepted the punishment I received. If I was punished for something I didn't do, well, that was a whole different matter, as you shall see. You could call me a lot of things, but you couldn't say I was a hypocrite. Most of the people who were spreading untruths about me were.

Business also fell off during this time. WCW was putting the clamps on WWE, and quite honestly, they were more with the times during this period. As the champion and the face of the company, the blame fell on my shoulders. I responded by doing the only thing I could do. I worked my tail off and put on great match after great match. It didn't matter though. Our product was not connecting as well as WCW's.

The downturn in business fed my detractors' seemingly insatiable desire to destroy me. Unfortunately, I let them get to me and lashed out even more. I'd yell at Vince and his right-hand man, Pat Patterson, who had always been so good to me. It was a horrible cycle that was destroying me inside.

As if all this wasn't enough, a whole series of crazy things started happening. The power would go out at a Pay-Per-View, a doctor would tell me that my knee was so badly damaged that I could never wrestle again, and then of course, there was Montreal. I tried to escape it all by taking vast quantities of painkillers. They could mask the pain for a short time, but in the long run, they nearly ended my life.

Two years after I first became champion I was completely broken—emotionally, spiritually, and physically. Randy Savage had once told me to slow down in the ring because he thought I'd never last. "I'm Superman," I told him. "I can do anything."

I wasn't Superman anymore. I was a thirty-two-year-old man with a back so messed up that I couldn't get out of bed in the morning without taking pain pills. All I ever wanted to do, all I knew how to do was wrestle. And now, I couldn't.

I retired from the ring, went home, and wallowed in my misery. I was angry, confused, and wracked with guilt. So many bad things had been said and written about me that I wasn't sure who I was anymore. I was raised in a decent family, and I always thought I was a decent guy. I wasn't sure of that anymore. Part of this feeling came from taking too many pills. Was I a bad guy because I was taking drugs? Or, was I taking drugs because I was a bad guy?

One thing I did know was that I was not a quitter. I never had been. Sometimes my never-say-die attitude led me into trouble, but I was never one to say, "I give up." I wanted to be a better person. I wanted to kick the pills.

Eventually, the darkness subsided. I met the woman of my dreams, my wife Rebecca. We had our first child, our son Cameron. To the outside world, I had everything: a loving, gorgeous wife, a beautiful son, and a lot of money in the bank. But there was still something missing.

I had never been a very spiritual person, but I began to feel that the Lord was calling out to me. I began calling out to him. He opened my heart and I became born again. I accepted Jesus Christ as my personal lord and savior and I began living a spiritual life.

There was now an unspeakable joy in my life, and I became the man I should have always been. Thanks to the good work of doctors and the healing power of the Lord, my back healed. I thought about wrestling again, and four and a half years after I was forced to give up what I love doing more than anything else, I returned to the ring.

When I came back, I apologized to Vince and Pat and everyone else who I had wronged or made life difficult for. The old-timers who were still there saw I was a different person. The young guys had probably read about me and weren't quite sure what to make of me at first. It wasn't long, though, before they saw that I was much different from what they had heard about me in the past. From the moment I came back, work has been nothing but fun.

The fans too have seen that I am a better person. They have been nothing short of wonderful. They have been cheering me nonstop for the past three plus years despite the fact that my gimmick is more hateable than ever. I repay them the best way I know how. Every night I go out, I try my best to make them yell the loudest for the longest.

| | |

I suppose history will ultimately judge my place in this business, and I'm sure nearly every time my name is mentioned, Bret Hart, Montreal, and the match that changed the course of this industry will come up. (And I'll get back to Montreal, I promise.) But there is a lot more to my life and career than my relationship with him and that day in 1997.

You've never heard my side of the story, but now here it is. It has Kliqs and Curtain Calls, vacated titles and unwarranted suspensions. I'm going to tell you about tearing down houses and tearing up hotel rooms. You'll read about Vince McMahon, Marty Jannetty, Kevin Nash, and a whole lot of people you may not have known who have helped me along the way. I'll take you inside a Ladder match, a Hell in a Cell, and a Bloodbath in Vegas. I've even tossed in a little rock 'n' roll and Graceland. You'll also learn about my family and friends, and how cultivating a personal relationship with Jesus Christ changed my life.

Trust me, it's been one crazy ride. Then again, what else should I have expected? I wasn't supposed to be here in the first place. And right after I was born, my mother didn't even want to see me.

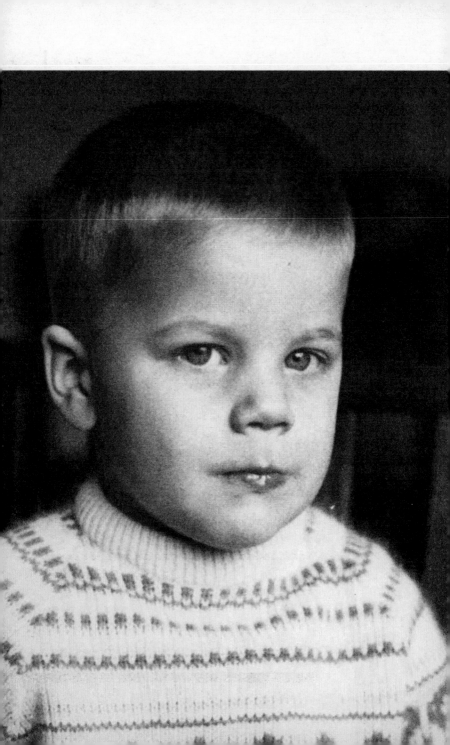

1
roll call

My mother didn't want to see me . . . at least that's the story she loves to tell.

Now before you start thinking bad things about my mom, or wonder how she could say something like that, you really have to know her. She is and always has been very over-the-top, and even though she sometimes pretends to be an angry lady, she's incredibly sweet, and I don't know if more than two weeks have gone by in my entire life that I haven't spoken to or heard from her. I am, and have always been, a momma's boy.

The truth is, though, I was not supposed to be here. I

wasn't planned. My parents already had my older brothers Randy, who is ten years older than I am, and Scott, who is six years older, as well as my sister Shari, who is four years my senior. They were a happy family and didn't plan on having a fourth child. But, I came along.

My mom wasn't angry that she became pregnant with me, she was more like, "Unbelievable! I'm having another child!" Plus, if she was going to have another child, she wanted it to be a girl. After all, she already had two boys.

Well, she got another boy, and I ended up being born Michael Shawn Hickenbottom on July 22, 1965, at Williams Air Force Base in Chandler, Arizona. And no, my mom didn't want to see me. Shortly after I was born and taken to the nursery, the nurses asked her, "Do you want to see the baby?"

"No," she replied, "because he's not supposed to be here."

They were a little taken aback by my mom's comments and couldn't quite figure her out. A little while later, they figured they could break her down and told her this story about a beautiful baby in the nursery who was all alone because his mother didn't want to see him. "Can you believe that?" they asked her.

My mom couldn't. "Who is this woman who would do such a thing?" she asked.

They just looked at her for a second and then said, "You!"

She felt awful, of course, and asked the nurses to bring me to her. They brought me in, and try as she might to pretend that she didn't love me, she couldn't keep up the façade for long. As I sat there cooing and looking up at her she fell in love with me, and I've been spoiled by her ever since.

| | |

My dad was an officer in the air force at the time, and it wasn't too long after I was born, just six months in fact, that he took part in an exchange program with the British Royal Air Force. So Mom packed up the family, and we moved to England. It was the first of many moves I would make as an air force child.

We lived near Reading, England, for two years. Then Dad volunteered to go to Vietnam, and Mom took the family to Storm Lake, Iowa. This was where she grew up and where her mom, my Nanna, still lived. We moved into a house down the road from Nanna's and lived there until my dad came back to the States a year or so later.

I was just an infant when we lived in England and only three when we were in Storm Lake, so I don't really have any recollection of time spent there. I do have great memories of Iowa, but those are from years later when our family would visit Nanna for a few weeks during the summertime. I was Nanna's little

My dad is the pilot on the left.

boy, and we would spend time together in the kitchen making grebbles—fried dough and sugar. I also got a glimpse of farm life, driving the tractor and being outdoors a lot. It was always a lot of fun, and I looked forward to visiting her every summer.

My first real memories start when I was four and my dad came back from his overseas tour. Besides being a pilot, he was also an expert on the Middle East. He began working at the Pentagon, conducting research and preparing position papers for the Defense Department, the State Department, and even the president of the United States. We moved to Camp Springs, Maryland, which wasn't too far from the Pentagon.

I don't remember the actual move, but I do remember my first impressions of the house we moved into. To me, it seemed like the biggest house in the world. At four, everything seems big, and looking back now as an adult, I realize that it wasn't a mansion or anything, but at the time, it just seemed huge.

One great thing about our house was that it was situated in a really neat neighborhood. At the end of our block, the neighborhood ended and it was all woods and forest. For a little kid who liked to run around and play, we couldn't have lived in a more perfect place.

When I turned five, my parents threw a birthday party and set up a treasure hunt for me and all my friends. It may have seemed like a small thing to them at the time, but it's one of my fondest memories. My parents placed clues all around the house and up and down our street. We would find one clue, my older brother Randy would read it to us, which would lead us to another and then another. They put clues under rocks, on trees, anywhere that five-year-olds would like to look. At the end of it, there was going to be this great treasure that we would find.

The clues took us up and down the block and into the woods where there was a big oak tree in which the local kids had put a tree house. We followed the clues past the tree house and then along a stream that ran nearby. At one point, we thought we had spotted the treasure. We ran across the stream with great big smiles on our faces, thinking we would soon be opening a secret chest. It turned out to be just a bunch of rocks, but that didn't deter us one bit from continuing the hunt.

We kept collecting clues and eventually made our way back to my backyard.

And there, sitting before us, was a big trunk stuffed full of toys. We were all so happy. We had found the treasure and there was something there for all of us.

I've lived a pretty crazy life and been through a lot of stuff, but I've never forgotten the treasure hunt. Now as a father of two beautiful young children, I'd like to be able to put together a treasure hunt for them on one of their birthdays. I only hope it will be as fun and as memorable as the one my folks gave me.

| | |

Football played a big part in my childhood and teenage years, and it was in Camp Springs that I began playing. My older brothers played, and I thought it seemed like a neat thing to do. I started out by playing with my brothers in our basement. We had this little rubber grip toy that we used as the football. I would start with the ball on one side of the basement and have to fight my way through them to get to the other side and score a touchdown. I think they had a blast picking me up and tossing me about. Unbeknownst to me, I was already learning how to take bumps and fly around.

I started playing organized ball, Pop Warner, when I was six. I was a stocky little boy who liked the physicality and contact of the sport, so my coaches started me out as a fullback. I was pretty good, but I did have one major problem that limited my enjoyment of the game. I had a hard time telling my right from my left. When they called a play that went right, I often went left, and when they called a play to go left, I often went right.

You might be thinking that a kid my age ought to know the difference between his right and his left, but there's a reason I had a bit of difficulty with this. I'm ambidextrous, and while this can be advantageous in many ways, for a six-year-old trying to learn his right from his left, it can be quite a source of frustration.

When a coach explained a play where I was supposed to go right, he would tell me to run between the guard and tackle on that side. When I asked which was right, he would tell me it was the side of my writing hand. When I asked another coach, he would tell me it was the side of the hand I drew with. Well, I wrote with my left and colored with my right, so I'd get confused. To try and help matters, one coach had seen me placekick, and he'd tell me it's the same

I've already been playing for a year.

side that you kick the ball with. Normally this would have helped, but while I kicked the ball off the ground with my right foot, I punted with my left. Unfortunately, his instructions only confused me more and I became very frustrated.

The coaches told my parents that if I wanted to play I needed to work on knowing my right from my left and where the holes I was supposed to run through were. So my dad and my brothers went to work to straighten me out. In our yard, they set up trash can lids where the offensive lineman would be and pointed out where all the holes were. We practiced a lot, and thanks to their patience I learned where to run.

Once over the right/left hurdle, I started doing pretty well. Then, I ended up hurting my leg. I'd like to say I pulled my hamstring, but I'm not sure if that's possible for a six-year-old to do. In any event, I hurt my leg somehow. We were at practice running laps. I was limping, crying, and just trying to make it around the field as best I could. I could hear my dad yelling, "C'mon Shawn, you're not hurt. You can do it!" So, I gutted it out and kept running.

I can also remember my mom then turning to my dad and really laying into him for pushing me like that when I was obviously injured. She couldn't stand to see her baby hurting, so she really gave my dad a piece of her mind. She also went over to my coach and told him in no uncertain terms, "You get him off the field!"

Well, Coach came over to me, picked me up, and carried me over to my mom. She took me right home. The next year, I played defensive lineman. Not so much running, and plenty of contact.

There were no great lessons that I learned from getting hurt, but this is a good example of how my parents related to me as I was growing up, my dad forceful and pushing, telling me to gut it out, and my mom not wanting to see me hurting at all.

| | |

At the time, I didn't really understand what my dad did for a living. He was always in his uniform, and he looked sharp all the time. He was very clean, very strict, and very proper. People saluted him a lot, I remember that. It seemed like a pretty cool thing to have people salute you. He worked a lot and wasn't home much, but if one of us was playing sports, he was usually there.

Later on, I would find out that he was a pretty good athlete in his day, and a great amateur wrestler, having wrestled for the University of Iowa, one of the top programs in the country. As a kid, though, I didn't really talk that much with my dad. He was from the generation where the father went to work and came home, had something to eat, and then relaxed on the couch. He basically kept to himself and would go to bed pretty early. I can't remember many intimate conversations I had with him as a kid.

My mom, on the other hand, took a very active role in raising the kids, and she was always very protective of me. She could get angry like all moms do, but when push came to shove, I was her baby and she almost always sided with me. One thing I learned very early on was that being a full-time mom is a real job, worthy of as much respect as a husband who works full-time outside the house.

My brothers were a lot older than me, and we didn't really have much of a relationship until recently. Both are college graduates and both are smart men. I always felt a little inferior to them, first because they were so much older than me, and then later on because they went to college and earned degrees. I felt they were smarter than me and that we would never have anything in common. I especially felt that way about Randy because he was a real brain. I was more of a jock, and because of my insecurity, I felt like a dummy around him. It used to drive him crazy, and that more than anything kept us from having a real relationship until very recently.

These days, because I've lived such a different life than my brothers and have gone through so much, I find myself giving them advice. For the first time, even though I'm their little brother, they make me feel their equal.

While I had a distant relationship with my brothers, I was real close to my sister, Shari. I thought she was the cat's meow and I just loved her so much. With my brothers out doing their own thing, we grew up together. She used to comfort me all the time and watch over me. Every night I would snuggle in bed with her. She provided a great sense of comfort.

| | |

We lived in Camp Springs until I was eight years old and there was really only one aspect of my life that I didn't like: school, or at least the first day of school. Not my actual first day in kindergarten, but every first day after that until seventh grade. It wasn't the classes that bothered me, or even meeting new kids when I changed schools. It was roll call, and sitting in my seat, dreading the moment my name would be called. With a name like Hickenbottom, it's not hard to figure out why. It is a funny name, and kids would make fun of it and me all the time.

I also didn't like the name Michael. My parents thought about naming me Shawn Michael Hickenbottom, but they decided Michael Shawn rolled off the tongue a bit better, so that was my official name. Everyone who knew me, though, called me Shawn.

I can't honestly say that I remember my first day of kindergarten at Middleton Valley Elementary, but I have no doubt that I cried leaving my mom for the first time to go to school. I also know that I got over leaving Mom real soon when I met my kindergarten teacher, Ms. Musgrave. She was spectacular and I adored her. She was my first love. When I went to first grade, she became my first grade teacher, and I couldn't have been any happier. My only disappointment with her was when she got married. I was heartbroken, but somehow I pulled it together and managed to move on with my life.

Before long, the local school district started a busing program. Rather than put me in a bus and have me attend school in a different neighborhood, my parents decided to enroll me in St. Joseph's, a private Catholic school. This was where I had my first of many uncomfortable experiences of being the new guy in school.

The very first day I was there, the teacher called out my name during roll. "Michael Hickenbottom?"

Everybody in the class started laughing. I can't remember the kids at Middleton Valley laughing at my name, perhaps a few snickers, but I sure remember these kids doing so. I felt terrible and if I had had one wish in the world at that time, it would have been to get out of that classroom. At Middleton Valley, I would yell out "Shawn" when they called my name and I would be called Shawn from then on. I felt so uncomfortable here that I didn't even tell the teacher to call me Shawn instead of Michael. For the rest of the year I was called Michael, and I hated every minute of it. I don't remember making one friend during that year at St. Joseph's. Thankfully, I still had the kids in the neighborhood that I played with.

By the time third grade rolled around, we had moved to Laughlin Air Force Base in Del Rio, Texas. My dad had been transferred there to be the base commander and once again the Hickenbottom family was on the move. Even though we had moved two thousand miles, my next first day at school would be just as bad.

That fall, I started at another Catholic school, Sacred Heart. This time the laughing and teasing would lead to the first of many fights I would get into. I was by nature a pretty shy boy, and I think I fought mostly out of fear. I can't ever recall wanting to fight. I fought because I thought I had to. It was just that I got picked on and picked on and picked on some more. I got so tired of it. It takes a lot to make me mad, but once I get mad I have a pretty bad temper, and I was about to unleash it on a kid who teased me at Sacred Heart.

During my first day there, a bunch of us were outside by the basketball courts and a boy starting making fun of my last name. I didn't like it and I went at him. When you are eight years old and you get in a fight, you're not going to do much damage, but I did pretty well for myself. We scuffled for a bit before we were separated and marched off to see the principal. Although they gave out spankings at the time, we weren't spanked. We were reprimanded and shown the paddle, but that was it. The punishment certainly didn't scar me or deter me from getting in fights in the future.

I stayed at Sacred Heart through the fifth grade. Then, my dad was transferred to Randolph Air Force Base right outside San Antonio. He went to live there while the rest of us stayed in Del Rio. At the time, my brother Randy was already off in college. Scott, however, was going to be a senior in high school. He was a real good football player and had been at the same school for three years. Starting anew as a senior would have been tough and a bit unfair to him. Shari also had a lot of friends in Del Rio and didn't want to move either. So my parents decided that my mom would stay with us in Del Rio for one more year while my dad lived up at Randolph, 150 miles away.

My dad made a pretty good living as a colonel in the air force, but maintaining two homes, sending a son to college, and sending me to private school was a bit much. So for sixth grade, I went back to public school. Sure enough, I got in a fight the very first day.

It was the same old story. The roll call, "Hickenbottom," the snickers, and then later the teasing. This time it was a boy named Steve who was doing the teasing. He was lipping off to me at recess, and I really let him have it. By this time I was big enough to do some real damage, and I bloodied him up pretty good.

I must admit that my pugilistic prowess got me over with my classmates right away. They were pretty impressed with how I beat the tar out him. I think it was a respect thing, the other kids were like "Whoa, don't mess with Shawn, he's real tough."

We were taken to the principal's office, but just like at Sacred Heart, we didn't really get into any trouble. Back in those days, schools wouldn't immediately call home and tell your parents that you were in a fight, so the only reason my folks ever knew I was in fights was if I told them.

Steve and I quickly made up. We soon became friends and ended up being teammates on our football team. Later in the year, he died in a tragic accident when his mother ran him over by accident while he was on his bike. I ended up being one of his pallbearers. The whole football team wore our jerseys to the funeral. This was my first experience with death and just a really sad moment.

Now that I have kids, and I'm not saying you have to have kids to realize what a tragedy that was, but nonetheless knowing what it's like to have kids and just thinking about them dying in such a manner, it's almost too much to imagine. My heart still goes out to his mother and family.

| | |

As you go back and review your life in the attempt to figure out how you became the person you are and why you acted in certain ways at various points in your life, you often come upon episodes that simply indicate: I was as I was, or, I just always was this way.

This is certainly true for me when it came to being punished for something I did not believe warranted punishment. Later in life during my wrestling career I would often be accused of doing awful things and/or breaking rules. I'll be the first to admit that I pushed buttons and could be difficult. But one thing I *did* do was own up to my shortcomings. If I did something wrong, I admitted to it and did not fight the punishment. When I was disciplined for something I did not do wrong, though, I fought the punishment and often made life as miserable as possible for those who I thought were wrongfully punishing me.

My internal sense of justice could be seen shortly after we moved to Laughlin. I had gotten in trouble for something—something that wasn't that serious, like forgetting to tell my mom where I was going that afternoon. If you ask my mom today, she'll even tell you that it wasn't that serious. But that day for whatever reason, maybe Mom was in a bad mood, I was going to get "the switch." My parents didn't spank us with their hands, they did it with a riding crop. It was my mom that called the crop "the switch."

Now I was a good kid for the most part and didn't get the switch very often. I learned real quick that it didn't pay to get in trouble where the switch was concerned. And more importantly, I was a sensitive kid and it bothered me to do something wrong to my parents or my family. It really hurt my feelings.

On this day, whatever I did, I didn't think I deserved to get it. My mom thought otherwise. She started getting on me, and despite my telling her that I was sorry and it would never happen again, she was adamant. I meant what I said, but the words were not good enough. I pleaded one more time with her.

"I'm sorry. I promise I won't do it again. Please don't," I said.

"Put your hands on the counter," she replied as she readied the switch.

I did exactly as she said. But still defiant and believing I didn't deserve the switch, I bolted out of the kitchen before she could hit me.

My mom couldn't believe I had run off. None of my siblings ever had the gumption to run from her. She was yelling at me to come back, but I just kept running and running and running. I ran past the officers' area, past the noncommissioned officers' area, through yards and down streets. I ran by the pool and all the youth fields.

Meantime, my mom and my sister had jumped in our truck and started following me. My sister could run like a deer and periodically my mom would pull up close to me and my sister would jump out and try and chase me down. She couldn't catch me on this day, though.

Eventually, I ran all the way to the end of the base. I was way out in the desert with only another big fence separating me from a vast, endless wasteland. My choices were either to stop and confront my mom, or try and climb the fence and head to Mexico or Del Rio. As I stood next to the fence, thinking what to do, my mom stepped out of the truck. I could tell by her expression that she was no longer mad, only concerned and a bit amused by the entire episode. She quickly said, "Baby, come here."

"I won't do it anymore," I said, obviously exhausted and a bit scared.

"I know you won't," she answered.

Then my sister came over and gave me a big hug. Later, my mom told me that Shari was really sticking up for me, pleading my case and telling her that I would never run like this if I had really done something bad. I think my sister standing up for me softened up my mom, and knowing this made me love Shari even more. That was the last time I was ever threatened with the switch. It wouldn't be the last time I ever ran from a punishment that I felt I didn't deserve.

| | |

Shortly after we moved to Laughlin, I was spending nearly every day at the pool. I was a big diver and spent hours diving off the boards. I wasn't afraid to jump off either the low or high boards, and before long I could do flips and even a backflip.

My dad took notice of my diving and one day told me to go up on the high dive and do a two and a half. I had never done this big a dive before, but I didn't want to disappoint him, so I climbed up the diving board and gave it my best shot.

It turns out my best shot wasn't good enough. I didn't make it and landed straight on my face, about knocking myself out. I was crying and selling my pain like nobody's business. My poor dad, he must have felt awful. And these are the memories I have of him! In any event, it didn't deter me from getting back on the board. Before long, I was back up jumping for all I was worth, although it's safe to assume that I didn't try another two and a half.

I also made friends with a boy who lived near us named Andrew. We were into superheroes and played together all the time. He ended up leaving the next year, and I remember being real sad when he did. Before long, however, I was making new friends and starting to experience the Texas lifestyle. We had moved off the base and I started hanging around with Donny Fletcher and the Sullivan boys. Donny and his family wore boots and Wranglers and drove pickup trucks. They were real country folk. As I made my way through elementary school I was becoming a full-fledged Texan. I spent a lot of time riding dirt bikes and going to the 4-H club and watching the kids there raise animals. I also tried chewing tobacco for the first time. I really didn't like the taste of the tobacco, but older kids chewed it and I just imitated them.

As far as academics were concerned, I was an average student who didn't try very hard and wasn't that interested in any of the subjects we studied. Nowadays, I read a ton of books, but back then, despite my parents' wanting me to, I wasn't into reading. I earned mostly C's and a few B's. Every now and then I would get a D and be told that I had to "bring those grades up." My parents never said that my future would depend on my education, and I never felt pressured to do well in school.

One other thing that I discovered in Del Rio was girls, or more exactly, that there was something pretty cool about them. Of course, I had no idea how to act around girls. I was shy and totally unsure of myself. One time in the sixth grade, we were at a party playing truth or dare and I was dared to go into a closet with this girl. We went, but we had no idea what we were doing. We just stood there and stared at each other, completely innocent and completely clueless.

A couple of weeks later I was at another party and a game of spin the bottle broke out. This night I turned out to be very "suave and debonair." A lot of the girls picked me to kiss them. Again, I had no idea what I was doing, and truth be told, I would have no idea all throughout junior and senior high school and really for a long time after that. But at this moment, it felt pretty darn cool to get picked to be kissed.

| | |

The summer between sixth and seventh grade we moved to Randolph and were reunited with Dad. By this time, moving was no big deal. Everyone in the air force seemed to do it, and I found it easy to make friends at Randolph. I had the summer to settle into life on the base, and by the time school started things were going pretty well. I met a new friend, Tim Roubelard, and was having a good time playing with him. Then it was time for school to start, and I began to brace myself for roll call. My last name was an albatross I couldn't get rid of.

The first day in seventh grade, I was nervous and dreading the moment when the teacher would call out my name. Fortunately, someone intervened and saved me the agony of a full-fledged heckling. He had black hair and the biggest buckteeth you ever saw. His name was Darren Sutterfield and he liked to go by the name of Scooter.

"Darren Sutterfield?" our teacher called out the first day.

"You can call me Scooter," he replied.

I guess we all thought that was pretty funny because the whole class broke out laughing. Whether they were laughing at him or the name I'm not sure, but by the time the teacher came to me there was already a bit of levity, and I definitely felt better. I got a few chuckles when my name was called, but it was nothing like the past. I guess Scooter took the heat off of me.

Junior high school turned out to be a really good time. I spent a lot of time riding bikes and skateboards with my friends and hanging out at the base youth center where we would play pool or Ping-Pong. I played football for our base team, the Randolph Rangers, during the fall, and I played baseball in the spring.

This was also about the time I started feeling peer pressure or at least realizing that it existed. There were different cliques, so to speak, at school. There was the "cool" group, the "nerd" group, the "goth" group, and then there were "the others." I didn't really run within in any one circle. I was sort of an in-betweener, which was fine for me.

Some of my classmates liked to talk about what they were doing with girls. Rumors would start flying around about so-and-so and so-and-so. I assumed they were true because I didn't really know any better. Later on I realized that there was a lot of lying going on, but at the time I just took what people said as the truth.

Elizabeth was the name of my first girlfriend. She lived off base and didn't go to Randolph. This sort of raised my profile at school. I was "going with" someone from the outside. In our small world, I had gone big time.

I met her at an arcade, and we spent a fair amount of time there. Sometimes my mom would give me a ride to her house and we'd hang out and be awkward with each other. I certainly liked her, but I was so intimidated around her. I was afraid of doing something that she didn't want me to do. My shyness made me feel awkward, but in a strange way, I think she and other girls kind of liked me for that.

It's funny because later on in my career I was known as such an egotistical brash guy because that's what I put out there for everyone to see. Inside, I was still the shy little twelve-year-old who didn't quite know how to act and who was afraid that people wouldn't like me if I showed who I really was.

2 my little world

In between seventh and eighth grade we moved off base, and one Saturday night I was at home sitting around with nothing to do. I decided to turn on the TV to pass the time. I wasn't looking to watch anything in particular. I don't even remember flipping the channels to see what was on. I just turned on the television and there it was: Southwest Championship Wrestling (SWCW).

I had never seen or heard of wrestling before, but I was immediately and completely captivated by it. I saw wrestlers like Tully Blanchard and Wahoo McDaniel. Wahoo was the big Indian and Tully was the number one bad guy. There was action, there was fighting, there was competition. It seemed like the coolest thing in the world. I watched the entire hour and then walked off to the kitchen where my mom was.

"Mom," I said to her with as much conviction as I could muster at the time. "I want to be a professional wrestler."

"That's nice, honey," she replied in an offhand manner, never dreaming that I was serious and that our lives would be changed forever that night.

Pretty soon, watching SWCW became my little thing every weekend. It was on pretty late, but my folks let me stay up to watch. One night I was watching and they were cutting promos about an upcoming show at the HemisFair Arena in San Antonio. When I realized that I could see this live, I became really excited. I asked my dad if I could go see the matches and he said yes and took me to the HemisFair Arena for my first show.

I'm sure if I looked back at that show now, it would seem so nickel-and-dime. At the time, however, it was huge and colorful and larger than life. Our seats were pretty high up, but that didn't detract at all from the grandeur of the show. They had this big ring light that shined on the wrestlers and made it all seem like a great spectacle. At that time, the wresters bled often, and when they bled that day, it was as if their blood was the brightest red there was. Tully and Wahoo were in the main event. They brawled and the crowd went nuts. It was just a great, fun experience. If I wasn't completely hooked before, I was now.

When school started up in the fall, I was the only one I knew who watched wrestling. Then I found out that a boy, Lorne, who I didn't hang out with, also liked to watch. We fast became wrestling buddies, practicing moves on each other and having matches outside his house and in the base gym. He had a mask and sometimes he would put that on and we would pretend we were certain wrestlers and go do our thing.

We followed the feuds that were going on in SWCW, and I rooted for the good guys for the most part. I also learned about guys like Ric Flair, Dusty Rhodes, Harley Race, Nick Bockwinkel, and Bob Backlund from Lorne. He had quite a few wrestling magazines, and through these, I realized that there was a whole 'nother world of wrestling outside of San Antonio.

In my mind, Bob Backlund was the number one champion. He wrestled in

New York, and I figured that meant he must be the best. Nick Bockwinkel, the American Wrestling Association (AWA) Champion, carried himself real well. He had a presence to him, and I would have ranked him right behind Backlund. Harley Race, who was the National Wrestling Alliance (NWA) Champion, maybe because of his old rugged look, seemed to me a bit behind those two.

This is by no means to imply that I was smartened up to the business. Heck, I wasn't even smartened up by the time I had my first real match. It's just that I began to look at the business and try to figure out how it all worked. There was no Internet, there were no newsletters or "dirt sheets" that I knew of, and the business was real protected. I observed what I could and tried my best to put two and two together.

Mr. Sifuentes, my social studies teacher, was a big wrestling fan. Sometimes he would give the class an assignment and sit up in front of the class and read a book. He was actually reading wrestling magazines he slipped inside his book. After Mr. Sifuentes discovered that I liked wrestling, he would occasionally look my way and let the wrestling magazine slip out. He was really cool, and Lorne, he, and I would discuss what was going on in SWCW before class a lot.

| | |

When I started high school, wrestling took a bit of a backseat to football. To say that high school football is big in Texas would be a huge understatement. Football is *the* thing in Texas high schools. It certainly was at Randolph, and I was eager to play.

The man who ran our program was Coach Mickler, and he ran it with an iron fist. There was no doubt that he was "the man" at school, and everyone did whatever he said to do. He won eighteen district championships, and he commanded a lot of respect in the community. He was, in fact, the de facto head of the entire school.

Coach Mickler looked straight out of central casting. He was a huge man with a pockmarked face, gravelly voice, and old and leathery skin. He smoked a lot, but you never saw the smoke come out of his mouth. It was as if he was so tough, he just swallowed it. He wore coaching shorts, his three-button

Ro-Hawks (our nickname) polo shirt, and a Ro-Hawks hat, and he always had a whistle around his neck. The only other thing he did besides coach was teach golf, and he did that because he liked to play.

Coach really wasn't much of a teacher on the field. Everything was about him. He called me either "Guy" or "Hick," and referred to other people as "Stupid" or "Ignoramus." Coach Mickler verbally brutalized a lot of players, including my friend Scott Marie. Coach was so hard on Scott that Scott jokingly claims he went to Mickler's gravesite five years after he had died just to make sure Coach was still there.

It was around football that I formed the core group of friends who I would hang out with throughout high school. Pat Ahman, Paul Silvestri, and Gavin and Troy Rose were four guys I became pretty close with. I still hung out with my wrestling buddy, but that was kind of separate from my jock friends. They weren't into wrestling.

Our school had a freshman team, so in ninth grade I played on that team and escaped the wrath of Coach Mickler, who concentrated his time on the varsity squad. I played offensive tackle and linebacker and was one of the better players on the team.

In all, my first year of high school was fun. I was running with my friends, starting to get into music a little, mostly bands like KISS, Van Halen, and Rush, and I had a few little girlfriends here and there. But it was going into my sophomore year that things began to really pick up.

We lived off base and whenever I needed to get to base or go to school, I could catch a ride with my sister or one of my parents would drive me. That was fine, but I was fifteen now and wanted to have some freedom. In Texas you only had to be fifteen to get a motorcycle license, and I knew some other kids who had one. So, I asked my folks if I could get a motorcycle. They gave me the big responsibility talk, and I agreed to everything they demanded. They had friends who had a Honda dealership in Tyler, Texas, so my mom, dad, and Scott went up there and came back with a red Honda 100. I loved it and couldn't have been any happier.

I also started working the summer before tenth grade. I was going to wrestling matches and I had my motorcycle now. My parents felt it was time I started paying for my own things. Gavin and Troy were working at a local pizza place called Mr. Gatti's, and they put in a good word for me. Before long, I was making pizzas, cleaning the restaurant, and pulling in the minimum wage, which was $3.35 an hour. I worked a couple of nights during the week and on Friday and Saturday nights, which were the busiest times.

When I began working there, my friends started coming in. And my friends were slowly turning into a bigger crowd, mainly because of Pat Ahman and the other football players. Everyone knew Ahman. He was a great athlete and was going to be the future of our team. Before you knew it, we had a dozen or so of us that would hang out there till the end of our senior year.

It was at Mr. Gatti's that I started to drink beer. I vaguely remember trying a beer in ninth grade, but it was brutal. I didn't think it was cool, and I just wasn't into drinking as a rebellious act. At Gatti's, I felt differently. I was a bit older, it was a cool place to be, and Gavin, who was like a forty-year-old guy in tenth grade, helped bring out that side of me.

We wouldn't drink during business hours. We were too young for that. But after we closed up, our manager would let us have a pitcher or two— nothing crazy, but definitely enough to catch a buzz. Being young and dumb, we would then drive home. I had my motorcycle, and Gavin had his '73 Super Beetle with a semi-black hood. We always called his car by its description. It sounds kind of goofy, but that's just one of those things we did.

| | |

I was one of three sophomores to make the varsity football team that year. The others were Pat, who was the starting quarterback, and Derrick Terrell. Derrick and Pat played a lot more than I did, but just being on varsity in tenth grade was a pretty big deal, and it helped my standing in the school's social scene.

Tenth grade also happened to be the year I met my best friend Kenny Kent. Kenny was new to Randolph, and we just sort of gravitated to each other. I noticed how the girls were attracted to him and that he was a nice guy. Kenny was easy to talk to, and we became good friends real quick. Most of the guys in our little gang thought he was soft, but I think they were jealous that he was comfortable in his own skin.

Kenny was different from my other friends. He wasn't afraid to admit that he didn't know everything. He didn't pretend to be cool as a way of hiding his true feelings, and he was fun to hang out with. I was never comfortable pretending to know everything, as I did with my other friends. With Kenny, there was never a problem saying, "I don't know what in the world is going on." I never felt pressured to do anything or be anyone but myself around him. We did goofy stuff that we knew was goofy and we laughed about it. Our other friends thought it was dumb, but we didn't care. We were just two teenagers living a pretty cool life, in no hurry to grow up. I broke Kenny into wrestling, which he liked, and we did just about everything together. The only thing we didn't do together was draw and paint. That's because I couldn't. Kenny, however, was a great artist. My other friends would make fun of him for that—I guess they thought it was soft or something—but I thought he was really good.

Barbara was the name of my first serious girlfriend. She was in eleventh grade, was real cute, and had quite a nice figure. We started talking at school one day and took a liking to each other. Eventually, despite my discomfort at uttering the words, I asked her, "Will you go with me?"

She liked me, and I knew that, but I was still afraid I would get turned down. Later on, in the midst of my wrestling career, this same fear of rejection would drive Marty Jannetty, my tag team partner, nuts. We would go into a bar and girls would be looking at me and giving clear signals. Yet I would never make a move until I had a few drinks. Marty would yell at me, "You are on TV! People know who you are. Would you please go over and talk to them?" He could go up to anyone and start talking. I couldn't do that. It wasn't in my personality. I was shy and afraid of being rejected even when there was zero chance I would be turned down.

Barbara and I had a lot of fun. She could drive and had a green MG. That's really when I became "the man." Pat might have been the best football player in school, but I was dating an older, good-looking woman that had a car. We ended up dating for most of the year. Then I decided I wanted to run around with the guys and have my freedom—whatever that means to a sixteen-year-old. I had no idea how to break up with someone, and I don't remember being too good at it. We fought over little things for about two weeks before we moved off in our separate directions.

I continued to live a typical high school life in eleventh and twelfth grade. I played football, I was a co-captain my senior year, and I found a new girlfriend named Chimane, who seemed very exotic at the time. Chimane's parents had been stationed in Germany, and she seemed very mature and worldly. We dated our whole senior year, and then she went off to Texas A&M and broke my heart.

We didn't have a wrestling team at our school, but between my junior and senior year two new kids came in who were amateur wrestlers. They formed a small wrestling club that competed in tournaments and when they asked me if I wanted to participate, I jumped at the chance. I had my mind set on becoming a pro wrestler, and back then you would often hear the TV announcer, in trying to build someone up, say, "He's got an extensive amateur background." So I thought this would be a great opportunity.

Unfortunately, my amateur wrestling career didn't last very long. I ended up wrestling in only one tournament because when Coach Mickler found out I was wrestling, he ordered me to quit immediately.

"You are not doing that junk!" he told me in no uncertain terms. He was afraid I might get hurt, as two-a-days were coming up and the season would start soon thereafter. I did win that one tournament, although I have to admit there were only three guys in my weight class, so winning wasn't that big a deal to me. It was a different story for my dad. I've won championships, headlined shows that drew 60,000 people, and become one of the greatest wrestlers alive, but I think my dad is more proud of that amateur win than anything I've done professionally.

| | |

When I was growing up, I always thought of my dad as the colonel, and I treated him like one. He worked a lot, wasn't around much, and we just weren't that close. There were, however, two important incidents in high school, each quite different from the other, that brought us a little closer together.

I was sleeping in one Saturday and my dad came in to wake me up. I didn't have anywhere to be or anything to do, but he wanted me out of bed and he told me in no uncertain terms to get up. He had been waking up at 5:00 A.M. his entire life, and it drove him nuts if anyone stayed in bed past nine o'clock. It was about eleven o'clock now and he wanted me up. I said, "All right," but didn't get up. I had been out late and I was tired. I wasn't doing anything wrong, I just wanted to sleep. When I didn't get up, he became real angry and started getting on me again. He didn't call me a lazy bum, but it was implied.

After he had yelled a bit, he yanked on my hair. I snapped and at this moment made the decision that I was no longer going to treat him as the colonel. I had been treating him like that my entire life. I loved him and I respected him, but now he had gone overboard. I felt he wasn't showing me any love and respect, and I had earned that. I sprang up out of bed, grabbed him by the throat, and yelled, "Don't touch me!"

He fired up and yelled back. "Don't you touch your dad!"

I let him go and headed straight for my parents' bedroom to see my mom. When I got to their room, my mom was there and I screamed, "Tell him to leave me alone!"

He had followed me in, and right after I said that to my mom, he grabbed me, spun me around, and started to say, "Don't you—" He never finished his sentence. I was a bit bigger than him by now and I threw him up against the wall and punched a hole in the wall right next to his head. Then I grabbed him and threw him across the bed.

My mom was screaming now and my brother Scott, who was in town visiting, came running into the room and pulled me out into the hallway. Scott had been in a few tussles with my dad years earlier, and he took me out for a drive. "I always wondered if this day would come with you," he said. "That's the way Dad is. He's your dad and you can't do that." His words didn't sit too well, and I went off again. He looked at me and simply said, "Shawn, you have a temper. You need to learn to control that." To this day, I hear my family say, "You have always been like that, Shawn. You are so good, but when something happens that you can't take, you just click into someone else and someday you are going to hurt someone or yourself."

Eventually I calmed down, came back, and told my dad I was sorry. He forgave me and soon everything was fine between us. This was a day we both learned a lot about each other. He learned not to treat me like that, and that the way he had done things before was not the way to do it with me. I learned that no matter what your father does, he deserves your respect and love. After all, my dad was doing the best he could.

Dad was raised by his mom and grew up in Clinton, Iowa. I don't know much about his childhood and suspect that the first chance he had, he was going to get out of Clinton. He went to the University of Iowa and then enlisted in the air force. That's all I know of his early years. He never told us about anything in his life till he started wrestling at the University of Iowa.

| | |

The second incident occurred during my senior year after my buddies and I began stealing signs. We thought it was a cool thing to do. Some guys began the trend by taking a Hamburglar from a local McDonald's and sneaking it into the atrium at school. Everyone thought that was the greatest thing in the world, and soon stealing signs became the thing to do. We'd steal anything we could get our hands on, although we specialized in nabbing mile marker signs that corresponded to our football numbers.

One night during the winter, when football season had already ended, Gavin, Troy, myself, and our friend Amy decided to steal a sign from our big rival, Cole High School. It was a brand-new one with a big Golden Cougar, their mascot, on it. Not being the swiftest fellow in the world at that time, I decided to wear my football jersey with its big number 63 on it. As we were taking it, a girl came by and asked what we were doing. We told her we were just waiting for a ride. She left, and we didn't think much more of the encounter. We took the sign and brought it to my house. On the way home, it fell off the top of my car and skidded on the road and got all banged up. We just laughed and put it back on the top of the car and held it there with our hands till we made it to my house. When we arrived, we told my parents what we had done. They thought it was pretty funny. Even my dad, who is Mr. Nothing Is Funny, got a kick out of it.

The next day during second period, Gavin and I were called into Principal Hall's office. We came out of our classroom and saw Amy and Troy in the hallway walking from their classroom. We knew we were getting busted. Coach Mickler was in there with the principal, and they asked us if we had stolen the sign. We denied it. Then Mickler blurted out, "You idiot! You wore your jersey! That's how they knew it was you. Don't lie." The girl who had seen us had told on us. So we went to my house, retrieved the sign, and brought it back to Randolph. Principal Hall then escorted us over to Cole, where we apologized and returned the sign.

Later that day during gym class, Coach Mickler called me into his office. He verbally tore me apart from one side of the room to the other. He called me white trash, a vandal, and a criminal. He also told me to bring in my letterman jacket the next day because I didn't deserve to wear it. Letter jackets at Randolph were very big, and to those of us that had them, it gave us an air of confidence and served as a symbol of our social standing. To lose it was a big deal. I didn't want to give it back, but Coach Mickler was Coach Mickler and even though my senior season had already ended, I was still going to do as he said. So I brought it in and gave it to him.

A couple of weeks later it was really cold. I was going out and my dad saw that I wasn't wearing my jacket. "Where's your letter jacket?" he asked. "How come you're not wearing it?"

"Coach Mickler took it away," I replied.

"Why?"

"For stealing the Cole sign."

"What? You got in trouble for that?"

"Yeah. He called me white trash, a vandal, a hood."

"What did he call you?"

"White trash."

"Coach Mickler called you white trash?"

"Yeah, and he took my letter jacket."

"I'm going to school to see him."

Now my dad never once took my side when I got in trouble. If I made a mistake, he would say, "You made a mistake. You deserve what you got." This time it was different. To begin with, he didn't think that stealing the sign was all that bad. He looked at it as the high school prank that it was. What really set him off, though, was the white trash comment. He was probably called that growing up, and he fought real hard to get away from that stigma. He was a colonel in the air force and was not going to have his son called white trash. It was a reflection on him.

He took me to Mickler's office and for the first time in my life, I was about to see this big tough coach be humbled. My dad told him in no uncertain terms that he needed to apologize to me for what he had said and that he needed to give me my jacket back. "Now you get that jacket, and you get it now and give

"The Colonel."

HICKENBOTTOM, RICH
1ST LT. 28651 A

it back to my son," he told Mickler. "And you apologize to Shawn for calling him white trash."

"Yes sir, Colonel, I'll do that right away," Mickler answered my dad. Then he turned to me and said, "Shawn, I'm sorry I called you white trash. It will never happen again."

I looked over at my dad and couldn't have been more proud. I thought what he had just done was huge, and I felt real proud to be his son. Stealing the sign was just good fun, but Coach Mickler had called me a vandal, a hood, white trash. He made me feel like a criminal.

Suffice it to say, my relationship with Coach Mickler changed that day. I didn't treat him with any less respect, but I knew that he knew that I knew. There was a little bit of uncomfortableness between us, but it was senior year and I'd be gone come June. And yes, I proudly wore my letter jacket the rest of the year.

| | |

In between football, girls, Mr. Gatti's, and the occasional fight I would get into, I was immersing myself further and further into the wrestling world. I watched SWCW every week on television and went to see it live when they came to the HemisFair Arena.

Southwest had a lot of interesting characters. Tully Blanchard's father, Joe Blanchard, owned the promotion, and Tully was portrayed as the owner's son who had gone bad. He drew a ton of heat. There was Scott Casey, who played the good guy cowboy. He kind of looked like Tom Selleck, and if he wrestled today, he'd get booed out of the building, but back then, wrestlers like him were very popular. Eddie Mansfield, the Continental Lover, was our Ric Flair rip-off. Mansfield was so good on his promos that even though he was a bad guy, I kind of took a liking to him. One time he and Scott Casey became involved in a program that ended in a Hair vs. Hair match. Mansfield would step up to the microphone and lead off with something outrageous like "Let me tell you something, you Rexall ranger, you drugstore cowboy!" He'd get Casey so riled up, and they built a nice little story that culminated in the Hair match. There was no way I was going to miss this, and I saw it in person at the HemisFair Arena. Scott Casey ended up beating Mansfield and cut off all Mansfield's hair.

Ricky Morton was another guy who was really good. He was full of fire, and fun to watch in and out of the ring. He and Ken Lucas had a great feud with Tully and Gino Hernandez. They were the top two tag teams for a while, and a big match between them was set up for TV. The match was supposed to start and Ricky was nowhere to be found. Lucas put up as good a fight as he could against the other two, but he lost. Then right before the show went off the air, Ricky came stumbling in on the promo set. He was all beat up and said he was attacked in the parking lot. He didn't know who had done it, but we knew it was Gino and Tully. They let you tie the story together. That's why he wasn't there for the match!

They were doing this to plug another live event at the HemisFair Arena, and you better believe I went down to see how this one played out. I've always loved those kind of story lines. They're simple but effective. I guess it's the old southern wrestling that I was brought up on.

Cable TV came to our area around this time, and soon I was able to watch the World Wrestling Federation on MSG and WOR and the National Wrestling Alliance on TBS. I locked into the TBS scene because there was that southern twist to it. It was like SWCW, only bigger. They showed a lot of blood, there were street fights, and I could watch Ric Flair.

Ric Flair was the end-all and be-all as far as I was concerned. He didn't wrestle that much on TV, but his promos—the whole limousine riding, jet flying, kiss stealing, wheeling dealing, son of a gun thing—were the greatest thing I had ever seen. Kenny and I would pretend to be Ric, cutting his promos to each other and whoever would listen as often as we could. To us, Ric Flair was the coolest guy in the world. He had it all. They would show clips of him and you would see the limousine, the jet, and the women.

I didn't know it at the time, but the reason he was so good at being the Nature Boy was because he really *was* the Nature Boy in his everyday life. That came across and you could feel it. That's the difference between guys that get over and guys that don't. When it comes from within, it's powerful and it works.

Ric had such presence. The way he talked, his robes, and the way he carried the championship belt. He told everyone that he was the greatest and you believed him. Even when he would lose the title, he still carried himself like a champion and you thought he would get it back soon. Ric Flair is the greatest wrestler I've ever seen. I thought so in high school and still do today.

As I continued to watch more and more wrestling, I began to study it. I tried my best to figure out how things worked and why they did, and I approached the business more as a student than as a fan. I understood there were different territories and that wrestlers in one territory wouldn't wrestle guys from another. I couldn't have told you the exact geographical breakdown of all of them, but I knew that the World Wrestling Federation was up east, the NWA Champion traveled all over, and that the AWA was up in the Midwest.

I also started to understand that only certain guys got to be the world champion and that wrestling was part performance and part athletics. The whole "Is it real or fake?" question never bothered me. I didn't think about that. I knew it was part performance. I also knew that I saw guys really smack each other in the ring. I just thought it was awesome and something I could do.

The Casey/Mansfield Hair match sparked my interest in thinking about what story lines work and what don't, because two weeks after Casey cut Mansfield's hair off, Eddie returned to TV, beat Casey up, and poured a bunch of horse manure on him. This set up a Horse Manure match. To me, this seemed like overkill. The story had played out with the hair and should have ended there. I had no urge to see the Horse Manure match, and I didn't go to the arena to watch it.

The more matches I went to, the closer I sat to the ring and the dressing room. I never made it to the first row, but I did make it to the second. I didn't realize the wrestlers were communicating with each other in the ring, but I realized what was going on was a real art form. I could see that this was something that takes time, effort, and athletic ability. I had all of these things and I knew that I could do it. The thing that was most puzzling was, how in the world do you get into wrestling?

I noticed that many of the same people were at all the shows, both fans and officials. I understood that there was this separate world of wrestling, and that somehow these people made it all work. The business was very protected back then. There was no going backstage and there was no one I knew who I could ask and who would tell me how the whole thing worked. I just knew that there was a secret world and I wanted to get in on it.

For all the shows I went to, I never hung out where the wrestlers parked their cars and asked for any autographs. I thought about it, but I was too afraid to approach anyone. I did, however, manage to get some of Wahoo McDaniel's blood once. He had finished his match and was walking back to the dressing room. He was bleeding pretty good, and I ran up to him and swiped a piece of paper I had picked up off the floor against his bloody arm. When I returned home, I stapled the paper to a picture I had of him. Please don't ask me to explain that one. I was a teenager completely taken with the business. It seemed like a neat thing at the time.

After the matches were over at the HemisFair Arena, it became a tradition for all the kids to run into the ring before security would come and kick them out. Kenny and I did this once and I ran in and jumped off the second turnbuckle. Needless to say, we thought that it was supercool.

Kenny and I also spent a lot of time imitating moves of our favorite wrestlers. One of our favorites was a guy named Bruiser Bob Sweetan. He was the first wrestler to come in as a bad guy, act like a bad guy, and be turned good guy by the fans. He came out to the song "Bang Your Head" by Quiet Riot and would finish his opponents off with the piledriver. That got over like a million bucks, and the fans couldn't help but cheer for him. One day I got into a bit of a tussle at school and—stupidly, I might add—piledrove a kid, just like Bruiser Bob would have done. Fortunately, I didn't hurt the boy. A piledriver is a very dangerous move and no one should ever try to execute it on another person.

By my senior year, wrestling was real big in our school and everyone was at least checking it out. It was common knowledge that I loved wrestling and watched it all the time. My buddies and I would knock each other into lockers all the time and try moves on one another in the hallways.

Kenny and I even put on a match for the talent show. I was the champion and a bad guy. Kenny was the challenger. We did hip tosses, arm drags, and a few other simple moves. We were wrestling on an elevated stage, and our plan called for him to knock me off the stage and hit me with a chair. I would fall down, slide under a table, and pour red food coloring all over me, pretending it was blood. Kenny would win the match and become the new champion. Yes, I was doing the job, and no, I didn't have any problems with that.

We pulled it off, and the audience really liked it. People thought it was hilarious, and we won second place in the show. The cheerleaders who lip-synched to Loverboy in their tight spandex won first place. It was a way unfair advantage. We never stood a chance.

That's Kenny on the left.

Kenny and me at spring break our senior year.

|||

My senior year was now drawing to a close. We had our skip day, our trip to the Gulf Coast, and the prom. I could feel that the end of this chapter of my life was near. Chimane broke up with me, saying that I would meet other people. I didn't want it to end, though. I loved my little world. Why did things have to change?

Every now and then I would tell my parents that I wanted to be a wrestler. I think they assumed I was going to college, because that's what most people do. Kenny had plans to go to Southwest Texas State, located about forty-five minutes away in San Marcos, and study graphic design. He was going to commute. Scott Marie was going to go to Southwest too. I guess I figured that I would go there as well. To be perfectly honest, I was not enthusiastic about it. In my mind, I had just gone through twelve years of school. I didn't want to go through another four, and I wasn't the kind of person who couldn't wait to leave home. I certainly wasn't the type who wanted to go to college and "grow."

I took my SATs without studying for them. I'm not proud to say this, but I cheated off the kid next to me. Unfortunately, he was no Albert Einstein, and I scored a 750. Fortunately, that was enough to qualify for Southwest.

The idea of being stuck in a room with somebody I didn't know didn't appeal to me, and I definitely didn't want to live in a dorm. I discussed this with my parents, and my dad and I made a deal. He would buy a trailer that Scott and I could live in, but in return, I had to promise that I would follow through with my education. Buying the trailer was a big investment for him, and he needed to know I was serious. I agreed and told him that I would finish school.

In the meantime, I kept telling my parents that I wanted to "do that wrestling." By this time, Southwest Wrestling was pretty much done, but World Class Championship Wrestling (WCCW), run by Fritz Von Erich, was coming to San Antonio fairly regularly. I was going to their shows and drifting as close as I could to the locker room.

My dad used to play a lot of golf, and one day he came home and mentioned that he played golf with a man who said he knew the person who ran the wrestling thing, a used car salesman down at North Central Ford. I believe he was saying this in a sort of off-the-cuff manner, but I also couldn't help but think that maybe he wanted to check out how legitimate the wrestling business was. I don't think he understood my fascination with it. He was more in the mode of, why would you want to do something so stupid?

Other people were asking me that as well. Some of my friends thought Kenny and I were idiots for being so into wrestling. Perhaps if I had had to go through that myself, I would have thought it was stupid. But Kenny was a perfectly normal guy with a good head on his shoulders, so him liking it made me think that there wasn't something wrong with me.

I asked Dad about the guy from the Ford dealership, and not too long afterwards, he came home and told me that he had set up a meeting with him. We drove over to San Pedro, where the dealership was, and I met my first wrestling promoter.

His name was Fred Behrend. Fred was a heavyset guy with yellowish hair, a sweet watch, and a big old diamond ring. He told us he owned World Class Championship Wrestling. Like most small-time promoters, Fred wasn't afraid to stretch the truth. The fact was he promoted matches in San Antonio, Laredo, and South Texas for WCCW. He didn't own the company. I didn't know any better at the time, so I believed him.

Fred listened as I told him how much I wanted to be a wrestler and then asked how old I was. I said I was eighteen, and that's when he broke the news to me that you had to be nineteen to obtain a wrestling license in Texas. My dad then jumped in the conversation and said I was going to school. Fred thought that was a good idea. He said, "In four years when you are done, you come on back and we'll try you out." That's where we left it. When he heard I was going to college, he probably thought he could say anything and it might as well be encouraging. After all, he probably figured he would never see me again.

| | |

So I was off to Southwest. Scott and I moved into our trailer and I began taking classes. I didn't like them. I didn't make many friends, and I just didn't fit in with the whole college scene. Sometimes our high school buddies would come visit, and I went home pretty often, but for the most part we hung out, drank beer, and watched a lot of TV.

I finished up the first semester with a 1.4 grade point average and was placed on academic probation. Dad was not pleased. He told me that he and Mom weren't spending all this money on me for me to do so poorly. I had made a commitment, he was paying for me to go to school, and I needed to step it up.

I told him that I wanted to wrestle. We had a big long talk about me really wanting to try wrestling. He said that I had made a commitment, but if I pulled my grades up to 2.5, he would take me back to Fred Behrend. We could then revisit wrestling and see how realistic it was. I thought that was great and headed back to Southwest looking to get my 2.5.

Kenny and I reconnected about this time, so when Scott decided to drop out of school, Kenny came up to be my roommate. He blended in real well at college. He made a lot of friends and was into his design courses. I still didn't fit in that well, but I had a little better time than I did my first semester. I took a psychology class that I really liked. It was taught by an old friend of my mom's, and I did pretty well in it. I also took a speech communication course, figuring that since I one day hoped to cut promos in front of an audience, it would be useful. It turns out the class wasn't that great, but at least I was thinking of the future.

I wish I would have taken some drama classes. The problem was I didn't understand the correlation between acting and wrestling at that time. If I had, I

My room in the trailer. That's a drawing of Tully Blanchard on the wall.

would have jumped all over it. One of the things that I've come to like about wrestling is that I've been able to pretend to be something I'm not. In this business, you are allowed to be someone you are not, but would like to be. I think all of us would like to be the toughest, coolest guy who always wins in everything he does. That's something few if any get to experience in our daily life.

Around Easter, Kenny and I decided to throw a party, and some old buddies from home came up for it. Everyone was having a good time, and then Gavin started getting a little obnoxious. I tensed up and was about to waffle him when I decided I would first show him and everyone else there that I was a real tough guy.

Gavin and I fought a couple of times during high school. He would get obnoxious, I would punch him, he would go down, and we'd be fine the next day. This night, I wasn't going to hit him—not right away, anyhow. I was sick of him doing this. I was like, "You do this all the time! You need to stop!"

I turned away from him, walked into the bathroom, picked up my electric razor, and headed back to the party. I pulled up the beard trimmer, turned it on, and pressed it against my forehead. I started to bleed, and cut a wrestling promo. Then I waffled him and knocked him down. Why I cut myself open with the razor, I'm not completely sure. I was like the idiot in a bar who gets all worked up and smashes a bottle over his head, saying in effect, "I want to show you that you shouldn't be messing with me because I am about to drop you." There's always that one stupid obnoxious guy, and that night it was me.

Kenny was a bit freaked out by the whole scene and was afraid that I had completely lost it and might really hurt Gavin. He ran out of the trailer and said he was going to call my parents. I took off too, but couldn't catch him. He was much faster than I was, and he made it to the pay phone at the little Sac-N-Pac down the road well before me. "Mrs. Hickenbottom," he shouted into the phone. "Shawn's cut his head and he's going crazy! Shawn and Gavin were getting into it and he's bleeding pretty bad, and he hit Gavin!"

Just then I made it to the Sac-N-Pac and grabbed the phone. "It's okay, Mom. Nothing to worry about," I said.

"Honey, are you okay?" she asked.

"Yes, I'm fine."

"I think you need to come home, honey, we need to talk." She was concerned. "Have you been drinking?"

"Yes."

"Just take it easy, you're just upset. Is your head okay? Is it bleeding? What did you do?"

"I cut it with an electric razor."

"Are you sure you're okay?"

"Yeah, I'll be fine." Mom was worried, and she talked to me for a while. By the time she was done, I had calmed down and the whole episode was over.

I wish I could say that whenever anything similar occurred in the future, I avoided conflict and handled it in a much more mature manner. The truth is, it didn't change me at all. I had my temper and although I was generally a nice guy, if you pushed me too far the gloves came off. It happened with the kids who teased me in elementary school, with my dad and Gavin in high school. It would

It was a really good thing my mom couldn't see us.

also happen with Jimmy Jack Funk the first time I came to the World Wrestling Federation, and later on with Bret Hart.

Despite my best efforts to pay attention in class and study as hard as I could, I ended up the second semester with another 1.4—but that was only because I hadn't dropped a course that I thought I had. If you took the F out that I received because I didn't fill out the correct paperwork when dropping the class, I would have made the 2.5. I explained the situation to my dad and he understood. He told me that I had lived up to my end of the bargain, and he would set up a meeting with Fred Behrend. My dream of becoming a professional wrestler was about to come true.

3
keep your mouth shut and your ears and your eyes open

If Dad said he was going to do something, he did it. He

called Fred Behrend up, told him how serious I was about

trying to become a wrestler, and arranged a meeting for us to

go down and meet again. This time when we went to see

Fred I felt different. I felt like becoming a wrestler was a real

possibility. I still had no idea what training for this entailed or

how the whole thing would work out, but I felt like I was

going to get an opportunity. We met Fred at his office,

exchanged pleasantries, and cleared up the age issue. I was

going to turn nineteen in a few weeks, so that was no longer

a problem.

Then, in walked a stocky, older-looking Hispanic man. He was about 5'10", with jet-black hair. He wore glasses and had the one big gold nugget ring on his finger. He also had scars all over his forehead. He was wearing jeans with a belt buckle and boots.

"This is Jose Lothario," Fred said, introducing Jose to my father and me. "He can train you."

I had never heard of Jose. He had wrestled for a long time in the area, but by the time I started watching he was mostly involved in behind-the-scenes activities. I introduced myself to him, and we shared a little small talk before Jose got down to business. "I can train you for three thousand dollars," Jose said in his heavy Mexican accent. "I can't guarantee that you will make it, but I will train you."

"All I want is a chance," I answered.

And that's where we left it. He didn't ask me many questions or try to dissuade me from trying to become a wrestler. At this point he didn't know if I could walk and chew gum at the same time, but training me was a chance for him to make some money. It was only after he started to work with me that he realized, "Oh my goodness, I have something here." So we took Jose's phone number, and my dad told him that we would think it over and be in touch. As we were about to leave, Fred asked me if I wanted to go see the World Class show that was in town that night.

My dad was fine with that, so he left to go home, and I went with Fred in his green Mercedes to the HemisFair Arena. On the way there, Fred started talking to me about the business. "There's not bad money in wrestling," he explained. "You can do all right. But you want to know where the real money is? It's in promoting. That's what you ought to do."

I told him I wanted to be a wrestler, and that I didn't care about money. He shook his head and kept telling me that the real money was in promoting and that's what I should get into.

Fred took me backstage that night and I met Kerry Von Erich and some other wrestlers. Boy, did Kerry look big! I didn't get to stay in the back for long, though. They weren't about to smarten me up even a little. I was just some kid with Fred, not a person to whom the business should be exposed.

Fred drove me home after the show, and when I walked in the door, it was obvious to me that my parents had been discussing Jose's offer. Three thousand dollars was a lot of money for us. Once again, my dad gave me the commitment speech. "Are you going to stick to this? You said you would with college, and that didn't work out." He had to sell the trailer to try and recoup some of his money. He didn't want to throw away $3,000.

This is what I *really* wanted to do. I understood it was a big commitment and I was going to see it through. I said, "I will train every day for as long as it takes, if that's what Jose says I need to do." And I would have. The idea of being a wrestler didn't seem so far-fetched anymore. I was chomping at the bit wanting to find out what it was all about.

| | |

Dad ended up taking out a $3,000 loan to pay for my training. He and my mom met with Jose and his wife, Jean. My parents told them how much I wanted to do this and how I needed to find out whether or not I could do it. I was a good kid, they told them. "If he can't do it he'll know, but you need to give him a fair shake." And that's exactly what Jose did.

My father understood that I would not be able to move on with my life if I didn't get to try and become a wrestler. Years later, after I had made it in the business, I asked him why he took out the loan for my training. I was hoping to hear, "I knew you could be the greatest," but what he told me was more meaningful. "Son," he said, "the idea of walking up to you when you were thirty-five with a wife and two kids and having a job you couldn't stand and having you look at me and say, 'You never let me try. I know I could have done that wrestling stuff.' I couldn't live with that. I couldn't have lived with myself if I never gave you that chance."

A few weeks later, Dad gave Jose the money. Jose told me to meet him at one of the tin buildings next to the Joe and Harry Freeman Coliseum that were used as storage facilities. That was where we were going to train, three times a week, until I was ready to move on or quit.

It was the middle of the summer and over one hundred degrees in that tin shed the day I started, but I didn't care. I wanted to wrestle. Jose was already there, and he had brought someone else. He was a big guy named Ken Johnson who was an underneath worker for SWCW. Ken was going to be the guy who did the physical work with me while Jose coached from the outside.

Jose didn't start me off with any kind of big pep talk, lecture, or explanation of what the business was and what training would entail. He was extremely old-school when it came to talking about the business with people who were not in it. His job, as he saw it, was to work me out in the ring, teach me a few basics, and then if I was good enough, I would learn by actually wrestling. This is the way people had broken into the business for years.

I was getting my training in San Antonio, which wasn't a real hotbed of wrestling like Minneapolis, where Ric Flair, Ken Patera, the Iron Sheik, and many others had broken in. Until I came along, Tully Blanchard was the only guy from San Antonio who had made it on the national scene. So, there wasn't anyone to talk to and find out how things worked. Jose was my trainer, and I was going to do whatever he said. I wasn't going to ask a lot of questions—at least in the beginning.

We started off doing Hindu squats. We did maybe twenty-five or fifty. Jose wasn't out to kill me the first day, he just wanted to let me know that this wasn't going to be a walk in the park. After the squats we did some tumbling in the ring. We did four corners around a couple times and then moved on to some hopping exercises. He explained that I was going to need to have good balance in the ring, and he wanted to see how I moved. Our first day of training consisted entirely of exercises and drills.

At our next session he had me run the ropes. He warned me that my back was going to be sore the next day, and boy, was it. When I told him my back was killing me, he chuckled. I think he really got a kick out of that. Welcome to the wrestling world, kid!

Pretty soon, we started going over the basics: proper positioning, takeovers, headlock takeovers, arm drags, and hip tosses. I was taking to it like a duck takes to water, and Jose couldn't believe that I had never done this before. He asked me if I was sure I had never wrestled or trained before. I told him all I had done was fool around with my buddy Kenny.

We never went over punching or kicking. Jose stuck to fundamental wrestling moves. He would stand on the outside of the ring and bark out instructions to Ken and me. If Ken had me in a headlock, Jose would yell, "Shoot him off!" and I'd learn to take tackles and bumps. We also did a lot of drills where I'd learn how to fall.

Ken was a good instructor in the ring. He was fairly physical—what we call snug—but I loved the contact. I loved being physical. The hardest thing about being in the ring with him was that he was hairy and sweaty and it was always so hot in that building. But you get used to that, and there wasn't one aspect of my training that I didn't enjoy. The only thing that was sort of bothering me was that we never worked on—and Jose never explained to me—how you put all these moves together to make a match. We did move after move after move, but I still had no idea how to actually wrestle a match. Jose never smartened me up.

About a month into training I was doing really well and Jose thought I really had a chance to make it. He came up to me and said, "You know something? Only one guy I've ever seen do this in the business. You do this and you be huge. Nobody can do it."

"What's that?" I asked.

"A backflip off the top rope."

I was like, "Are you serious?"

"I know you can do this," he said all excitedly. "You do this and no one can stop you. We work on this next time."

"How are we going to do that?"

"Don't worry, I take care of it."

So the next training session, we went to work on the backflip off the top rope. He told me to climb up on the top turnbuckle and fall backwards. He said, "You fall backwards, you go right over and you land on your feet. Just don't stop, you just keep going, okay?"

I was thinking, "You've got to be kidding," but he put his hands on my butt to give me an extra push, and I fell backwards and flipped over. I landed right on my feet. I got a real charge out of that and climbed back up and we did it three more times. The next time, I did it all by myself. Flipping off the rope reminded me of diving at the pool, and it came rather easy.

After I showed Jose I could do the backflip, he began taking a whole new approach to our training. He stepped it up a notch, and we started working on combination moves and *luchador* sequences. He wasn't teaching me moves now, he was teaching me a style.

Still, we never went over how you put together an actual match. We never went over selling or anything like that. He was concerned only with the physical aspects of working. I assume he thought I would get the other when the boys in the business smartened me up.

| | |

After only two months of training, Jose knew that I was ready to move on. He came up to me and told me that I had the hang of it and that I just needed to get in there and wrestle.

He was still wrestling at the time, working a couple of Fridays a month down in Houston for Paul Bosch, the longtime promoter there. When he wrestled in Houston, I would drive him back and forth. One time, he introduced me to some of the guys from Bill Watts's Mid-South territory, which ran shows in Louisiana, Mississippi, Oklahoma, Arkansas, and parts of Texas. Bill and Paul had some type of arrangement where Bill's guys would work some of Paul's shows in Houston, and a few were there that night.

I didn't know it, but Jose had a relationship with Bill and had probably mentioned me to him. I think Jose wanted to get me around those guys and see how I would react. He wanted to tell them in person that I was a good kid and that they should take care of me when I started working with them. I was completely clueless, though, and had no idea when or if I would go anywhere to wrestle. I had just started training and didn't know that Jose had set the wheels in motion.

Jose was a great teacher and always looked out for me. He was a nice, wonderful man, not that grumpy, mean, aggressive old-timer that you hear about in this business. He really believed in me and he was very encouraging. Only a month into our training, Jose was telling people that I would be a champion some day. However, he didn't say that much about how everything worked. We would talk a little, but mostly he would tell me old wrestler jokes. Whenever I asked how matches were put together or how should I act in certain situations, he would say, "What you need to know, I'll let you know." That was his answer for just about everything.

We did discuss what name I would wrestle under, because Shawn Hickenbottom wasn't going to do. Jose liked the name Shawn Michaels, and he called me that half the time anyway. My mom liked it too. She didn't want me to be somebody that I wasn't. "Don't you dare be Bill Hughes or something like that," she told me. "I gave you those names and you are going to keep them forever!" I wasn't entirely psyched about the name at first. It sounded kind of plain to me, but that might have been because of my dislike for the name Michael. But I had nothing better, so that's the name we decided to go with.

Jose also helped me get my ring attire. He wanted to dress me up like a flashy *luchador* and actually took me down to Mexico to get some fancy boots from a man he knew. Had I been Hispanic, I'm sure they would have been white hot. But I'm a white middle-class kid, and these black boots with a silver snake-skin design looked pretty ridiculous. I wore them once and then I sold them to Brickhouse Brown when I got to Mid-South. They were the ugliest things I ever saw, but Jose sure did love them.

I I I

In the beginning of October, Jose informed me that he was sending me to Mid-South and that I would be starting in two weeks. I was excited. I had wanted this day to come for so long, and now it was finally here. But there was also some trepidation. Would I make it? Would it be everything I dreamed it would be? And more significantly, what was I getting myself into? I still had no clue how anything worked. The business end, the performing end, nothing. His only instructions were, "Keep your mouth shut and keep your eyes and your ears open." When I came home and told my parents, they hit me with a barrage of questions. Where will you live? How much will you get paid? How long will you work there? How will you get to all the towns you will work in? I had no answers. I couldn't just tell them, "I'm going to keep my mouth shut and keep my eyes and ears open." That wouldn't quite cut it.

So I went back to Jose and asked him a bunch of questions. He told me of a hotel in Alexandria, Louisiana, where some wrestlers stayed and where I could get a weekly rate. He explained that I would get paid the week after I started, so I needed to have enough money to carry me through that week. He also told me I would be starting in Lake Charles, Louisiana, on October 16, that the show started at 7:30 P.M., and that I needed to be at the building an hour before the matches were set to start. Those were all the instructions I received.

My folks would have liked to know more, and so would have I, but that was all the information I was going to get. I told them, "We've gone this far and Jose's let me know when I need to know things, so I guess we just have to trust him."

| | |

On October 14, 1984, I set off for Alexandria, Louisiana. I had a duffel bag full of wrestling gear, another bag full of everyday clothes, a 19-inch television, $300 worth of traveler's checks, and not a clue in the world what I was getting myself into.

As I left San Antonio in the copper Toyota Celica hatchback that my dad had given me, I was not dreaming of wrestling Hulk Hogan in Madison Square Garden or Ric Flair in the Omni. My dream was to come back to San Antonio some day, walk through the Windsor Park Mall (our local shopping mall), and have people recognize me and maybe even ask for an autograph. Wrestling in New York and squaring off against Flair was so far beyond my imagination that even the thought of dreaming about this never entered my mind. My more immediate concerns were what was I going to do for the next two days and what in the world was going to happen when I arrived in Lake Charles for my first match.

I was driving into the great unknown. I had never really been on my own before. I don't even remember there being a time when I packed my own bag when I went on a trip. My mom had always done that for me. How does one live on their own, get an apartment, set up utilities, and just live? How would I spend my time? Where would I spend it? I didn't even know enough to ask some of these questions.

More intriguing, and definitely more frustrating, was not knowing how the wrestling business worked. I couldn't visualize my first match, my first trip with the boys, or anything wrestling related. I was two days away from my first match and I had nothing to grasp on to, nothing to occupy my mind, nothing to mentally rehearse and allay my fears. I was scared. Scared and intimidated. Frightened of not having any idea in the world of what to do.

I didn't make it to Alexandria that day. After about four or five hours I pulled over in Beaumont, Texas, and called it a day. I figured a drive like that equaled a good day's work. I paid for a motel room and called home.

"Hi, Mom, it's Shawn."

"Oh, hi, honey. You're in Alexandria already?"

"No, I'm in Beaumont. I think that's pretty good for today. I'm going to sleep here and head on to Alexandria tomorrow."

My mom got a good laugh out of that. She was probably thinking, "C'mon, Shawn, it's only five hours to Beaumont! My boy has no idea what it's like out there in the real world."

I thought it was perfectly reasonable to call it a day in Beaumont. So I ordered a pizza and settled in for the night. When I woke up the next day, the fear of the unknown was still piercing through me. I called Jose and asked him again and again, "What do I do when I get to Lake Charles?"

In his strong Mexican accent, he told me, "You go there. You get to the locker room an hour beforehand. You sit there, you shut your mouth and you open your eyes and you open your ears and you just listen."

"That's it?" I asked one more time.

"You just listen."

"All right."

So I took off from Beaumont and headed to Alexandria, one hundred and fifty miles separating me from a whole new life. I turned the radio on, but all I heard was silence. There was still nothing to grab hold of.

Three hours after I left Beaumont, I pulled into my motel in Alexandria. It wasn't the Ritz-Carlton. It was one of those one-story motels where you drive in under the underhang and pray that the rooms are somewhat clean. It cost me $114 for the week.

I brought my belongings into my room and then sat there for a while trying to figure out what to do next. I didn't think that maybe it would be a good idea to check out the town, find some restaurants, and see if there was a gym I could start training at. I was so naïve. I had no information and no ideas of what to do. I spent the rest of the day at the hotel just trying to pass the time.

My first moment of relief came when I saw Dennis Condrey, who teamed with Bobby Eaton as the Midnight Express, and a guy I would later find out was

Carl Fergie, a referee. Condrey gave me a little wave and I waved back. I don't know if he knew I was the new guy or if he was just waving at some kid. He was a heel and I never really got to know him. In those days, heels and baby-faces didn't travel together and used separate locker rooms. A young rookie like me wasn't going to be hanging out with a successful heel.

Seeing him there did make me feel a little better though. Jose had told me that this was where the guys stayed, so I had envisioned the place being filled with wrestlers hanging out by the pool. Of course, there was no one there when I arrived, so when I saw Condrey, I at least knew I was in the right place.

The next morning I woke up and tried to figure out what to do. I knew I had to be at the building in Lake Charles at 6:30, but that meant that I didn't have to leave until about 4:30. I tried to kill some time in Alexandria, but I just became more and more antsy. I ended up leaving about 1:30 and made it to the building in Lake Charles at 3:30. No one was there. The parking lot was empty and the building was locked.

Desperate to kill some time, I drove around Lake Charles for the next cou-ple of hours, periodically coming back to the arena and sitting in the parking lot. I knew that the wrestlers went in a back door, but I thought there had to be a way, a wrestler way, of parking and entering the building. So I watched from a distance, hoping that some wrestlers would pull up. I figured I would follow them and do what they did.

As the hours slowly ticked by, I became very restless. I was tired of driving around and I had eaten all I could. I just wanted to do *something*. It seemed like forever, but eventually the ring truck pulled up to the building. I went up to one of the crew, told them that I was new, and asked him where to go. He pointed to a dressing room and I went in there and sat by myself for what seemed like an eternity. Occasionally, I'd get up and walk around the building. I watched the crew set up the ring, looked around, and then went back to the dressing room.

Finally a big burly man with a beard, smoking a cigarette, came up to me and asked in a deep voice, "What's your name?"

"Sh-Shawn Michaels," I responded nervously.

"Oh, you're starting tonight. You're Jose's boy. Grizz Smith here." He didn't introduce himself as the agent, the person who was in charge of the show, but I understood that he was an official and at least helped run things. He asked me if I had ever worked before.

"No, sir."

"This is your first match?"

"Yes, sir."

"Your very first one?"

"Yes."

"Okay." He then left and went to check on things in the heel locker room.

A short time later, the wrestlers started coming in. I just sat there quietly. I remembered that Jose did tell me to introduce myself to people, so I prepared myself to do that. These guys were veterans, however, and they could see immediately that I was new. They started to come by and introduce themselves to me. Robert Gibson & Ricky Morton, the Rock 'n' Roll Express, Terry Taylor, Jim Duggan, Magnum T.A. They were very kind, but I was intimidated. They were all such men! They looked like men. I was a nineteen-year-old kid with no hair on my body and plenty of baby fat. These guys had such presence. Even though they were very friendly, I felt like I was a million miles from them.

When I told them that I was going to have my very first match tonight, they all sort of broke out in this inviting grin. I think they were getting a kick out of seeing this young greenhorn get his start. It was getting closer to showtime now, and Grizz came up to me and said, "You are going to be in the first match, and you'll be working with Art Crews. Art's a good kid. You just go out there and listen to him. Art will talk you through it. He'll beat you with a spinning neck breaker."

"Okay." I went back and sat down wondering, "What am I going to do? What am I supposed to do?" This was well before the days when wrestlers went over matches beforehand. You were given a finish and you made the match out in the ring, calling it on the fly. I wasn't going to be able to talk with Art before our match and figure everything out.

Completely clueless about what was going to happen in the ring, I started to get dressed. That's when I had my first experience with ribbing. Despite Jose wanting me to wear flashy *luchador* ring attire, I decided that I would go with a white vest that my mom had gotten me, some white boots, and a pair of black

Ricky Morton & Robert Gibson.

spandex pants. Most guys wore wrestling trunks, but I liked the spandex. The thing was, that's what Ricky and Robert wore. In the wrestling world, you didn't steal someone else's gimmick.

Duggan was in the dressing room and he saw me put on my tights and called out, "Hey, Rock 'n' Roll, we have somebody stealing your gimmick over here."

I was thinking, "Uh-oh. What have I gotten myself into now?"

Ricky heard Duggan and he came over, looked me in the eye, and asked, "You doing the spandex pants?"

"It's all I have," I answered very sheepishly.

He hesitated for a minute before smiling and said, "It's all right, kid." They were just kidding around, having a little fun with the new guy.

So I got dressed, started stretching a little, and then Grizz said it was time. I took a deep breath and headed from behind the curtain and into the arena. There was no entrance music or anything like that, and I remember walking to the ring and the whole building being completely silent. No one knew who I was and I wasn't physically imposing, so people just stared at me.

As I was walking to the ring, a million different things flew through my head at once. "How should I act? What do I do? Why is it so quiet?" It became one big jumble. My mind was completely clouded and overwhelmed.

Despite the uncertainty, I made it down to the ring and climbed up on the apron. Art was already in there and he was introduced first. I saw him raise his arm when the ring announcer called out his name, so I did the same thing. I think two people clapped when I did that. They must have been nice folks who recognized this was my first match and felt like giving the new guy a hand. I then took my vest off, and the bell rang.

Art started circling around the ring, and I followed him. Then he came to me and we locked up. "Take it easy," he told me. His words put me at ease, and we went on to have a very basic match. I was able to get in a lot of offense, hip-tossing and shoulder-tackling him, as well as nailing him with a drop kick. Every time I did something, he would tell me, "Good job." Seven or eight minutes into the match, he stopped me, slammed me a few times, hit me with the spinning neck breaker, and then pinned me. After our match was over, I started to leave the ring and the ref yelled, "Sell your neck, sell your neck." So I grabbed my neck and walked back behind the curtain.

A lot of the guys had been watching, and they couldn't believe that was my first match. Everyone said it awesome. I was ecstatic. I had had my first match, the other wrestlers liked it, and now I had some idea of how things worked.

Terry Taylor even took the time to pull me aside and explain how I needed to show a little more emotion in the ring, how I needed to remember to "fire up," as he called it, when I would make my comeback. Every one of the guys was encouraging and nice.

While I was watching the rest of the matches, Grizz came over and gave me my booking sheet for the next couple of days, and Ricky and Robert asked me if I wanted to ride with them tomorrow to the next show. I thought that was really cool of them, and I said, "Yes." They told me to meet them at the Popeye's in Alexandria, and I don't ever remember riding alone again in the six months I spent in Mid-South. During the drive back to Alexandria that night I stopped and called my parents to tell them how well things went. They were excited for me and told me to keep in touch.

| | |

I met Ricky and Robert at Popeye's the next day and hopped in their car. We shared a little small talk and then I received the "what happens with the boys, stays with the boys" talk. In other words, you don't stooge on a fellow wrestler.

Back then, you took a new guy and you taught him the ways of a wrestler. If you were a partier or a carouser, you said, "That's what I am. Now don't go telling people." It would be wrong to say that it was a code of honor among the boys, because oftentimes it served as an excuse for behaving badly. To me, it seemed that wrestlers had two separate lives: one with each other, and another with the rest of the world.

In the coming weeks, Ricky and Robert would teach me many things while we drove from town to town. This was where I began to learn about the business. This was my classroom. People didn't show up early to arenas and practice like they do now, and there weren't coaches, agents, and writers there to help you out. Just like Jose said, you shut up, observed, and listened to advice from the veterans.

They taught me about ribbing, they taught me verbiage, and a lot of general principles about the industry. And they explained some of the stranger customs that wrestlers observed. One of these customs was chipping in four cents a mile for gas, or "trans," as people in the business called it. Why was it four cents a mile? Probably because some wrestler twenty years before came up with the number and it just stuck. I was learning that's the way a lot of things were. We have many urban legends in this business, a lot of customs and practices that I, and many others, have no idea how they came about.

One of my very first times in Houston.

One practice that I found really unusual, they did have an explanation for. That was the loose handshake. Every time you would see someone you would shake their hand, and ninety-nine percent of the time, guys would give you the limp fish handshake. This was because people shook hands how they worked: loosely. Back then one of the keys to being a good wrestler was to make it look physical out there without actually killing your opponent. That was the art form. Today, most guys just club the heck out of each other.

The soft shake didn't bother me at first, but after a while I couldn't understand why grown men wouldn't shake hands like grown men. Many guys did it without actually knowing the reason for it. It was one of the things the boys did, so that's what they did. I did it for years but it always felt stupid. Then one day when I was in WWE, I thought, "That's just dumb. I'm not going to do that anymore. We're out there beating the heck out of each other and we're shaking hands like this?" Hunter, Kevin Nash, Scott Hall, Kid (Sean Waltman), and I started shaking hands like men with one another. Undertaker was doing it too. The loose handshake turned out to be something that ran its course.

Ricky and Robert, and really all the guys in Mid-South, made me feel comfortable and wouldn't make fun of me when I didn't know something. That second night, I was wrestling Art again. I was told I was "going Broadway." I had no idea what that meant, so I asked what that was. Grizz explained that I was going ten minutes through to the time limit. I was also told that since we were going Broadway, we'd have to do a lot of false finishes. Of course I had no idea what that meant, but they explained that to me as well. It turns out that I did know how to do a lot of things they talked about, I just didn't know the terminology, but no one mocked me for that. They expected me to not be smartened up, and I believe they kind of enjoyed having a curious, decent young guy there. Plus I was a natural in the ring, and I think they saw something in me right from the very beginning.

That second night's match was a lot different than my first match with Art. I felt so much more comfortable and it showed. When I got to the back, they all told me, "Way to go, kid." I was on cloud nine.

Ricky and Robert also saved me from getting in some trouble early on. I had received my booking sheet from Grizz the first night and I saw my name next to a whole bunch of towns, so I figured if my name was next to a town, I would be working there. We shot TV every week in Shreveport, and my name was listed next to the first Shreveport TV booking after my first match. I went there, had my match, and thought everything was fine. I also had a chance to thank Art for all he had done for me in my first few matches. He was kind and very complimentary towards me.

Well, I got my next booking sheet there and my name wasn't listed for the next taping. I figured I wasn't supposed to be there. The day after the taping I went to meet Ricky and Robert at the Popeye's to ride to the next town, and they asked me why I wasn't at the taping.

"My name wasn't on the booking sheet," I said.

"Shawn," they said with their country accents. "You are full-time. Everyone who is full-time's got to go to TV. The guys whose names are on the list are extras who are just being brought in for that one TV."

"I didn't know." Bill Watts fined me $50 for that mishap. It was the first of many fines I would get in my career.

I was so green. The first time I wrestled Jake Roberts during a TV taping I messed up the match. Whenever he put me in a hold, he wrapped his fingers around my wrist or forearm and squeezed. Every time he did this, I yelled and screamed real loud. He eventually beat me with the DDT, and then after the match he came up to me and said, "When I give you the office, you need to reverse it."

"What?"

"You don't know what the office is?"

"Yeah, that's where Bill is. That's where they do administrative stuff."

"No, when I squeeze your arm. That's the office. That means reverse it."

Wrestling with Jake "The Snake" Roberts.

"Oh, I didn't know. Nobody told me."

"Nobody told you?"

"No."

"Well, just ask. Don't be afraid to ask." Then he chuckled and walked away.

After a few weeks of riding with Ricky and Robert, Terry Taylor came up to me and said, "I know you are driving with Rock 'n' Roll, but if you want to ride with me sometime, I'd love to drive with you and help you out." Most people didn't get this when they broke in, but I did. That's why I think Mid-South was the greatest place to start my career. One of the reasons I was able to become so good so fast was because of the way people like Terry Taylor helped me.

Terry was what we called a "white-meat babyface," a young good-looking guy who fought from behind and needed the crowd to support him. I envisioned myself as eventually taking on that role, and looked to Terry for any advice he could give me.

While Ricky and Robert acclimated me to the wrestling culture, Terry helped me understand how to work in the ring. He explained how to be a babyface and when and when not to show emotion. According to Terry, it was important that I experiment and not get lured into being or doing one thing. "Mix it up," he told me. "Instead of you giving the other guy a tackle at the beginning of every match, maybe he gives you one first, then you bounce up like you didn't expect that. Keep the fans on their toes."

"But I'm the babyface. Isn't the babyface always supposed to be better than the heels?"

"Yeah, but you're going to get better. You're going to adjust. He's going to go for that tackle again, but you are going to drop down and when he comes by again, you are going to hit him with a hip toss and then hit him with a tackle and then another one and he's going to fall out of the ring and you are going to fire up and the fans are going to go 'Aaaaaah.'"

Terry had a real passion for the art of wrestling and it showed. I could see it on his face, and I felt comfortable asking him anything. When I was concerned that fans weren't making much noise when I was wrestling, Terry told me not to worry. "They don't know you yet. It's going to take time. Learn the business. Learn how to work. That's the most important thing."

I was wrestling every night and had plenty of opportunities to experiment. And there was no "How does that make me look?" attitude. I wasn't worried about a particular move making me look stupid. I looked at every move within the context of the entire match. Terry taught me to take everything in its totality. It's like scripture: if you take passages out of context, they don't make sense. "Judas went out and hanged himself." That doesn't mean go out and hang yourself.

| | |

Good advice can come from the most unexpected sources, and I listened to everyone in Mid-South. Tony Falk was a job guy and the most through-and-through country bumpkin you ever saw. He was out of shape and balding, but God bless him, he was just the sweetest guy in the world. Tony not only taught me carny—wrestling speak—but he also let me in on the key to the future of this business that no one else was talking about.

I was riding with him one day, and he blurted out, with the biggest country accent I'd ever heard, "We're going to the Shizow."

"What?"

"The Shizow."

"What?"

"You don't know carny? Listen up, Shawn, I've been doing this for a while now and in this business you always talk like that. You don't know carny? You got to learn carny."

I had actually heard it before but never asked about it because I figured someone would eventually tell me what all these z's in the middle of words were. Up to now, everything had been "When I'll need to know, I'll know." Every day was a new revelation, and that's what my mentors said it should be. So right there in the car Tony started teaching me carny, and I finally figured out what those z's were all about.

That wasn't all Tony taught me though. Not long after he introduced me to carny, he enlightened me about the future of the business. "Shawn," he said. "You want to know the future of this business? Working out. This is going to be a body business. In five years, it's going to be all about the body. The hardest work you'll ever do in this business is keeping your body in shape. I'm going to start working out this week. I'm going to start training."

I tried not to laugh when he said this. With his delivery and look it was hard, but I never discounted anything anyone said. The idea made perfect sense. It's not strange to hear someone say, "I've got to start working out this week." It was just hearing *him* saying that. He was so out of shape and the exact opposite of what you think of when you hear "body business." But Tony was right. He knew what he was talking about.

A couple of years later, I saw him in Tennessee. He was just as out of shape as he had been back in Louisiana, but he came right up to me and said, "Shawn, it's a body business just like I told you. And this week, I'm going to start getting in shape."

"Tony, you were right, but you've been saying you're going to get in shape since I first met you." Tony was absolutely priceless. But it just goes to show you that you don't have to be on top to have a good idea or understanding of where things are going, and that it pays to listen to people. Tony was always an underneath guy, but he knew it would be a body business. I guess he just couldn't get off the couch.

| | |

The only person in Mid-South that I had a problem with was "Nature Boy" Buddy Landel. He was a heel, and when I wrestled him for the first time he really beat on me physically. It was the first time that someone had gotten rough with me. After the match, Ricky and Robert asked me what I thought of it, and I said, "I don't know. He sort of beat on me a little bit."

Ricky quickly pointed out, "He ate you up tonight. He was working real snug with you. Wasn't he?"

"Yeah."

"That's Buddy. If you hit him one time, he'll stop. But you got to keep fighting, Shawn. Start fighting with him a little bit and he'll call you a good match."

The next night, sure enough, Buddy waffled me a couple of times. So I started beating on him. I let Buddy know that I wasn't going to sit there and take his punishment. After I hit him a few times, he said, "Easy, kid," and everything went smoothly after that.

In this line of work, you give your opponent your body, and in turn, you take care of him. You don't jerk people around. That's something Ricky and Robert taught me. This is a very serious business, and you don't mess around with another guy's health. Other than that first match with Buddy, I've never had a problem with anyone getting unduly physical in the ring.

I was about five months into my wrestling career now and soaking up every bit of information I could. My matches were fun, even though I was losing all the time, and I was making what I considered to be pretty good money, between $400 and $700 a week. I didn't have many expenses, so that money would go a long way.

Occasionally, I would beat underneath guys like Art Crews, and every once in a while I would go to a draw with a mid-carder like Tim Horner. But I was never higher than the third match, and if I was in the third match, I'd be teamed up with someone like Horner and we would lose to another tag team.

Because I was so low on the card, I didn't get to cut any promos on TV. In order to learn about the verbal aspects of the business, I watched the other guys do theirs. Years later when Bill Watts came to work for WWE, he said that many of the veterans were impressed that a job guy like me stuck around to watch them do their interviews.

However, I did get to do my backflip off the top rope. The first time was when Bill sent me to Dallas to do a quick shot for WCCW. I was working a match against Billy Jack Haynes in the old Sportatorium. He came up to me before we went out and said, "Hey, brother, we're just going to have a match and I'm going to beat you with a full nelson. Is there anything you can do?"

"Don't let guys just beat you up," Ricky, Robert, and Terry had told me. "That doesn't do anyone any good. If a guy beats you too easy, then he's just beaten a nobody and he doesn't look any better for it. It's better if he beats someone who can fight. It makes him look stronger, and it makes you look stronger too. Don't just sit there and take a beating, give the guy a run for his money."

With their words in my mind, I told Billy Jack that I could do a backflip off the top rope. He was like, "Really?" I said, "Yeah." He said, "That's awesome. We need to get that in there." He figured a way to get me up to the top rope within the context of our match, and I did my flip. He may have beaten me with his full nelson, but all the people remembered was my backflip. World Class was on cable and the backflip was new, people weren't doing it.

The second time I did my backflip was special because it was during a match in Houston where I was teamed up with Jose against Chavo and Hector Guerrero. The Guerreros flew around the ring *luchador* style, but we were able to stay with them. It's hard to believe, but in just a few months, I could do a lot. All you had to do was tell me what to do and I would do it. I was comfortable, I was natural, I was smooth. I'm sure Jose was proud of me.

l l l

Not too long after that, Bill Watts had a talk with me. "Shawn," he said in his cowboy accent, "we've enjoyed having you here, but you've done all you can do here. You stay here too long getting beat, and the people are not going to buy you anymore. I'm going to send you to Kansas City [Central States Wrestling] to work for Bob Geigel. He's a good man. Go to the KC office and they'll get you set up there. They'll use you a little bit. You'll learn to win. There's an art to going over too. You just don't win matches. You got to learn how to win matches. You'll have a chance to do interviews. You take a hell of an ass-kicking, kid—if you're not careful, you'll be taking one your whole career."

Not many people liked Bill, but I found him to be brutally fair. He was hard, mean, and rough, but that's what I needed then. And I must admit, that's what I react to better. I think that's why Vince and I had so much trouble. Vince liked me a lot, he loved my passion for this business and things I did moved him. The more it moved him, the more I would push. Vince had a hard time saying no to me. Bill, on the other hand, was a no-nonsense, cold, rough man. He was very rigid. When I tried to get out of that fine for missing TV, Bill didn't budge. "Now you know how it works around here. That's the way it is." I got that. I never missed or was late to a taping again.

Right before I was set to leave for Kansas City, Bill put on a Pay-Per-View show at the New Orleans Superdome. The first *WrestleMania* had just aired, and this was his answer to the competition. It was no *WrestleMania,* but I'd say there were close to 15,000 people there. I was put in a six-man Tag match with

Brad Armstrong and Tim Horner. We beat Thor (Kevin Kelly), Edgar Thomas, and Jack Victory. I think Bill threw me in there as a thank-you for the work I did. It was nice of him.

I did two more shows in Mid-South, a double shot on Sunday in Oklahoma City and Tulsa, before heading off to CSW. My dad drove with me because he was going to help get me settled in Kansas City. We were at the Tulsa show when a young girl approached him. "Do you know Shawn Michaels?"

"He's my son," Dad answered.

"Wow! Do you think you could get his autograph for me?"

"I don't know, because I don't know if I'm allowed to go in the dressing room."

"Then can I have yours?"

"Sure." And he wrote, "Shawn Michaels' father." He still gets a kick out of that today.

After the show, I said my good-byes. The last one was to Terry Taylor. He, my dad, and I were sitting in a bar having a couple of drinks. When I left to ready the car for the drive to Kansas City, my dad stayed to have one more drink with Terry. While I was out, Terry told my dad, "Your boy is going to make it. He's got something special."

Dave Peterson.

4
something is dying
to get out

My dad helped me get set up at a hotel in Kansas City,

and then I went downtown to the Central States Wrestling

office to meet Terry Garvin, an agent who helped Bob Geigel

run the territory. Terry introduced me to Bob, and Bob

signed me to the standard contract. It said: You are going to

work here, we are going to do whatever we want with you,

and you can't do anything to us. I didn't even read my first

couple of contracts. I just signed them. Very few people had

guarantees back then, and if you did, you had to be a pretty

big star. I certainly wasn't going to get one.

My first match was a tag team affair where I teamed with

Dave Peterson against Scott Hall and Danny Spivey. It was in some little town with about twenty-five people in attendance. Since I was the new guy, I let Dave start in the ring. It was pretty funny to watch these guys wrestle. They were just doing random moves in the ring and going nowhere. Dave was a big muscle guy, and he would go down when Scott or Danny hit him, but he'd get right back up. There was no give-and-take. Nobody was selling anything. Nobody was registering. To me, it didn't make sense.

Now, I was green, but I knew how to work by this time. I knew putting on a good match meant telling a story and tapping into emotion. That concept had not even been broached with anyone in the ring. I'm not saying that I saved the match, because all the matches in Kansas City were bad, but I went in there and started calling things and made it passable. The boys were just stunned that I knew how to call a match.

❙ ❙ ❙

Marty Jannetty was the top young babyface in Kansas City. He worked a lot with Bob Brown, who was the booker of the territory. Teaming with Marty was Bob's way of keeping himself on top, and a fairly common practice among aging bookers/wrestlers. If they couldn't make money on their own, they'd make it off someone else. It made perfect sense from their perspective.

I first saw Marty in the locker room, where I introduced myself and shook his hand. Meeting new people was an issue for me, and there was a bit of tension when I walked into the Kansas City locker room for the first time. Even though I had been wrestling for a while, I didn't feel like a member of the fraternity *here*. It was like going into another new school. It doesn't matter how many times you know you'll make friends that first day, the first two weeks are sort of uncomfortable.

In about a week or two, Marty came up to me as I was dressing in the corner of the locker room and he said, "Hey, Dave [Peterson] and I have been talking. We see something in you."

"Thanks."

"Why don't you start traveling with us?"

"All right."

Then he looked at me and said, "There's something in you that's just dying to get out, and we're going to get it out."

I just laughed and said, "Okay." I didn't realize that this was the beginning of something that would forever change me personally and professionally.

In Mid-South, I'd drive back to Alexandria nearly every night after each show. Every now and then I would hear stories about guys going out, but I wasn't into that. With Dave and Marty, I now started to go out to bars after shows. I was only nineteen and sometimes I would be denied entry at the door, but Dave and Marty didn't care. They would leave and we'd go find a place I could get in. I didn't get busted very often though, because there was something about Marty that made me carry myself differently. He had a presence about him, and when I was with him, I had it too. If I tried to get into a bar by myself, you could just look at me and tell I was under twenty-one. When I walked in with him, I stood taller, looked more confident, and was rarely stopped by a bouncer. It wasn't that Marty was so old—he was only about five years older than me. It was simply the way he presented himself. It wasn't until years later that I finally realized that Marty was as much of a clod as any of us. He really didn't have anything under control. It just appeared that he did, sort of like my friends in high school who acted as if they knew everything.

We really didn't do anything crazy. (It was nothing compared to what we would later do in the AWA and WWE.) For me, it was my first time experiencing going out with the boys and having fun. None of us had any real responsibilities. Marty and Dave had girlfriends, so if we had to get back to Kansas City after a show, we did. But if we were wrestling a hundred miles out of town, we'd split a room, go out, and have some fun.

We worked seven shows a week and traveled all over Missouri, Iowa, Kansas, and sometimes Nebraska or Illinois for a spot show. When we were driving from town to town, we talked wrestling all the time. Marty had a passion for the business, as I did, and we did the best we could to smarten each other up.

| | |

Ric Flair had been my idol since I first saw him on television as a high school kid, and I actually met him while I was in Kansas City. He came in to defend his NWA

World Championship against Harley Race. I saw him at the arena, and I was like "It's Ric Flair!" He looked exactly like he did on television. His suit, the gold watch—he looked like a champion. Since there were separate dressing rooms for heels and faces, I didn't get to see him that much. I just passed him in the hallway and got the "Hi" and the handshake.

I watched his match and then headed to Diana's, a local bar. I was standing around with a few of the guys when Ric came in. He walked up to the bar and sat down. That's when I strolled over to him and said something like, "Good match tonight." I didn't give him the "I think you are the greatest of all time" stuff. I didn't want to sound like a big mark.

He said, "Thanks," and then asked if I wanted a beer.

"Yes, sir. That would be great," I said.

He bought me a beer, and then I went back to the group of guys I was hanging out with. I don't ever remember getting a bill that night. None of us did, and we drank all night, and Ric picked up the tab for all of us. That's the way he was: everything is on The Naitch, Whoooo!

One night, near the end of my stay in the territory, Marty and I wrestled together in a Tag match against Scott and Danny. We had never worked as a team before, but everything came together when we were out there. It was one of those things where you just say, "Wow! That felt nice. We really clicked." Sometimes you get in the ring with someone and it feels like a complete struggle. Then there are other times you know there is some magic going on. That's how I felt with Marty. We jelled. Our timing was in synch and we didn't have to think about what our next move should be. We knew what the other one wanted to do.

| | |

After only a couple of months in CSW, Jose called and asked me to come back to San Antonio. The Blanchards had sold Southwest Championship Wrestling, and Jose and Fred Behrend were booking and promoting what was now called Texas

All-Star Wrestling. He said they wanted me to be the "hometown boy" and that I was going to work on top with a $500-a-week guarantee.

Money was tight in Kansas City. I made anywhere from $250 to $350 per week. If I had a match in St. Louis, I earned a little more because that was the one town where we drew a bigger house, but even then, I still wasn't doing as well as I did in Mid-South. Five hundred dollars a week was a great deal, so I gave Geigel my two weeks' notice and said my good-byes. Back then, that's all you had to do. You gave two weeks' notice, put guys over on the way out, and headed on down the road.

Saying good-bye to Kansas City was not that big a deal. Even saying bye to Marty, who I had spent a fair amount of time with, wasn't difficult. We hadn't developed the kind of relationship where you got past the surface. In fact, it wasn't until I was in my late thirties and he was in his forties that we talked like men. It was just good-bye and see you later. There was no intimacy at all.

I had only been in the business nine months and I now was coming home to work on top and on television. I was ecstatic. In my mind, I had come a long way in a pretty short period of time. Looking back now, I realize that I had only made it to level 1 in this business. At that time, I felt like I had made it all the way. I was working on top in a territory. What could be better? Soon I figured I would get the reputation of being a top guy and would be able to travel from territory to territory, always working on top.

To show how far I had come, I decided to drive back to San Antonio all by myself. My folks offered to fly up and drive back with me, but I wanted to show them that I could do it on my own, so I turned down their offer. I made it in one day—fourteen hours of No-Doz and coffee. It was a really cool ride. I was at peace, there was a sense of accomplishment. I couldn't wait to walk through the Windsor Park Mall.

5 half a wrestler

At this point in my career, I wasn't aware of the politics

that engulfed this business. It wasn't unusual to put a young,

good-looking guy on top, but I wouldn't have had this spot if

it hadn't been for my connection with Jose, and Fred

Behrend for that matter.

They tried their best to hype me as something special.

In the little program they wrote up, they called me the

Dwight Gooden of wrestling. Jose and Fred told me to call

up all the people I knew and have them come to my first

TV taping. "We want all those people with signs," Fred

said. Well, I scraped up about fifteen folks and they all

came to the little studio where we shot TVs. My family was there, as were Scott Marie and Gavin. They had these simple signs where they had scribbled "Welcome Home Shawn," with a crayon or something. It was brutal.

We taped our weekly show at a place we called the Junction. It was next to the Blanco Café, and it probably seated seventy-five people. They had the ring and a little platform where you did interviews and they commented on the matches, and then maybe three rows of seats, two on the side where the hard camera was. This was the same place they taped SWCW, but I had never gone to see a TV taping during my high school years. It was a million miles from a *Raw* set, but at the time it seemed pretty cool to me.

I beat a Mexican extra in my first match. This was the first time I ever came out with entrance music. It was some slow hoedown tune—it wasn't good. The plan was for me to be a cowboy. Of course I didn't have any cowboy gear—I was wearing some blue tights that Terry Taylor had given when I wrestled in Mid-South—but it was San Antonio, and being a cowboy seemed like the thing to do. I had a lot of fun out there. The small crowd was yelling for me. They were holding their signs up for the cameras, and the hometown guy won. I was off to a very good start.

| | |

Chavo Guerrero was the top heel, and unbeknownst to me, very shortly after I arrived, he had pushed Jose out of his booking position. He came up to me and said, "We are going to get you over big-time." Hearing those words made me feel great. I didn't realize Chavo was just blowing smoke up my rear end.

Very shortly after my first match, I was set to wrestle him at the Freeman Coliseum. In the wrestling business, "We are going to get you over" means you are going to work with this top heel. But what Chavo decided was going to get me over was to go to a thirty-minute draw. I was fine with that. I didn't understand that I was getting the shaft. Obviously, I knew winning was much better than losing, but I didn't know that going to a draw was not necessarily good. You didn't ask, or I certainly didn't ask, "Where are we going with this?" I didn't know any of that. You did what you were told to do that night and that's what you knew.

So when I was told we were going thirty minutes through, I didn't complain. That was the longest I had gone to that point. I was excited. It was halfway to an hour, and at that time in the business, going an hour was, at least in my mind, what made you a wrestler's wrestler. So I was half a wrestler's wrestler, and that was great. It wasn't till after the fact that I understood that what Chavo did wasn't going to get me over.

Years later, I would laugh about it with him. It's the whole wrestling promoter's way: We're going to get you over, make you look like a million bucks. "Am I going over?" No, but . . .

At the next TV, I was put in a tag team with Paul Diamond, and at the following one, Chavo turned babyface. So much for my singles run on top. That was the bad news. The good news was that I would be teaming with Paul, a former professional soccer player who had played with the Tampa Bay Rowdies in the NASL. Paul was 6'1", 220 pounds, about the same size as me but leaner and more cut. I was still carrying some baby fat. Paul lifted, trained, and helped clue me in on the ways of taking care of my body. He was a good worker too, and we clicked well from a tag team perspective. And like me, Paul enjoyed talking about the business.

Here I am with Paul Diamond doing a backflip.

We were called the American Force and we won our first championship by acclimation: Chavo and Al Madril, a seasoned veteran who was in the twilight of his career, gave us the titles. So much for a big victory in your first championship. Paul and I didn't really care though. We liked wrestling, and having the titles was neat. We lost the championship to the Hoods, Ricky Santana & Tony Torres, about three weeks after Chavo gave it to us, but Chavo soon moved out and a man named Gary Hart came in to book. He was really into Paul and me, and he made us the number one tag team again.

Life wasn't bad. Was I wrestling singles? No, but I was getting my $500 guarantee, and most importantly, I was learning, working good matches, and having fun. Paul and I learned lots of tag team basics, combination moves, quick tags, stuff that Marty and I would eventually take to another level. I was learning the science of tag team wrestling.

Besides riding with Paul, I also rode with Al Madril. Al taught me two important things: wrestling psychology and an appreciation for Elvis Presley. To the untrained observer, Al could appear quite lazy in the ring, and I guess to be fair, he was. However, he could get a lot of mileage out of not doing that much. In Mid-South, everything was pretty much giddy-up and go. Al worked much slower. If Ricky Morton threw five punches, Al would throw one. He pulled people's hair a lot and worked methodically. He was over, though, and didn't have to do that much to stay popular. I couldn't apply what Al was teaching me then because I was a young guy on the rise, but I can now. That's one of the aspects I love about this business: there's something to learn in everything. I don't think that there's such a thing as bad advice, only advice that won't work at a certain point in time.

The best thing Al did for me was get me interested in Elvis Presley. He was a huge fan and played Elvis tunes in the car all the time. Riding down the back roads of South Texas, I hardly could have imagined that Elvis, or more significantly, Graceland, would end up playing an important role in my personal life many years later.

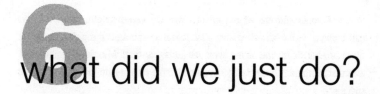

what did we just do?

When I first came back to San Antonio, I lived with

my parents. That was fine, but after a while my dad

brought up the point that I had saved some money, about

$5,000, and needed to invest it. He also pointed out that I

would probably be happier having a place of my own. He

said renting an apartment was a waste of money and

suggested I take the money I had saved and put a down

payment on a little house. That way I would have

somewhere to live, save money on taxes, and build up some

equity in the house.

It made perfect sense to me, so I bought a little house

in San Antonio and moved out on my own. I was just twenty years old and had a house with a waterbed and a TV. It was sweet. And to top things off, my older brother Scott was living with me. Imagine that! My older brother was a tenant of mine. To the outside world, I must have really looked like a real success.

I was working seven days a week and didn't have much time to hang out with my old high school buddies or make new friends away from wrestling. I was starting to get lonely. No matter where we wrestled—we even went as far as Odessa, which was six or seven hours away—I would always come home to San Antonio for the night. When I came home, I had nothing to do and no one to be with.

I told my mom that things would be better if I had a girlfriend, and one day she said, "What about the Wood girl? What about Theresa? She was always a sweet girl."

The Woods were family friends, and I vaguely remembered Theresa. The last time I saw her was two years before, when she was only fourteen. She would have been sixteen now but was still in high school. I didn't know if it was okay for me to be dating a sixteen-year-old. My mom told me it was fine. She and Joan, Theresa's mom, had obviously been discussing this. I asked Theresa out. We went to the movies and started dating.

Theresa would come to shows with me, but I never brought her in the back. No one brought their girlfriends backstage in those days, so she sat out in the arena before and during the shows. She didn't mind. She was pretty enthralled with me. I was quite a catch for a high school girl; and, I was thrilled to be with her. She was a sweet young lady, a terrific girl.

We had been seeing each other for a couple of weeks and Christmas was coming up. My mom asked me, "What are you going to get Theresa for Christmas?"

"I don't know."

"What would you like to get her?"

"I don't know."

"What about a ring?"

A ring sounded like a great idea. Jewelry was big in the wrestling business.

A lot of the guys had big nugget rings and bracelets, and their wives had nice things. Since wrestlers had nice things and I was a wrestler, I wanted to have nice things and I wanted my girlfriend to have them too.

"How about a diamond? You want to get her a diamond?"

"Sure, that's great." I had absolutely no clue what I was about to do.

I gave Theresa a diamond ring on Christmas day. She cried when she got it. I probably would have too had I known what I was doing.

My mom blurted out, "Oh my goodness, they are engaged!"

"Huh?"

To this day, my mom can't believe that I didn't know that giving Theresa the diamond ring meant getting engaged. I guess I was that clueless, because I was not thinking about marrying Theresa at the time. I just wasn't a very complex or thoughtful person. If my mom said, "Shawn, turn right," I turned right. If she said, "Why don't you get her a diamond ring?" I bought her a diamond ring. I honestly didn't know you only bought someone a diamond ring when you planned on getting engaged.

Then someone asked us when we were getting married. We sort of looked at each other because both of us were like, are we doing this? We thought fairly quickly and said that we weren't going to set the date, that I just wanted to let her know that she was the one. This was a promise ring.

Later that night Theresa and I discussed what had gone on, but we weren't mature enough to know what was right. She was still in high school and I was a pretty clueless twenty-year-old. We certainly had feelings for each other. Was it love? Neither of us knew, and neither of us had anything to compare it to. No one was asking us all the questions that needed to be asked: Are you sure? Have you thought about this?

Everyone figured we were engaged. I figured we were still boyfriend and girlfriend. She still lived at her parents' house. I'm not saying it all makes sense. I'd like to go on record saying it's been a crazy ride. Believe me, I've looked at my parents and asked them what in the world they were thinking, why they didn't say something. But they didn't, and for better or for worse, Theresa and I were embarking on a very strange, and in many ways unfair to her, relationship.

| | |

Meanwhile, on the wrestling front, things were about to pick up. Paul and I were having a nice run as American Force, but Jose thought my career was stagnating. Even though he had been edged out from a powerful position in the company, he was still aware of the politics that were going on in the promotion.

Jose was magnificent. Not too long after I came back to San Antonio, Fred Behrend wanted to become my agent. That wasn't what Fred called it, but he wanted to take ten percent of me. Fred was going to get me all the places I wanted to be. All I had to do was sign a piece of paper and give him ten percent. Jose told me not to do it, so I didn't. Jose was always looking out for me. He would let me learn and struggle, but when the time was right, he let me know it was time to move on. Jose didn't make a huge deal of the situation or tell me that I was being screwed out of anything. He just said it was time to go. One thing Jose didn't do was stir things up.

He told me we needed to put a tape together and send one to the World Wrestling Federation and one to the American Wrestling Association. Those were the places I needed to be. We knew the Rock 'n' Roll Express and a ton of young babyfaces were wrestling in the National Wrestling Alliance and I wouldn't have much of a chance of getting in there. So we made the tapes and sent them to the two other big organizations.

The AWA called back and told Jose they wanted me. They were losing a lot of their wrestlers to Vince, so they were desperate for talent. I was going to leave, but first I had to have a talk with my partner, Paul. When I told him I was leaving, he was a little hurt about being left behind, but he understood. I wanted to become a singles wrestler. That was my goal in going to the AWA. I had no idea that they wanted to put me in another tag team. Everything with Paul was on the up-and-up. It was a chance to work for a much bigger company on a much bigger stage. He knew I had to go.

Paul was a good wrestler and he eventually came up to the AWA while I was there. He teamed with Pat Tanaka and they did very well. He also came to WWE later on and worked as Cato in The Orient Express. Marty and I worked with him several times and enjoyed every minute of it.

7
rockin' to the dawn

Going to the AWA was a real step up. It wasn't the

World Wrestling Federation, but it was definitely a lot bigger

than Texas All-Star Wrestling, and it had national exposure

on ESPN. Jose kept telling me that if I wanted to make it

really big I had to get on cable. This was a huge break for

my career.

When my dad found out that the AWA was on ESPN, he

realized I was taking it up a notch and suggested that I lease a

new car. He was my financial adviser, and just like when he

told me to buy the house, he pointed out all the benefits of

leasing a car: I wouldn't have to make a huge down payment,

and I could write off my monthly payments. I ended up getting a maroon 300ZX T-top. The payment was about $300 a month, which fit within my budget. I didn't have a guarantee, but they told me that I was going to make something like $500 or $600 a week. The only other fixed expense I would have would be rent when I got up to Minneapolis. I was twenty years old, a wrestler, and driving a 300ZX. I thought I was pretty darn cool.

The AWA was centered out of Minneapolis. Verne Gagne, a former Olympic wrestler, had started it back in 1960, and it had been an institution in the upper Midwest ever since. Superstar Billy Graham, Ric Flair, and many others had come through the territory. Hulk Hogan made his name there before Vince snatched him up and revolutionized the business by going national just a little before I started wrestling in Mid-South. When I arrived in the AWA, it was definitely on the decline, but it was still considered one of the big three along with the World Wrestling Federation and the NWA. In my mind, this was a territory where you wrestled. It was old-school and cool. I was going to be around a whole new slew of talent, and I looked forward to mining their vast knowledge of the business.

Although Verne ran the company out of Minneapolis, the television tapings were held in Las Vegas, Nevada, at the Showboat casino. That's where I was being flown for my first match. It was the first time I had ever flown for business.

Ray Stevens met me at the airport and took me to the Showboat, where I dropped off my bags and then met with Greg Gagne, Verne's son, who was pretty much running things by this time. It was an informal meeting. Greg explained a few things to me and then I signed my contract. It was the same old standard contract that said I was guaranteed nothing and they could do what they wanted with me.

After meeting with Greg, I decided to take a walk through the casino. It was my first time in one, and technically, I wasn't old enough to be in there. I was walking through an area where they had a lot of slot machines and bumped right into Marty, who was sitting there pulling on a one-armed bandit. I sat down next to him and we caught up with each other, just small talk. After a couple minutes he took off and I decided to give the machines a try. I put three quarters into the machine he was playing and hit the jackpot. I made $750 my first day in Vegas. I told him what happened a bit later when I saw him and he was a good sport about it. He was very happy-go-lucky at the time.

Because I knew Marty, I felt a little less nervous in the locker room that day than I was on my first days in Mid-South and Kansas City. There were also a lot of extras there, one of whom I was going to beat. I knew that they were even more uncomfortable than me and that made me feel a little better.

The little nervousness that I had came from the fact that I always felt I was the youngest guy in the dressing room. Just like in Mid-South, everyone here seemed like such men. Even a guy like Curt Hennig, who was only seven years older than me, seemed like a real man. He carried himself differently than I did. His dad was a Minneapolis wrestling legend, and he looked liked he belonged with the other men there, such as Nick Bockwinkel, Buddy Rose, Doug Sommers, Boris Zukov, and Sheik Adnan.

Plus, I looked really young. We'd come back to Vegas every three weeks for the TV taping, and I'd get kicked out of the casino sometimes because I wasn't twenty-one. I eventually became good friends with a lady who ran the casino and I'd tell her, "I'm old enough to wrestle, I ought to be able to have a drink."

My match that first night against an extra went smoothly, as did everything else. About the only other thing of interest that happened was that Marty came up to me and told me I needed to do something about my short hair. I started growing it out that night, and I've kept it long ever since.

I I I

I wasn't sure what Greg and Verne had planned for me when I first came to the AWA. They had mentioned singles, and they had also inquired if I knew Marty. I guess they had some ideas of putting me with Marty. They were definitely going to do something with me, because they knew I could work. You never knew for sure though. There weren't any "for sure's" in the wrestling business. I was coming back to Texas to be on top and have a glorious singles career in my last stint, and I ended up being in a tag team.

After only two singles matches, Verne told Marty and me that he wanted us to be a team. I think they were thinking that we could be their version of the

Rock 'n' Roll Express. That was the first time I met Verne. Marty and I went down to his office to meet him to discuss our name, our image, and what we wanted to do.

Verne was not a big fan of young wrestlers. He was very much into the old, old-school style where guys mostly mat-wrestled. He was not happy that the business was taking a more entertaining than sports turn, but he recognized that he was losing talent. In his eyes, Vince was stealing all his talent that he got over. He seemed to be a frustrated man.

The first thing he wanted to know about me was if I had any amateur experience. I told him about my brief stint in high school. He sort of grunted and then asked if we had any ideas for our team.

Before this meeting, Marty and I had talked about teaming up and what we might do. I had moved into the same apartment complex where he was living, and we talked wrestling all the time. Greg Gagne wanted to call us the Country Rockers. After thinking about it, we both agreed that didn't work. I was still listening to my Judas Priest at that time, and really dug a song of theirs called "Living After Midnight." I told Marty this was the perfect music for us and maybe we should call ourselves the Midnight Rockers. I played the song for him and he thought it was cool. I was so into it. I was telling him you have to listen to the words, we are going to live this thing and we are going to do it.

Then we started to think about what we would wear. At the time, Marty was wearing long tights with fur tiger stripes, and a tiger stripe around his boots. I liked that and told him that's what we should go with. We were a little concerned that we might be seen as blatantly stealing from the Rock 'n' Roll Express, but we reasoned that since they wore spandex and didn't wear the tiger stripes, we were okay—right!

We told Verne what we had come up with, and I will never forget his response. If you ever want to know why Verne went out of business eventually, all you have to do is keep reading. "Do you think the people are going to confuse that name with rocking chairs?" he asked.

Marty and I were stunned. We looked at each other and said, "I don't think so." Verne just didn't get it. Then there was a minute of silence. We looked at each other again. Was he working us? Is he that big of an idiot? We walked out of the office, thinking, "How did he get rocking chairs out of that?" Verne's ques-

Me and Marty.

tion marked a turning point in my career. I began turning away from older guys, reasoning that they didn't understand us or where the business was going. There was a *huge* generation gap.

I felt badly for Greg during the meeting. Greg understood, but I think he was torn between doing things his dad wanted and knowing that they had to change with the times. It must have been a difficult time for him.

Marty and I started a short time later, and I have to admit that the first time we came out to our music, I felt a bit awkward. Marty could get out there and pump up the crowd and dance. He was already doing the "I'm pretty cool" gimmick. I couldn't dance, and I had always been the white-meat babyface. I remember being all over wanting to come out to the music, but when it first came on and I had to go to the ring, I felt like I had two left feet.

The awkwardness made me realize that there was more to wrestling than just working in the ring. I had to get into my character. It wasn't an epiphany where all of a sudden I started concentrating on absolutely every single detail of my presentation, but it planted a seed that I would cultivate later on. That night we wrestled a couple of extras and won. They were a little difficult to move around, and the match was just okay. We'd have very few "just okay" matches in the future.

||| |

Marty and I worked a couple of enhancement matches and then started wrestling with the regulars like Zukov & Adnan and Rose & Sommers. We didn't have a program with anyone, but people were coming out to see us. We were changing the face of tag team wrestling.

At this time, tag team wrestling was basically two guys who tagged in and out of a match. The only thing that made it different from singles was that there were four guys wrestling instead of two. No one linked move after move after move. Marty and I did. We executed lots of double moves and interwove them constantly throughout the match. Instead of just one of us leapfrogging our opponent when he dropped down, both of us did. Instead of single elbows, we gave double elbows. Sometimes teams would shoot somebody in and do a double hip toss. Well, we decided to do a double hip toss, a double elbow, and a double nip up and then punch the guy. Then as this guy was standing back up, we'd punch him again. We even did a double dropkick off the top. There's a lot of risk of getting injured and missing the move, but we didn't care. We wanted to tear the house down every night. We also did a little suplex maneuver where I would be suplexing one of our opponents and Marty would jump off the top rope and body-press the guy as I had him up in the air. There wasn't any aspect of working that we couldn't double, or combine after a little thinking.

We also utilized the five count. In technical terms, you have a five-second window after you tag to get out of the ring. We'd start tagging in the middle of moves so that we could legally have two guys in the ring. I'd tag Marty, shoot my opponent in and drop-toe-hold him. He'd stay down and Marty would drop an elbow on him. By today's standards, it's not real complicated, but this was fairly new back then. We were fast and in constant motion. There was no down time. With four people in the ring, there's no reason for the action to stop. Even from a psychology standpoint it makes more sense for a match to have a fast pace to it when there are four guys out there. Some people complained that we were doing too much, highspotting, but everything we did flowed within the story we were telling in the ring. We weren't doing crazy moves just to do them. Besides the athleticism, there was a real art to what we were doing. It wasn't that hard on our opponents either. We did most of the running. All they had to do was stand or lie there and take it.

Our work resulted in some newfound publicity. *Pro Wrestling Illustrated* wrote an article on us, and they used an inset picture of us on the cover. The title read "From Imitators to Innovators." It was an acknowledgment that we were not just ripping off the Rock 'n' Roll Express, but had developed a whole new style. That article was a very big deal. It told us, "We're making it."

I believe that Marty and I had a huge, if not the biggest, effect on tag team wrestling during that period and maybe ever. For all the screwing up we were doing outside the ring, we worked really hard inside. When we traveled up and down the road together, we spent countless hours trying to come up with new moves. We watched tape when we weren't on the road, and we were always writing ideas down. I don't want to give the impression that we were the tag team version of Ric Flair. It wasn't like it got over like gangbusters right away, but we did pretty well, and we were the only ones we knew of that were wrestling this style.

| | |

"Pretty Boy" Doug Sommers and "Playboy" Buddy Rose were the tag team champions. Both of them could bump around real well and were very good workers. Buddy was the ring general, and Marty and I learned a lot from him. Sherri Martel was their manager. She was great, just a super person.

When we started working with them, it wasn't one of those things where someone told us about this big program we were going to have. Back then it was, "You are going to work with these guys and we'll see what happens." Well,

Sherri Martel, Marty, Ed Wiskonski (Col. DeBeers), me, and Buddy Rose.

we ended up having a really good TV match with them. People now refer to it as *The Showboat Bloodbath*. Originally, we were going to do the old story where they beat Marty up in the parking lot, sort of like what I had seen with Ricky Morton and Tully Blanchard back in SWCW. Instead, we decided to get color in the ring. Everyone bled except for Buddy, and they bloodied us up pretty good. The match ended in a DQ. We went nuts, they went nuts, and we received a lot of national exposure because it was on television. It was rare to see blood on national TV, and even rarer in the AWA. Verne was very conservative.

This match showed that Marty and I had some fire and toughness. Up until this point, we were perceived as a cute little gimmick, a little bubble gummish. They'll draw the girls. They have a good spot on the card, and they have good matches. But, can they really mix it up with the big guys? That was the one question mark about us, and the *Bloodbath* showed that we had the mettle to become champions.

We thought we were going to do the parking lot scene for the next TV and then win the titles. Ricky Steamboat had once rubbed his face real hard with a towel—it's sort of like rubbing sandpaper against your skin—to produce a nice shiner. Marty decided to do this for the parking lot brawl and scuffed himself up real good. Then Verne, or Buddy, or whoever was calling the shots, decided not to do the scene. Marty still has the scar from that rubbing, and we ended up chasing those guys for the title for almost a year.

Despite not winning the titles, we were hot now, and our feud with Buddy and Doug was hot. We sold the Showboat out with a Cage match and drew most places we went, but we couldn't get the belts. Buddy and Doug realized they could keep themselves on top by working with us, so they strung out the chase as long as they could. We finally beat them in Minneapolis at a house show on January 27, 1987.

After all the chasing, winning the titles was a little anticlimactic. The fans had waited so long that our feud lost its edge, and they also would rather have seen us win on TV in the Showboat. We were very popular in Vegas, and it was our home crowd. We drew money with Buddy and Doug everywhere we went, but especially at the Showboat. When we started, the place was a quarter, maybe half full. By the time we were done with our program with those guys, the place was sold out. Now, sold out was probably 2,500 people, but that was a marked improvement over what they had been doing. This was the first time both of us could say we drew money.

| | |

Marty was a big ribber. He never stayed still and was always up to something. I actually wasn't that big a ribber, but I was his partner, and for the eight years I was with Marty, we were the Rockers. There was no individuality. I don't mean to imply that I was lily white. I enjoyed the ribs and probably would have done more if I had been better at pulling them off. I just wasn't that good at it, certainly not as good as Marty or Curt Hennig or Scott Hall.

Marty loved to pull ribs on the office. We would do interviews during the week in Minneapolis and whenever Larry Nelson (our announcer) would finish an interview, he would put the microphone down. Marty would then go over and disconnect the mike from the cord. Larry would come back to do another interview, and of course his mike wouldn't work. Larry never varied his routine, and Marty pulled the cord out every time. It's not that big a deal once, but after so many times, Larry would go, "C'mon! Jannetty! Rockers, stop it!" He'd do it every week, and every week we'd be laughing till it hurt.

We also liked to get Greg Gagne. Greg wrote with a pencil, and whenever he'd put one down, we'd take it and hide it. He'd bring out another one, and we'd take that too once he put it down. One day we got Greg so hot, he brought a whole big stack out. But we were determined, and we ended up taking all of his pencils, sharpening them down to half-inch nubs, and frustrating the heck out of Greg.

Most of our fun was very sophomoric. Marty and I had these crazy sunglasses that we wore as part of our gimmick. Every time we would do an interview, we'd put the glasses down. When we'd come back, Scott and Curt would have put a big lock right in the middle of the glasses. We kept having to break the glasses and put them back together again and again.

Hennig was big on locks. He'd put a padlock on everything. One time in Sioux Falls, Marty and I were on last. When Scott and Curt were on last, Marty would hide their bags. This time Hennig saw an opportunity for revenge. We came back after our match and couldn't find our bags. It turns out Curt and Scott had chained them to the pipes above the dressing room, and we had to get someone to cut them free.

All these pranks came naturally to Marty. He didn't have to think about it that much. There were times when I would be hanging out in the back and I'd hear Curt and Scott start cussing because he hid their bags. I didn't even know he did it. Everyone was always grilling me about what happened and I would honestly say, "I don't know." They wouldn't believe me. "You guys are too much," they'd say. I spent a lot of years saying, "I don't know." I'm not sure if people thought I was just lying.

One night in Milwaukee, Curt got Nick Bockwinkel pretty good. Nick wore these big old glasses that he actually needed to see. While he was out wrestling, Curt put a lock right in the middle of them. It's one thing to do it to our sunglasses, but it's another to put one on someone's real glasses. We wondered what he was going to do on the four-hour ride home, and we laughed, imagining him sitting in his seat and holding the lock up with one hand while he drove. Nick had to know that it was one of the four of us who did it, but he wasn't confrontational. He'd say something like, "Ah, Marty, very good, boys, very classy. We're all mature here. Way to go, very good."

If the padlock on the glasses was a borderline thing to do, what Marty did to Nick not so long afterwards definitely crossed the line. Curt had been AWA Champion and he was our friend. He deserved it and was doing well, but Nick wanted the title back and he got it from Curt.

It was about this time that Buddy Rose and Curt started teaching us about wrestling politics. We were now very anti-office. When we heard Nick wanted the belt back, we were like, "They're keeping us down! They are out to screw us!"

Of course, I had no basis for my complaints. But I had gone down the path of bitterness. I was going to complain about everything now. Verne wasn't a good guy to work for, and he was a mean-spirited man. I didn't have much interaction with him, but the few times I did, it wasn't very positive.

So we were angry now, and Marty decided to do something for Curt. It was wintertime, and we were doing our Wednesday promos in Minneapolis. Nick was there, and after he had finished a set of interviews, he set the championship belt down and walked away. Marty picked up the belt, rushed to the side door of the studio, and proceeded to heave it behind some bushes and into five feet of snow. When Nick came back and couldn't find his belt, he started complaining. Nick and Greg Gagne went right to Marty and told him in no uncertain terms that he better give the belt back.

Marty claimed that he hadn't done anything and didn't know what they were talking about. I hadn't actually seen him do it. So when they asked me about it, I told them I didn't know what happened. I asked Marty later if he had done it, and he 'fessed up. I think everyone knew Marty did it because no one else would have done something like that. However, he was never fined or suspended because nobody could prove anything.

No one ever found that belt, and Nick had to go around for at least a month as the champion with no belt. I think it made Curt feel good, though, because every night for a while Nick would walk out without the belt. I would like to make clear that stealing Nick's belt was wrong. The glasses were okay, but the belt was bad for business. When you do something that is bad for business, it's not a rib. We were so into "sticking it to the man," we didn't distinguish between the two, and that was wrong.

Nick will probably read this and think we had some vendetta against him, but we didn't. I didn't, at least. I had a great deal of respect for Nick. He helped me in many ways, including making sure that I worked for everyone in the arena, not just the people in the front row.

"You do stuff that is good," he said, "but you have to remember that guy up there in cheap seats may not be able to see real well. You have to overexaggerate a little bit. You may not be wrestling in front of many people now, but your goal is to wrestle in front of a sold-out place. You have to work as if you are there now, like there are people up in those seats."

Nick was helpful, but I have to say, when everyone decided that we were not likable, he joined in and became very condescending towards us. I didn't do anything to him. I just wasn't going to turn in my partner.

Sticking together no matter what was one of the things that Marty and I discussed when we started teaming together. We decided not to be like everyone else. We were going up together, we were going down together. Whatever happened, we would stick together. And considering all we were about to go through, we stayed together for a very long time.

| | |

Buddy Rose taught me a lot while I was in the AWA—some of it good, some of it not so good. He sort of indoctrinated me into the "screw the office" mentality. When business started slowing down in cities like Chicago because most wrestling fans were going to see Vince's shows, our payoffs started to drop drastically. At one point, we were only getting $100 for working there. We had to drive eight hours to Chicago, stay over, and then drive back to Minneapolis. Then they'd want us to work somewhere the next day. Economically, it didn't make any sense.

One day Buddy Rose told us, "I'm not going to Chicago. Let me ask you something. If somebody told you that over in Chicago there was a hundred dollars in a tree, would you drive eight hours to get the hundred dollars?"

"Of course not," I replied.

"Then why would you go there now, because that's all you're going to get?"

"You're right. That's stupid. I'm not going either." And Marty and I didn't go. We got yelled at for skipping the show, but we were getting yelled at on a regular basis. Even for things we didn't do.

Ribbing and refusing to go to Chicago weren't the only things that Marty and I were admonished for. Our penchant for being loud and occasionally tearing up hotel rooms didn't win us many friends in the office or among the older, quieter wrestlers. One episode ended up getting the whole company kicked out of the Showboat hotel. Marty and I were sitting in our room one night drinking beers. When we finished a bottle, instead of putting it aside or throwing it out, we decided to toss it at the door. The bottles broke all over the place, and before long the area near the door was covered completely with broken glass.

The next morning the maid tried to open the door, but it kept getting stuck on the big pile of glass. Eventually she pried it open enough to peek inside. "Oh my God!" she yelled, before running away.

It was a stupid thing to do, and thankfully no one got hurt. That was the last time we stayed at the Showboat. The next taping we were across the street at a little dive called the Lamplighter Inn. Everyone was mad at us for that.

| | |

I had changed a lot since I left Texas. I was no longer the innocent, bright-eyed rookie traveling down the primrose path. I was now twenty-one years old, had a cool car, and was on TV. I was feeling good about myself, and I wanted to live a little. In my mind, I was like a mini Ric Flair. My dream had been to be a wrestler. Now that I was one, I wanted to be one of those wrestlers that people wanted to be around.

We had a lot of time off in the AWA. We barely worked in the summer, because you couldn't get anyone to come inside when the weather finally turned warm. And we didn't work seven days week during the rest of the year either.

This meant I had a lot more time to occupy, and I ended up spending lots of it at bars.

Scott LeDoux, a boxer who did some special guest refereeing for us, had a place in Minneapolis called Jukebox Saturday Night, and we were there every Tuesday night. If we were working somewhere else that night, we would bolt back to get there before closing time. We had somewhere to go almost every night. Monday was a great night at Eddie Webster's. Tuesday night was the Jukebox, Wednesday night was the Cattle Company. Thursday's we'd take off, and Friday and Saturday we could go anywhere. Everywhere we went, we were the life of the party. Marty and I used to joke that if we drew as many people to our shows as we did at the bars, Verne might still be in business today.

Most of the time I was out with Marty. Sometimes others guys would come. The Nasty Boys—Brian Knobbs & Jerry Sags—came into the territory while we were there, and we ended up hanging out with them a lot. The first day they were there, they came right up to us and said, "We heard you guys like to party. We are going to hang out with you." A lot of guys didn't like them because they were so obnoxious. Marty and I got a kick out of them.

The partying did not affect my ring work, even though I hardly trained. If I went to bed at four, I usually didn't have to get up until eleven the next day. I'd wake up, go down to the Country Buffet, eat some breakfast, chill out, and be ready to get on the road around two to hit whatever town we were working at. At night, I'd just eat at Burger King. I could get away with a lot back then.

After a few months of success in the AWA, I was definitely feeling entrenched and part of the fraternity. In fact, in the AWA, Curt, Marty, Scott, and I *were* the fraternity. We were the group you wanted to be in with. So I was comfortable—at least on the outside. Inside, however, I was feeling very different.

I lived in the same complex as Marty and Buddy and Col. DeBeers, but I lived alone. Marty had a girlfriend he lived with, and Buddy and DeBeers were roommates. It didn't take me long to figure out why those guys didn't live alone.

Being alone was something I didn't deal with very well. I didn't have any hobbies and I didn't read. When the other guys would go home to be with their families or girlfriends, I had nothing to do. I had no interests, and to be honest, I didn't enjoy my own company. The toughest part of my day was figuring out how to kill time when I wasn't wrestling or out at a bar.

Unfortunately, and I only have myself to blame, I didn't do anything productive in my free time, and I didn't have enough courage to go out and go to a movie or restaurant without getting ripped. Instead, I tried to escape. I didn't know what else to do. I didn't make a life for myself outside of wrestling. I'd seen some of the guys throwing pills down, and I avoided doing that in the beginning. But eventually I succumbed to temptation, and before long I was downing pills just to get through the day.

My typical day consisted of waking up and eating. Then I'd get a workout in, if I felt like it, or maybe lie in the sun if it was summer. Then I'd pack, go to the show, wrestle, get a buzz on, and then start all over the next day. If I wasn't wrestling, I'd just get the buzz on. A day in reality made me uncomfortable and anxious. I just didn't know what to do with my time. So I escaped with pills. A day without escaping was a day I couldn't deal with.

I was fine as long as I was in the role of Shawn Michaels, the Midnight Rocker. When it came back to being Shawn Hickenbottom in the apartment, I didn't know who I was. So I just tried to make it like I didn't exist—pop a few pills and go to sleep. That was the easy way out.

Theresa would come up and visit me every once in a while. It didn't take her long to realize that I had changed, that I was now living in a different world. She was a very straight arrow and when she was with me, it was kind of like stepping into the *Twilight Zone*. We had plenty of late-night phone calls when I wasn't in the best shape, so it wasn't as if she was blindsided by it all. We had even discussed that we were going in different directions and maybe staying together wasn't the best thing, but we could never cross the breaking point. We'd eventually tell the other one that we loved them and we'd end up staying together.

I justified my behavior with the whole "I'm a wrestler, you don't understand, I'm a different breed" kind of b.s. that we say to people. What I was really learning to do was to live two different lives—one with the wrestlers and another with Theresa and my family. I didn't really feel bad about it because I was thinking, "I've never lived. I've never tried anything." I came from a really conservative upbringing, and now that I had my first real taste of success, I wanted to see what that was like and enjoy it. I thought that I ought to be able to do it. I have no problem admitting I wasn't a man then. If I had been, I would have broken it off with Theresa. At that time I didn't have the strength to end our relationship. Part of it was not wanting to hurt her feelings, and the other part was fear of being alone.

I really did care for her and I know she felt the same way about me. There was no malice in any of the things I did. I believe she enjoyed some of the aspects of being a wrestler's girlfriend, but in retrospect, I wish I would have had the guts to end it. It would have been much fairer to her. I didn't, of course, and instead of breaking up, we stayed together and continued to grow apart.

8
start spreading
the news . . .

Marty and I did well our first year in the AWA. I made about $39,000, but we could tell that the territory was struggling. The World Wrestling Federation was kicking the AWA's butt, and we were going to smaller and smaller arenas and working less. We did well in Minneapolis, Denver, Las Vegas, and San Francisco, but that was about it.

Everyone wanted to work for Vince. That was the big time. Curt had gone there. He walked into the locker room one day and started singing, "Start spreading the news . . ." with that huge smile of his. Scott had some talks with them too. Marty and I started thinking about how we could get there.

Terry Garvin was working for Vince now, and Marty had a relationship with him from his Kansas City days. We figured it couldn't hurt to call him, so Marty did. Marty handled all of our business back then. He acted like he knew what he was doing, and since I knew that I didn't know what I was doing, I trusted him. I couldn't tell you exactly how it came about that we got a deal to come to the World Wrestling Federation, or New York, as everyone in the business called it.

One day out of the blue, Marty just told me, "We are going to New York!" I was ecstatic, he was ecstatic. We couldn't wait to get to the locker room and start singing, "Start spreading the news . . ." We were not leaving humbly.

Years later, Pat Patterson told me that he had seen us on ESPN, thought we were talented, and even as word leaked out that we were trouble, continued to lobby for us. He told Vince, "They are working for Verne. They are just rebelling. You take them here, sit them down, and they'll do business." Pat figured we weren't dumb enough to screw up once we got the chance of a lifetime. Boy, was he in for a surprise!

| | |

Before I get to our brief yet very tumultuous stay in WWE, I would like to clear up a few things about Marty's and my reputation. We were known as young punks, and we deserved that moniker. The unfair thing was that we were no different than any other young wrestlers. We were never the first ones to do anything for the first time in the wrestling business; that, I am positive of. But we were like the guy in class who always gets blamed for whatever happened.

We were extremely talented, and our brashness made it look as if we didn't have a shred of humility. In this business, that's a one-way ticket to big heat. Everyone thought we acted the way we did—tearing up hotel rooms, ribbing, partying all the time—because we were really good. But that wasn't the case. Yes we were cocky, yes we tore up a hotel room every now and then, and we pulled a lot of ribs and partied excessively. But we weren't mean. We enjoyed our jobs, we enjoyed the people we hung out with, and we just wanted to have a good time. Our behavior never bothered any of the people we hung around with.

It sure bothered a lot of other people, though, most of whom had never met us. There are a lot of people in this business who thrive on rumors and gossip. Today, a lot of misinformation is spread on the Internet. In the late eighties there was no Internet, so I don't know how all this half-baked stuff was spread around, but something could happen in New York at noon, and everyone would know about it in Atlanta an hour later. Two hours later, not only would people in Minneapolis have heard about the "news," but the story would be ten times grander than what actually happened. The sad fact is, there are a lot of angry, bitter people in this business and I guess if they couldn't make it on their own, they figured they could tear others down. I never understood this and it frustrated the heck out of me. If someone has a problem with me, just tell me to my face. Don't go running around to some other guy or some dirt sheet reporter and start spreading untruths.

At this point in time, I was too into being cool to be angry, and Marty and I took it as a badge of honor that we had a reputation. We were of the mind-set that our heat had transcended the AWA. We had gone national! I remember when Jimmy Snuka came to the AWA and told us we had a reputation. Then he whispered, "Remember, brother, any publicity is good publicity." Now that's not really true, but at the time we ate it up. We thought it was cool to have the rep. We were going to find out nothing could have been further from the truth.

| | |

My adventures in the World Wrestling Federation began when Marty and I arrived in Buffalo, New York, on June 2, 1987. They were taping *Wrestling Superstars* that night and would be filming *Wrestling Challenge* in Rochester the following night. We weren't coming in with a lot of fanfare and they didn't have any great plans for us, so there were no meetings beforehand and no guarantees. They just told Marty that we should show up at the building by 2:00 P.M. and be ready to wrestle because they might use us.

We arrived at Memorial Auditorium full of excitement and a bit nervous. We were about to play with the big boys. We knew we had a reputation, and *now* that didn't seem so cool. We weren't sure how people would receive us. We also didn't realize that we couldn't have picked a much worse day to start.

A few weeks before, the Iron Sheik and Jim Duggan had been arrested for possessing drugs while traveling in New Jersey. Vince McMahon was furious when he found out: one, because they were doing drugs, and two, because they were working a program with each other and the company didn't want the public to know they were friends in real life. Even though Vince had admitted wrestling was sports entertainment, he didn't like rubbing it in the fans' faces.

The day we started happened to be the day Vince started drug-testing the wrestlers, and many of the guys were upset about this. Vince held a big meeting and told everyone that the company was global and had an image to maintain. Drugs would not be tolerated. Vince went on about how he loved Jim Duggan, but now Duggan was through. If you were caught doing drugs, you would be fired. I can't say how many guys were doing drugs at the time, but more than a few grumbled about the testing. I was so nervous that if Vince would have said we weren't allowed to drink water, I wouldn't have.

We walked into the building against this backdrop and went straight into catering. Everything seemed so big. It was a huge vast room and we saw all these guys that we had watched on TV and they looked huge. Because we were nervous, our senses were heightened. Every noise was louder, every color was brighter, and every eye in the place, at least it seemed to us, looked our way. And these weren't welcoming eyes. They were the kind that burned a hole right through you. Never in all my life, including all those first days of school, had I felt more uncomfortable. This was definitely not Mid-South. We could feel we were not wanted, and you could cut the tension with a knife. Our backsides were puckered.

We wondered if we were allowed to eat. No one talked to us, so we went and grabbed some food. Looking for a place to sit down was no picnic either. Everyone was staring. We simply put our heads down and tried our best not to be noticed until we found a table.

As if we weren't aware yet how everyone felt about us, Chief Jay Strongbow—who was working as an agent—came up to us and said, "I heard about you guys, and I don't think you should be here." Now that really made us feel welcome. They decided not to use us that night, and Marty and I watched the show by ourselves. We were uncomfortable, but we were in this together so we got through it.

Most of the wrestlers were staying at the Ramada Renaissance. Marty and I decided to stay at another hotel. We figured if we stayed away from them, we would stay out of trouble. Terry Garvin thought otherwise. We had asked him to come over to our hotel so we could thank him for getting us here. When he arrived, he told us that we needed to get in with the guys, that we needed to hang out with them at their hotel. We didn't want to go. We told Terry that we didn't want to start any problems, but he was adamant. "If you don't make the first move," he said, "they'll think you're prima donnas."

Terry pointed out that we hadn't introduced ourselves to a lot of people at the show. We should have known better and sucked it up and done it, but we were too scared after all the stares and what Chief Jay said to us. We had stayed to ourselves, thinking how could anyone not like that? Instead, our shyness was translated into "these young punks won't even introduce themselves."

After a little hemming and hawing with Terry, we decided to go and walked into the bar at the Ramada. What a scene it was! The nightclub was a very dark and cavernous place. The boys were all in little groups. There was the Samoan group, with Afa, Sika, and Tonga, in one corner. Paul Roma, Jim Powers, and Davey Boy Smith, the British Bulldog, were in another. The Superstars were on the road all the time, and everyone was strung out. It wasn't quite like walking into the bar from *Star Wars,* but describing it as an ominous sight would not be an exaggeration.

We took a deep breath and walked in. Again, all eyes were upon us. At the time, we didn't know any of them, so we thought they all hated us. Greg Valentine, I'd later find out, was just a quiet guy and that's why he sat and stared. But we didn't know, so when he looked at us and didn't say anything, we figured he didn't like us. Years later I asked Dino Bravo why he was staring at us that night. He told me that he was just trying to figure out why we had so much heat.

We made our way to an open section and stood there all by ourselves. We didn't go anywhere. We didn't say anything. Terry kept coming over and telling us to mingle, but we were afraid. Finally, we decided to introduce ourselves to Jim Powers and Davey Boy Smith. They were a couple steps down from us and we sensed a more jovial atmosphere there. No one else looked like they were having fun.

We started small-talking with them, and everything was going fine until

Jimmy Jack Funk (Jesse Barr) decided to come over. He was ripped and wanted to start some trouble. Slurring his words horribly and sticking his face in ours, he challenged us. "Hey, I hear you guys are big partiers. Let's see something."

We told him we didn't want any trouble, we were just here to have a good time and meet some of the guys.

"C'mon!" Funk yelled before picking up a glass off the table and chewing it up. "C'mon, you guys are big time, let's see it!" He picked up another glass and bit into it.

"No," I said. "We have a ton of heat, and we are just trying to fit in."

But he wouldn't let it go. He just kept bugging us and bugging us. If you remember, a similar thing had happened to me back when I was in college. Gavin had provoked me and I didn't react too well. It turns out that in the intervening four years, I hadn't changed much. I was furious and had to do something. So I grabbed a glass and smashed it over my head. That was all I did. Then I turned around and told Terry I was out of there. I jumped in a cab and went back to my hotel.

After I left, and I didn't know this until Marty told me the next day, Marty hooked up with a girl that Funk had been trying to hit on. What happened was that once I left, things cooled down a bit between Marty and Funk. Funk started working real hard on this girl and thought he had closed the deal. Unbeknownst to him, she had an eye for Marty. When closing time came, she pulled up in her car and Marty jumped in. Funk was left on the curb fuming.

The next day at Rochester when we came into the building, we could still feel some tension, but it wasn't as bad as the day before. I hadn't made a big scene when I smashed the glass, and the only ones who saw me do it were Powers, Bulldog, Funk, and Marty. We also went into catering early enough so that we didn't stand out when we came in.

We ate and were walking out of catering when Jimmy Jack Funk came by. "What's your problem?" he asked Marty.

Marty, thinking it was some kind of bonding ritual, laughed. "What do you mean?" he asked. I was confused because I didn't yet know what happened between the two of them.

"What's your problem, man?"

Marty now realized Funk wasn't kidding around. "I don't know what you are talking about."

Funk turned away from us, walked into catering, and started yelling. "Man, these guys last night, they were tearing up the bar, they were breaking bottles, causing all sorts of trouble."

I don't recall ever saying a word. I just left the room. Later I asked Marty if anything happened. He said nothing happened, and I implored him, "You have to tell me." Finally he told me about the girl. But that's all that happened. All the stuff Funk was saying was a lie.

You might be wondering, what about all the other people in the bar? Couldn't they stand up for us? Well, you have to understand something about some of the guys. Ten years later, Davey Boy was telling that story and describing how we had torn up the bar. I had to look at him and tell him that that stuff never happened. We even went to him and Powers that day and asked them if they could say something on our behalf. They knew what really happened, they were right there. They said, "I don't know, man. We don't remember." The next week, Powers and Paul Roma debuted as a new young tag team called the Young Stallions. You don't have to be a brain surgeon to figure that one out. People didn't want us there. We had given them an opening, and they were going to take it for all it was worth.

After Funk had made that scene—and I'm not making this up—we found out who we were wrestling that night: Jose Estrada and Jimmy Jack Funk! Wait, it gets better. Who's the agent for the match? That's right, Chief Jay Strongbow! I'd like to think that someone was playing a rib on us, but I've never heard anything to that effect. People have called me a lightning rod for controversy in this business, and I guess they are right. I was certainly starting off with a bang.

Marty and I were too nervous to be able to laugh at the lunacy of it all. We were talking about what to do if Funk started shooting on us. Do we fight? We decided that it would best to talk to Chief Jay. We went up to him and explained, "We know you don't like us and we understand that. We'll work as long as we have to to get your respect. But we didn't do anything last night and

Funk is stirring up this trouble between us and everyone. We are just trying to do our job and we have to work with him tonight."

"I'll take care of it," he said. "He'll do business. Don't worry about it." Chief Jay left and a minute or two later, Funk and Jose Estrada came over and we talked about the match like nothing happened.

Our match went really well. I came back through the curtain and Gorilla Monsoon said, "Good match." Jimmy Jack Funk shook our hands and said, "You guys are talented." Jose said thank you too. He was an extra at that time and he was very kind. He wasn't part of the angry mob. We breathed a big sigh of relief, thinking that we had buried the hatchet and that our work had gotten us over.

We showered, dressed, and were leaving the building when we saw Vince. We came over and said hello to him. Vince was friendly, and then in a very off-the-cuff manner said, "Hey, let's watch the old having fun." It was an acknowledgment that he knew what happened but that he wasn't hot about it. We were very relieved now.

"Yes, sir, it will never happen again."

That night, Marty and I talked about the situation. Obviously Vince knew, but he wasn't angry. He's the person that matters, and we didn't have heat with him. We felt like we had dodged a bullet. Sure, we had fences to mend with the boys, but we would do that over time. For now, we thought we were okay.

A couple of days later I was home in San Antonio when Marty called. "Shawn, they fired us," he said.

"What?"

"They fired us."

"Because of what they said happened?"

"I guess so."

"You have to call them back. You have to get a meeting with Vince. Did you tell them what happened?"

"Sort of."

I think he had just talked to Terry. "You have to get us a meeting with Vince."

He called back in a little while and told me we could meet with Vince at the company's headquarters in Connecticut. I was upset, nervous, and very afraid. I couldn't imagine that this opportunity could slip away. Hadn't Vince seen us in Rochester and given us his okay?

Who knew what Vince had heard, but I was going to tell him the truth. I had been broken in with the old "everything's a work in this business" attitude, but every now and then I felt the truth needed to be told. This was one of these times. We were talking about the chance of a lifetime here.

We flew up to Connecticut and were sitting on a couch outside of his office. We were nervous, but we thought once we cleared up what actually happened, everything would be all right. We sat for a while before Vince stuck his head out of his office and looked at us. Both Marty and I were wearing cowboy boots. "Nice boots," he said.

"Thank you very much."

"They are made for walking, you know." Then he broke out in a big chuckle. "Just kidding, come on in."

Then he fired us. We sat down and Vince said, "Sorry, but we are going to have to let you go." He said he still wanted to hear our side of the story, which we told him.

"I believe you," he said, "but the thing is, these guys don't want you here and they are not going to allow you to be here. They'll drive you out. You have to understand that we have a family here, and if they don't want you here, it's not going to happen." Vince also told us we were young, talented, and had a future. He told us to work somewhere else and maybe someday we'd try this again. "The door is always open," he said.

Pat Patterson was also in the room and he chimed in, telling us that we had so much talent, but with our reputation, we needed to really bend over backwards for the guys and we didn't do that. I think what he was telling us was that we had to grow up. We had to understand this business, and this was a huge opportunity that we had just blown. If we ever got another chance, we better ingratiate ourselves to everyone a lot better.

I really don't know why the boys hated us so much, even with our reputation. I understand that most of them had worked very hard and paid a lot of dues to get where they were. They weren't going to give that up to some young punks, but we were only a tag team. It wasn't like we were coming in on top and going to be taking a large slice of the pie. Had we come in and shaken every hand, it might have been different. I don't know.

Vince told us the door was always open, but I figured that was something he said to be nice. All my dreams vanished instantly. Now, I would never get the chance to prove that I could be a great wrestler at the highest level. My career was over, and since I didn't do or like anything but wrestling, my life was over. I was only twenty-two years old.

9
down and out

I left Vince's office a broken man and returned home to San Antonio. I didn't know what I, or we, were going to do. Marty and I couldn't go back to the AWA. We were fairly obnoxious leaving there and had burned that bridge. We didn't know anyone down in Atlanta, and Rock 'n' Roll were working there besides. We had heard good things about Ron Fuller's Pensacola territory. It wasn't New York. However, if you worked there, you could live on the beach, make about $700 a week, and the longest trip you'd have was about three hours. At least this was the information that Marty told me. He had even mentioned to me that Fuller wanted us and had offered us a $700-a-week guarantee.

So Marty and I talked, and he said he would call Fuller. Again, Marty handled all of our business back then because I figured he knew what he was doing. It wasn't too long afterwards that Marty called back and said we had a job. The only thing was, the territory was no longer operating out of Pensacola. Fuller had moved it to Birmingham, Alabama. Also, there was no $700-a-week guarantee. In fact, there was no guarantee at all. We went from living in paradise and making a good living to residing in Birmingham and not knowing how we'd get by. Things couldn't get any worse, or so I thought.

Marty arrived in Birmingham first and made arrangements for us to live in an apartment complex where we each had our own place. My apartment was on the first floor of the complex. It was situated on a hill, though, so my window was at street level. It felt as if I were living in the basement. I had a TV on a little stand, a couch, and a small table, and I slept on a mattress on the floor. The place was dark and dreary and felt like a dungeon. Perfect for my mood, but the exact opposite of what I needed.

By the time we arrived in Birmingham, everyone knew that we had been fired, and the stories of what we had done to get canned were growing by the minute. We walked into the dressing room our first day and Tony Anthony, who was working as the Dirty White Boy, saw us and immediately started bellowing, "Oh my God, there they are! What a bunch of stupid idiots! The chance of a lifetime, the chance to grab the brass ring and they messed it up in one night! There are guys in this business that wait for a lifetime to have an opportunity like that. You get it and you messed it up!"

Well, that made us feel welcome. We just stood there and took it. What were we supposed to do? Say "Hi, Tony. How's it going?" I was thinking I couldn't get any lower than this. We're not in Pensacola, and within the industry, we were basically mud.

Tracey Smothers came up to us and with his big southern accent asked, "Is it true that y'all went into the bar with a shotgun and shot up the place, set a couch on fire, and threw it into the pool?"

"No! I broke one glass over my head, that's it!" I'm not sure what they believed or how much ribbing was going on. We just admitted that we had screwed up and that helped us weather the initial storm.

III

We were working now, which was good, but the crowds were tiny and there was nothing to do in Birmingham. In Minneapolis, I'd go out, get wasted, and have fun. In Birmingham, I stayed in my dreary apartment, got wasted, and tried to forget. I was spiraling downwards in a hurry, and thoughts of suicide began to creep into my head. Maybe it was the drugs, maybe it was just weakness, but my spark had disappeared. My sense of self-worth was tied up in being a wrestler, and I was wrestling in front of twenty-five people in small towns in Alabama.

I remember sitting alone in my apartment one day and thinking if I had a gun, I would have done it. I knew it would hurt my mom, I knew it would hurt my family, but I was so depressed. When I was a kid, I was afraid of getting in trouble because I thought it would hurt my family. Now I was teetering on the brink of not caring at all.

Thankfully, the Lord was looking out for me, and I made it through that day, but I continued to struggle with the drugs and the depression. One big problem that I had was that I really had no one to talk to about this. I called my mom almost every week, and she even came to visit to try and cheer me up. She's my mom, though, and there were certain things I just couldn't tell her.

Marty and I didn't have the kind of relationship where we could talk about our feelings. I could never get below the surface with him. Kenny, my best friend from high school, was someone I might have been able to call, but I was living in such a different world then. He was a normal guy living a normal life. I thought he might freak out if he knew what I was up to. Jose and I weren't talking much at this point, and he tended to stay out of my business. He wasn't nosey, and it wasn't his nature to get so involved. It seems obvious that I would talk to Theresa, but I just couldn't. Part of it was that I was ashamed to admit to her what was going on. In addition, we weren't really close. We had talked a few times about breaking it off, but just like in Minnesota, I'd talk her into staying together for fear of being alone, of not having a safety net. So I struggled on, making enough to get by, to get my drugs, pay my rent, and eat some food.

My work in the ring was still pretty good. I was blessed with enough talent that even if I were operating at less than one hundred percent, I was still better than most others. But my attitude stunk. I was an angry man, and I took this anger out on others. Eventually, it ended up getting Marty and me fired.

One day at a television taping a girl came up to me and asked me for an autograph. She wanted me to put it on the back of her jacket and turned around so that I could sign it. Instead of writing my name though, I wrote in big letters, "I am a dyke." At the time I thought it was funny. The truth is, everything that I was doing at that time that I said was a joke wasn't a joke. What I did was cruel and mean, and I'm sorry I did that.

Fuller was trying to sell the territory, and one of the guys he was trying to sell it to was at the taping. The girl must have noticed what I wrote and told him because he came over and started reprimanding me. I lost it and started tearing him from one side to the other. I gave him the self-righteous promo about how I was giving up my body and making him all this money and how he couldn't even take a joke. I really let him have it and then walked away.

The next day we had a spot show, and Bob Armstrong, who was running it, came up to Marty and me and said, "Hey boys, they told me to let you guys know that they are giving you your two weeks' notice. They are letting you go."

"What? Because of what happened yesterday?"

"I don't know."

"We don't need two weeks, we quit now!" And we left. Marty walked with me. I have to give him credit. He stuck with me.

10

graceland

Since I had gotten us fired, I decided that this time I would make the calls to get us a new gig. We thought we ought to try Tennessee, so I called Jerry Jarrett, who ran the territory. He said he'd love to have us and even agreed to the $500-a-week guarantee I requested. I felt better. This was the first time I had done the work to get a job and I secured a guarantee. Two weeks later we were up in Nashville working for Jerry, and things were starting to look up.

The Nasty Boys were working there, and we ended up moving in with them. It wasn't pretty, the four of us in a one-bedroom apartment, but they were a lot of fun and they helped me start having a good time again. They also were

extremely obnoxious and took a lot of heat off of Marty and me, which was a nice change.

Our five-hundred-dollar guarantee ended up lasting only a few weeks, but we didn't really care. What were we going to do? Leave, and go where? We figured whatever we were going to make, we were going to make. My spark was back, and I just wanted to have fun and work. And I did, running around with the Nasty Boys and Jeff Jarrett.

One of the really neat things Marty and I were able to do there was turn heel. We had never done that before, and we asked Jerry Lawler, who ran the Memphis part of the territory, if we could. He liked the idea and we ran a program where we turned on a team called the Rock 'n' Roll RPM's, Mike Davis & Tommy Lane. The fans were great in Memphis, and they took to hating us right away. We played cocky young heels. We had to keep our characters within reason, and what else would the Rockers be as heels? We weren't going to be angry brutes. No one would buy that. But we were young and cocky, and our gimmick fit perfectly. We ended up winning the titles there and even had the chance to work against the Rock 'n' Roll Express when they came in for a bit. That was a blast. It was very neat to work with the guys who had helped nurture me in this business.

Marty and I loved working as heels, and we were really good at it. We liked bumping all over the place, cutting heel promos, being sarcastic, and expanding our repertoire. When you are a heel, you have a lot of freedom in and out of the ring. You are able to do and say all the things that you can't say as a babyface. You can have a bad day—heck, you're encouraged to have a bad day. You don't have to sign all the autographs, and you can tell people to get lost. What's the worst that can happen? I say no to an autograph and make somebody mad? I'm a heel. I'm supposed to. Being a heel was like being set free.

In the ring, it changes your psychology because you can be more aggressive. It gives you the option of trying different moves because you are a different character. If you switch back to babyface, you can keep the new moves and mannerisms you developed. It really allows you to grow as a performer. I know I got a lot better.

I I I

While Marty and I were growing together in the ring, the first cracks were appearing in our relationship outside it. We had spent nearly every single day together for the past couple of years, which is rare for a tag team. Most married couples don't spend as much time together as Marty and I did. We didn't have many problems for the most part because we were so similar, living to party and wrestle, but about this time some tension was surfacing. It wasn't like we were fighting all the time. It was simply that it was no longer fun to be around each other *all* the time.

In Memphis, we worked live morning TVs, and one night before one of the shows, we stayed out a bit too late. When it was time for our match, we were not of sound mind. We went out and worked but were awful. We were stumbling around, and we started arguing. Then we came over and cut some kind of brutal promo. Missy Hyatt was doing the commentary, and she actually said, "Looks like the Midnight Rockers were out a little later than midnight last night."

Coming to the ring while not of sound mind is a big no-no. The guys you are working with have to be able to trust you not to hurt them. What we did was wrong, but we weren't the first ones to do it. In that company at that time, it happened. The attitude was, "If I can deliver in the ring, then don't tell me what to do in my personal life."

| | |

About the only other significant thing that happened in Tennessee was that I snuck into Graceland one night and kissed Elvis's grave. We were working in Memphis and Knobbs asked me, "You a big Elvis fan?"

"Yeah."

"Let's go to Graceland."

We went in the middle of the night. We had a few beers first and we walked up to the gate. The guard told us it was closed. So we walked maybe fifteen feet down the street, climbed over the wall, and started walking up Elvis's driveway.

The same guard saw us and kicked us out. We walked around the corner to where there is only a brick wall separating Graceland from the rest of the neighborhood, climbed on top of it, and jumped into the grounds. Then we snuck up to where Elvis and his mother and father are buried, climbed over the little fence that separates the graves from the rest of the grounds, and kissed his grave. We were lying there staring up at the sky when we realized, "We better get out of here!"

I hopped the little fence around the graves and Sags followed me. Knobbs then tried to get over the fence, but he caught his foot on the top, took a big bump, and made a lot of noise. Sags and I took off sprinting to the brick wall. Knobbs was huffing and puffing behind us. It was quite a sight to see, if you can imagine Knobbs chugging along. He made it, though—we all did. I never wanted to go back and take the tour after going in that way, and I didn't know that many years later, I would have an even cooler experience with Graceland.

| | |

Word starting spreading that Marty and I were doing well as heels, and it wasn't long before Verne Gagne ended up calling Jerry and asking if we could come up to Minneapolis and work a few shows there. Jerry was fine with it, so we started traveling back and forth between Minneapolis and Tennessee.

When we walked back into the AWA offices, Greg had that half smile on his face that says, "I bet you wish you weren't so cocky when you left now." However, he didn't say anything. He didn't have to. Greg had been in the business long enough to know that you never say never. There were no ill feelings. We both needed each other now.

I saw Greg at *WrestleMania XX* for the first time in many years and said hello to him. He smiled again and said, "You've done pretty well, Shawn."

"Thank you," I said. "You know, I'm sorry for the way we acted when we worked for you. I know we were a big pain."

"Ah, don't worry about it. You were young, Shawn." I really was sorry, and Greg was a really good sport about it.

We got over real quick again in the AWA. We worked as babyfaces there and heels in Tennessee. You could do that then, because neither area saw the other's television. We started taking more and more trips to Minneapolis, and before long, we were back working full-time in the AWA.

We beat Randy Rose & Dennis Condrey on December 27, 1987, to win our second AWA tag team titles. It was good to get the titles, and it gave us a lot of confidence. We knew we were good and we were doing well, outside of the world of WWE. After all that had happened, this was verification that we were now back. We held the belts for about three months before dropping them to my old friends Paul Diamond & Pat Tanaka.

The Nasty Boys had moved on up to the AWA a little before we did, and Curt was still there, so I had a good time traveling and hanging around with them. I was living at Brad Rheingans's house. Brad was a former Olympic wrestler who trained guys who worked for Verne. The Nasty Boys lived with him too. Things were cruising along smoothly, but, after a while, the whole AWA scene began to get a little stale. We had already lived that life, and we needed something more.

We had heard that Verne had given Curt Hennig a guarantee. We reasoned that we had been with Verne awhile, were consistent, and deserved a guarantee too. We needed something to keep us happy. So we went in to Verne and asked for a guarantee. We figured, what's the worst he can do, turn us down? And then what? We'll be where we are now. We told him we were the most over guys he had and that we deserved a guarantee. He proceeded to tell us how we were young punks who would never draw a dime.

We got in a big huff about this and decided to quit. We didn't have anything lined up but figured we could go to Japan and work. Wrestlers made a good living there, and with our style, we thought we would do well in Japan. It was risky to quit without a job, but we were fed up with the AWA, and nothing positive was going to come by staying there. Our time there had run its course.

Unbeknownst to us, Pat Patterson had been going to Vince and asking if he would bring us back. Pat told Vince how we had turned heel and done a great job. He thought things would be different if we were given a second chance. I think he worked on Vince for a while. Something Pat said must have worked, because shortly after we quit the AWA, Vince called and told us, "I'm bringing you back. I'm getting a ton of heat for it, and if you do absolutely anything

Me and Marty with our second AWA Tag Team title.

wrong, you will be gone forever." He let us know that we were on double, double secret probation.

I couldn't believe it. We were getting a second chance. Less than a year ago, I thought my life was over. Now I thought, "It's just beginning." There was only one thing I had to take care of before I headed back to the World Wrestling Federation: my wedding.

11
wedding bells

Theresa had come to visit me in Tennessee, and we
had yet another very serious talk about how us being
together wasn't the right thing. She was having a hard time
dealing with me and she wasn't comfortable around the
other wrestlers. Theresa said everything except "I want to
break up."

I was confused. I still cared a great deal for her. I also
knew I needed some stability, but I just didn't want it right
then. What I really wanted to say to her was, "Can you wait
until I've made it big in the business, lived a full life as a
single guy, and then we'll hook up at the end of all that?" I

wanted to have my cake and eat it too. I was afraid I wouldn't meet someone else who I really liked and wanted to settle down with. It was similar to how I felt when Vince let us go. "I'll never have another chance. My life is over."

Breaking up might have hurt a lot in the short run, but it would have been better in the long run. I just wasn't a strong enough person, and I had never been good at breaking up. I was terrible with Barbara in high school and I was no better now. At one point in our conversation, I yelled, "I don't know anymore!"

But now we were getting married. I had officially proposed to her during my second run in Minnesota. Our wedding date was three weeks before I was going to start for Vince. Perhaps this was meant to be. Things were looking up. I was going to have a new wife and start a new career in WWE.

I moved back to San Antonio for our wedding. The Nasty Boys came, even though they weren't invited. When they found out I was getting married, they decided they were coming and there wasn't a way to stop them. I tried to make them understand that this was my home and they had to take it easy. It was like that *Seinfeld* episode where George was engaged and lived in two different worlds: one with Susan, his fiancée, and one with Jerry, Kramer, and Elaine. If the two worlds mixed, there would be a lot of trouble. That's what I was afraid of with the Nasty Boys coming down: the wrestling world and my family world colliding in one big, bad explosion. It turned out that my fear was misplaced. Not because the Nasty Boys acted like the Brady boys, but because they were so crazy that my dad actually got a kick out of them. They stormed into my parents' house, jumped on my dad's bed while he was sleeping, and woke him up. I couldn't imagine anyone doing this to the colonel, but he seemed amused by it all.

Theresa and I were married in a Catholic church. My dad was my best man, and Kenny, Scott, Gavin, and Pat, my high school buddies, were all in the wedding party. Marty was not there, and the Nasty Boys were the only wrestlers in attendance. The wedding came off without incident, except for the lighting of our unity candle. It fell down after we lit it—talk about a bad omen—but we just shrugged it off. We honeymooned in the Caribbean and two weeks later I was back in the World Wrestling Federation.

12
graduation

My second stint in the World Wrestling Federation

began on July 7, 1988, at a house show in Toledo, Ohio. It

was a much better situation than the first time in Buffalo.

This wasn't a televised event, so there weren't nearly as

many people there. Second, there wasn't anything else going

on, like the beginning of drug testing. And third, we were

keenly aware of how we were perceived and how we should

act. We were quiet, cordial, and we wrestled Jose Luis

Rivera & Jose Estrada, the Conquistadors. Everything went

smoothly. Two days later at the Boston Garden we wrestled

the Conquistadors again; everything went well once more.

The following day, we had another house show at the Meadowlands. After the show, everyone was going to go to the bar at the hotel. We hadn't been out with the guys at the previous shows, so we decided we would try and mingle. This bar wasn't as crowded as the bar had been in Buffalo, and there was a more relaxed vibe. When we walked in, Dynamite Kid came right over to us and in his thick English accent gave us some advice. "You guys got a bunch of heat," he told us. "You've got to go in. I don't give a damn what you've done or who you are, but the boys don't like you and you have a ton of heat because you don't talk to anybody. You've got to come in and shake hands and say hello to everyone."

"We don't want to cause any problems," I replied.

"That's just the way it is. They think you are cocky. They think you are prima donnas. They are not going to let you in unless you at least show the initiative and come up and shake their hands. You have to do that. You do that and you don't owe them a thing after that. But you can't just come in and not talk to people."

"Sorry, we didn't know."

We shook everyone's hand that night. Some of the guys still didn't like us, but we had done what we should have done a year ago in Buffalo. We paid the guys the proper respect.

A couple of days later, we had our first television taping and there was a whole new slew of guys, including most of the top guys, that we had to introduce ourselves to. One of them was Andre the Giant.

Andre was always playing cribbage with Arnold Skaaland, a founding father of the World Wrestling Federation who now worked for Vince in an administrative capacity. Andre would sit and play all day until his match. While he played, everyone would come to him and shake his hand. Even the big stars, like Hogan, Randy Savage, Jake Roberts, and "the Million Dollar Man" Ted DiBiase, would pay their respects to Andre. Hogan may have been the main-event guy on TV, but Andre was the main event in the locker room.

Everyone would come by, saying, "How you doing, boss?" and extend their hand. He'd look up and shake their hands. It was almost like a Mafia don greeting line. I thought it was very cool. After what Dynamite told us, we figured we better go pay our respects to Andre. We were nervous, though. Were we allowed to call him boss? We didn't want to mess this up. So we went to him, stuck our hands out, and said, "How are you doing, boss?" He wouldn't even look up. We just shuffled off with our heads down like sad puppies.

For almost two years, I came up to him at every show we worked together, stuck my hand out, and said, "How are you doing, boss?" Not once did he acknowledge my existence. Marty gave up after a while. It was driving him nuts. He told me, "Everyone else has accepted us, I'll just eat the heat with him. It's never going to happen with him." But I still wanted him to accept me, so I kept trying.

We were on a European tour, and Marty and I were teaming with Andre in a six-man against The Orient Express and Mr. Fuji. This was the first time we were in the ring with him. He was old-school and didn't talk over matches before, so we didn't speak to him before the match. After the match everyone was shaking hands, as is the custom. Those guys said, "Thank you, boss," and he shook their hands. Now it was our turn. Andre stuck his hand out! What a relief that was.

Later that night, I saw him at the hotel bar. He waved me over. "Have a beer," he said.

"Yes, sir." Then I sort of whispered, "I know you don't like us."

"When you first came in, I didn't like you. But after that you're okay."

"But you never shook our hands?"

"After that, I was just ribbing you then."

"For a year?" He just laughed and went back to his beer.

| | |

Our first few months there, we worked a lot with the Conquistadors and had really good matches. In less than two months, we were going on last at a lot of the shows. Normally, the main event would go last, but Hogan always wanted to go on fourth so he could get back to the hotel while they still had room service. Both of us were pretty low on the card. However, our matches were exciting, and the office put us in that slot, which was a nice compliment.

We were winning everyone over with our work. Guys figured out that we could make them look good, so people wanted to work with us and welcomed us into the fold. We only had trouble with a few teams—like Demolition—who were too worried about looking "strong" to put on a great match. This was our first experience with the whole "how does that make me look" attitude. Before, our main concern was having a great match. We didn't know there was any other concept except trying to tear the house down. Rock 'n' Roll, Terry Taylor, and Ted DiBiase taught me that in Mid-South, and Buddy Rose taught both Marty and me that in the AWA. We believed, and I still believe today, that if you have a great match, everyone looks strong. That's how I got over in my career. No one in this company ever had a plan to go with Shawn Michaels as their number one guy. My work put me into that position, and Marty's and my work made us a great tag team. "Strong" to us was people yelling loud. Demolition's definition of strong was how few times you went down. They were more concerned with getting themselves over than having a great match, and that's not right. We still had good matches with them, but they weren't as good as they could have been. We'd hit them with double dropkicks and they'd stagger. We'd have to hit them with two or three before they would finally go down. We knocked everyone else down with one.

Our very first match at Madison Square Garden was against Demolition. Wrestling in the Garden was a huge milestone for me, something I had dreamed of since high school. We wanted to have a *great* match that night, but it was just good. They just wouldn't give enough. But we had a nice little spot in the company and we weren't about to say or do anything that would stir things up. We knew what would happen if we did that.

| | |

My first few months in the World Wrestling Federation were a big adjustment, not so much because of the wrestling or the culture, but because of the travel. We were on the road all the time, and every day was like *Groundhog Day*. We'd fly into a town, get our bags, go to the car rental counter, drive over to the hotel, check in, find out where there was a gym, and change into our gym clothes. We'd have a protein shake on the way to the gym, work out, tan, eat, come back to the hotel, shower, and head to the arena. After our match, we'd shower and go back to the hotel or to a bar, and then we went to sleep. We'd get up the next day and do the same thing, day after day after day. Worse, there didn't appear to be any rhyme or reason to the towns we went to. We could be in Chicago one day, Los Angeles the following day, and Miami the next. Everyone used to comment, "Do they just throw a dart at a map to see where we are going?"

We were like a traveling caravan of gypsies coming through airports, and with guys like Hillbilly Jim, One Man Gang, and the Honky Tonk Man, we certainly turned a lot of heads. Hogan and Savage would get stopped by fans asking for autographs. I'd see that and hope there would come a day when people would stop me and ask for my autograph. The top guys also flew in first class and were sitting there comfortably while we shuffled into coach. That was another thing I wanted some day: to be one of the guys flying first class.

| | |

Our first Pay-Per-View match was at *Survivor Series 1988*. That was yet another milestone. Being on a Pay-Per-View meant that you were a solid part of the team. It's true a lot of people were on *Survivor Series* because of the team format, but it felt like a major accomplishment to us. We were teamed with The Powers of Pain, The Hart Foundation, The British Bulldogs, and the Young Stallions against Demolition, the Conquistadors, The Rougeaus, Nikolai Volkoff & Boris Zukov, and the Brainbusters—Arn Anderson & Tully Blanchard.

Our mission was to get in a scrape outside the ring with Arn and Tully because we were going to start a program with them. It wasn't going to be a huge deal with tons of vignettes, but you really didn't have to do that back then to get people into a feud. A simple thing like a fight resulting in a DQ was good enough reason for a program. Arn and Tully had just come from WCW, where they had been founding members of the Four Horsemen with Ric Flair and Ole Anderson. Both were great wrestlers. I was a huge Tully Blanchard fan, and it was neat to be able to wrestle one of my boyhood heroes. The best thing about them, though, was that they were great teachers. They were firm believers in "the match" and were eager to help Marty and me out. They wanted to work with us and were adamant that we could tear the house down together.

I put the headlock on Arn Anderson.

There's an art to a Tag match, and Tully and Arn taught Marty and me the nuances that can turn an ordinary match into a great one. They would take control of our matches from the start so that we would have to fight back from underneath. This allowed Marty and me to show some toughness and allowed the crowd to rally behind us. Sometimes a babyface is in control for the first five or ten minutes of a match and then all of a sudden he gets stopped. If you are smacking someone around for ten minutes and then your opponent stops you, how does that make you look? You beat him up for ten minutes and you couldn't beat him and then he punches you one time and down you go?

Tully and Arn helped us much in the same manner that Buddy Rose and Doug Sommers had in the *Showboat Bloodbath*. They gave us grit, and that was essential for our young, white-meat, good-looking babyface team. People have to believe that behind all the flash, you will fight. Fans will get behind a fighter. Those guys taught us that.

Because Tully and Arn's offense was so good and intense, I looked tougher when I made my comebacks. Arn would snapmare me over, grab the rope, and then lift his leg high in the air before smashing me in the face with his boot. It looked vicious and I fed off the emotion that he put into his kick. If you get kicked in the face, you don't just yell, "Oh!" and put your hand up there. You have to feel the pain.

This is one of the things that is missing in the business now. Too many guys go out there and go through the motions of being a wrestler. I always tell the guys, granted I took it to a dangerous level, but you have to emotionally immerse yourself into this business. If you don't feel the pain of a kick or the joy of winning, the fans aren't going to buy it or you.

I gravitated towards Tully because we were both from San Antonio, and I know he liked having me as his student. He was still a "territory guy" who believed that when young guys came in, you got hold of them and you taught them how to do things the right way. During our program, he gave me some of the best advice I've ever received. After we had wrestled only a few matches, I came to him and said, "I'm learning so much from you guys, and my psychology is getting better."

"Shawn," he replied, "let me tell you something about psychology. Psychology is about who can make them yell the loudest the longest. That's all it is. From the time you walk out till the time you leave, it's about making them yell the loudest for the longest."

It sounds *too* simple, but that's the basic philosophy I took into my singles career. I was going to try and make the fans yell the loudest for the longest every time I stepped into the ring. It's still my goal every time I go out into the arena.

On January 23, 1989, Arn & Tully beat us at Madison Square Garden. Tully pinned Marty after Arn had knocked Marty's leg out as he was attempting to suplex Tully. The loss didn't matter because we really tore that son of a gun down that night. When we came to the back, Hogan looked at all of us and said, "How am I supposed to follow that?" He wasn't mad. He said it with a complimentary tone, and we were flattered.

Tully and Arn were so efficient and polished. At that time I can remember thinking, what an honor it was to be working with these guys. Both Marty and I did. We were so fortunate because they took us to a higher level. We didn't have to rehash anything that we had learned before. Every day we worked with them, we learned something *new*, and after our program with them ran its course, I felt I now knew how to have "the" Tag Team match. I believe I had finally graduated and earned my "tag team degree."

| | |

The next major milestone in my career came at *WrestleMania V* in Atlantic City, New Jersey. I was very excited to be there. Theresa came up for it, and Marty brought his girlfriend too. We were all staying at Trump Plaza, and the night before, we went out for a couple drinks. Marty and I wanted to do something special for our first *'Mania* and had talked about doing a double dropkick off the top rope. While we were out, I suggested that we give it a shot tomorrow against the Big Boss Man & Akeem—the Twin Towers. We were having a good time, everything was positive, and we decided that we would try and get it in the match.

The four of us stayed out for a while, and then we went back to our rooms. I ended up getting in a fight with Theresa. I became so angry, I left the room and headed down to the lobby to cool off. I came out of the elevator, and at the very same time, Marty came out of another elevator. It turns out he had a fight with his girlfriend. We just looked at each other, headed to the bar, and drank till four in the morning. I managed to get about four hours of sleep. When the alarm went off, I thought, "Great, my first *WrestleMania*. I have a huge hangover and I'm going to be working on practically no sleep."

I don't remember much about getting ready for our match except being extremely hungover. I can recall popping some Fastins, pills that were supposed to get you going, and drinking tons of coffee. The match itself turned out pretty well. We took a pretty good beating and managed to get in the double dropkick. We weren't perfect on it, but the fans screamed for it. It wasn't a positive thing, but back then I felt like I could stay out all night and still tear it up at a *WrestleMania.*

We lost the match and I began to wonder if we were losing too much. I know I've said it's not necessarily the 1-2-3 that counts, but at some point, you have to start winning. If we kept losing, would the people ever buy us as champions? There is an argument to that way of thinking. If we get beat every day for

Drop-kicking the Big Boss Man.

twenty years, and then they put the titles on us, we are not going to draw money.

At the same time, I also knew that we had to have patience and that we were still progressing in our career. We had a good thing going. We were just trying to seek that balance between knowing where you are, appreciating it, having patience, and still moving forward.

Heaven forbid we expressed our thoughts because then we would be labeled troublemakers, which of course was not the case at all. We simply wanted to win, and who doesn't? Is it really fair to call someone trouble when he wants to win a game he is playing? You are only difficult or trouble when you demand to win or place ultimatums. Then you are not only trouble, you are a spoiled brat.

| | |

Soon after *WrestleMania,* we asked Pat Patterson if we could do an angle with interviews and vignettes. The program we did with Tully and Arn resulted from a brawl outside the ring, and we wanted to do more. At the time, we were working with Jacques and Raymond Rougeau. Pat came up with the idea of them hitting me with their manager Jimmy Hart's megaphone. The Rougeaus did an interview with Tony Schiavone and started claiming that we weren't in their league, we had copied them, and we were nothing more than two wannabes. Marty and I took exception to their remarks and rushed out onto the floor and started brawling with them. During the brawl, I was struck in the throat with the megaphone and coughed up blood. Eventually we went so far as to say I lost my voice, and we worked the angle all the way to *SummerSlam.*

The general line on The Rougeaus was that they could do anything but were a little lazy. We were working something like two hundred and fifty days a year, and they decided that they were not going to kill themselves every night and risk their careers. I believe their mind-set was, we'll work hard at the Pay-Per-Views and the major towns, but we are not going to kill ourselves in Moline, Illinois. You could call them lazy, and that was fine with them. The Rougeaus thought they were being smart businessmen.

Now, I see their point. Then, I was so gung ho on tearing down the house every night, I considered them to be lazy. I was working with Randy Savage a few years later and he was telling me that I couldn't go all out every night. "You've got to pick your spots."

"Randy, I'm Superman. I don't have to."

He just looked at me and said, "I don't know, you might be."

Marty and I adjusted to The Rougeaus' style and came out much better for the experience. Shortly after we started the program, Pat came to us and suggested that we do a series of Marathon matches with them. A Marathon match meant we would go an hour and whoever wins the most falls wins. He

wanted us to do this at every house show. Going an hour in the ring really clicked with me. It was a badge of honor in the business. It's one of those things that when you are a hundred years old, and no one knows who you are, you can proclaim, "I went an hour with The Rougeaus back in '89." We did, and we learned about pacing. Our style was very quick and fast paced, but you can't do that for a whole hour. Even for young hotshots like us, that was impossible.

Jacques, bless his heart, came up with a brilliant idea where we wouldn't tie up for the first ten or fifteen minutes of every match. We'd have a little contest of who could top whom instead. We'd start the match like we were going to lock up, but Jacques would stop right before we got to each other. He'd walk away, do a nip-up, and then make a grand gesture, saying, "Now let's see if you can do that?" We'd nod our heads and do the nip-up. The fans loved it.

We'd go to lock up again, but Jacques would stop again, and this time Raymond would springboard over the ropes. Then they would point to us, challenging us to do a springboard. We'd do it and the fans would yell again. We'd go to lock up a third time, but I would pull away. I'd go to the corner, do my backflip off the top, and challenge The Rougeaus to do that! The people would really scream for this. The Rougeaus couldn't do it, so they'd wave their hands like they were frustrated and the whole thing was stupid. They would start to leave the ring and head to the back. They would come back and then leave again. Finally Jacques would whisper to Raymond that he could do it. He'd climb up to the top and milk it for a bit. Then either Marty or I would shake the top rope, Jacques would fall on it, and Raymond would prance around all frustrated. The fans really ate it up, and we were a quarter through the match.

Our program concluded at *SummerSlam*. They added Rick Martel to their team and we added Tito Santana. Rick and Tito had a little angle going on, and it gave our match a little more juice. We lost and were basically in cruising mode at this point. Marty and I were comfortable in our jobs and we were having fun on the road. Yes, the little guy in the back of my head would pop up every now and then and wonder about the losing, but it wasn't that big a deal. The biggest thing for us is that we now felt like a part of the family. We no longer felt like we were on probation, and that was a huge relief. I had been in the World Wrestling Federation for a year and made $118,000. I was very happy.

13

broken ropes

Marty and I stayed in the same spot for the next year.
We worked with a lot of teams, including The Powers of
Pain, The Hart Foundation, Andre the Giant & Haku, The
Rougeaus, and The Orient Express, who we wrestled at
WrestleMania VI. I also wrestled in the *Royal Rumble* for the
first time. I figured I could gauge how my career was going
by how long they let me stay in the *Rumble*. I soon learned
that the amount of time you spend in there has no bearing
on how your career is going, but that's how I felt in 1990. I
entered twenty-seventh and lasted about a minute. Thank
God it didn't have any bearing on my career!

At *SummerSlam 1990,* Marty and I were going to wrestle Paul Roma and Hercules. A couple of days before the show I was home in the Tampa/St. Petersburg area—Theresa and I had moved there because a lot of other guys were living there. I was riding my motorcycle to the gym, going about forty miles an hour down the road, when an old lady driving in front of me stopped completely out of the blue. I slammed on my brakes and the bike locked up on me. It slipped under me and as I pulled it back up, I jarred my knee. It wasn't hurting too bad, so I didn't worry about it. I even went and trained. The next day, the day before *SummerSlam,* Marty and I had a match against the Honky Tonk Man & Greg Valentine in Hartford, Connecticut. During the match, I went to kick Greg and my leg buckled under. Somehow I made it through the match, but my knee was killing me.

When I arrived at the Spectrum in Philadelphia for *SummerSlam,* I told Pat Patterson that I could barely move. He asked me if I could just get to the ring. I couldn't. There was really nothing I could do, but they told me that they couldn't cancel the match because we had advertised it. Animal from the Road Warriors claimed that he had taped knees before and he did some sort of tape job on me. That along with a bunch of pain pills allowed me to run to the ring where Hercules attacked me with his chain. The attack forced Marty to wrestle alone and lose. It also provided the explanation for me being off television for a while.

It turned out I had blown out my ACL and torn my medial meniscus. The doctors told me that it would take nine months to come back from surgery to repair the ACL. I wasn't going to get paid if I didn't work, so I told them that I couldn't take nine months off. I decided to only have the knee scoped. The doctors cleaned out all the loose cartilage, and despite not having an ACL, I was back in the ring in six weeks, just enough time to prepare for our first title reign—or what I thought was going to be our first title reign.

Marty and I were ecstatic when we found out we were scheduled to beat the Tag Team Champions, Bret Hart & Jim Neidhart, at a television taping at Fort Wayne, Indiana, on October 30, 1990. I think the story was they had tried just about every other tag team in the company as champions, so they might as well give us a shot. We were going to go two out of three falls, splitting the first two and winning the third. Unfortunately, everything fell apart.

We were wrestling the first fall and the top rope broke off right in the middle of the match. Bret and I were in there, and I yelled, "Grab a hold!" and he put me in a chin lock. We knew it was a TV taping, so we figured if we just sat in the hold someone would come down and fix the ring. It wouldn't be pretty for the live audience, but we figured they would edit it in the studio and make it look decent.

We were yelling at the referee, and he was yelling at us. We were all wondering why no one was coming down to fix the ring. The refs didn't wear earpieces back then, and we couldn't get anyone to do anything. So we continued the match with ropes hanging down. It was brutal. We won the first fall when Marty blocked Bret's attempt at a sunset flip.

No one came to fix the rope after the first fall, and the second turned out to be even more of a disaster. Bret tried to apply their normal finisher: Jim holding me up and Bret hitting the ropes and nailing me with a clothesline. We should have done something else. Bret hit the ropes and it looked awful. It was such a disaster that I couldn't tell you how we won the third fall. The broken ring took the air out of everything. We won and we tried to put on a celebration in the ring. I just hoped they could fix the match with the magic of television.

It turned out that they couldn't. A couple of days later I was over at Marty's house in Orlando and the phone rang. I heard Marty say, "It's okay. We understand. That's fine." They couldn't fix the match, and instead of doing it again, they were going to leave the belts on Hart and Neidhart. I was like, "You've got to be kidding me!"

We understood why they didn't want to air the match, because it really was that bad, but we couldn't understand why we couldn't just do the match over. Later on, we heard that Jim and Bret had politicked to keep the titles, but I don't know whether they did. I still can't tell you exactly what happened. We were bummed. We figured, well that sucks, let's go get ripped. There was nothing we could do about it.

Tag Team Champions—for a day, at least.

If the revoking of the titles did anything for us, it gave us the sympathy vote in the locker room. Marty and I were consistently having good matches, and guys liked working with us. They thought it was cool that we were going to get our pat on the back. When it didn't happen, they felt for us. The business isn't always fair, and everyone knew that.

14
the end of an era

Marty and I had been wrestling as a team for five years, and by the summer of 1991, the strain of spending so much time with him was starting to get to me. When you spend so much time with one person, you are bound to have days where you want the partnership to end, but I always got through those and we'd settle right back into having fun and doing our thing. However, there was now some serious friction between the two of us.

Marty was getting to be all about the partying. This is not to say that I wasn't partying, but it was getting lopsided with him. There's a difference between partying and losing one's balance, and he was losing his balance. He wasn't just partying to have fun, he was doing the freaky kind of partying that I had done in Birmingham. Marty was laying down and sleeping in the dressing room all the time and looking haggard.

In May, Marty and I were in a Denver hotel room getting smashed with Roddy Piper. Right in front of Marty, Piper started talking about how *I* had a great future in the business and that *I* had all this talent. The next thing I knew, Marty was challenging me to a fight. I told him I wasn't going to fight him, but he hit me anyway.

I told him again, "I don't want to fight you."

He hit me again and then charged at me hard. I had to defend myself, and we scrapped for a bit before Piper eventually pulled us apart. I passed out right after the fight and woke up the next day with a big shiner. I was mad now and wanted to fight him. I went looking for him, but he had already left for Phoenix, where we had a show the next day. When I arrived in Phoenix later that day, I was still hot. I went straight to the hotel. I knocked on his door and yelled, "It's me, open up!"

Marty opened the door and then backed up. I had planned on rushing in and punching him, but he said he was sorry before I could. When we drank, we became stupid sometimes, and that was what happened. We talked about the whole commitment thing to each other and tried to patch up our differences.

I think Marty was frustrated. He and I had never discussed breaking up and going single, but I think he began to sense that me going on my own was a real possibility. It came up a lot when I was around Piper and Teddy DiBiase. I would grill them for advice just like when I was nineteen and in Mid-South. I don't think Marty liked that because I believe he was worried what would happen to him once we broke up. The shame of that was, Marty was, and still is, incredibly talented. He had the ability to be a great singles wrestler.

Roddy was a wild man, but I don't believe he was trying to stir things up. He was always very helpful and gave me two of the best pieces of advice I ever received in this business: Don't ever stop being who you are—don't ever let them turn you into a character like the Hijacker—and don't ever ask anybody else how your match was. I had come back from the ring once, and I asked him,

"How was it?" He yelled at me. "Come here! You know how it was. You ought to know how it goes."

By asking other people, I was showing that I was not confident in my ability. The top guy in the main event doesn't ask how it's going. He knows it's going well, he's in the main event. You can't let other people in this business know that you don't have confidence in your ability. They'll eat you alive if they sense weakness. Roddy was right. I stopped asking after that.

| | |

Things between Marty and me finally came to a head that fall. We were at a photo shoot for a Wheaties box along with Brutus Beefcake, the Road Warriors, and a few others. Everything was going well, but we had been there for a long time. Joe Laurinaitis, Animal of the Road Warriors, came over to us and said, "This is hardly worth five grand."

"You guys are making five grand apiece?" I asked.

"Yeah."

"That sucks. We're only getting $2,500. That doesn't seem fair."

I told Marty, and he was even more upset than I was. We talked about it, and decided that he should call WCW and see if they had anything for us. Before the photo shoot Marty had mentioned to me that the Rock 'n' Roll Express had left WCW and there might be an opportunity for us. He told me Magnum T.A., who was doing some booking down there, said we could get $150,000 guaranteed and up to $200,000 with incentives. We were making around $180,000, so it sounded like a good deal to me.

While we were still at the shoot, Marty said, "I'm going to call the office. Are you with me no matter what?"

I said yes, but I really didn't mean it. I never seriously thought about going anywhere else. I figured Marty would tell Vince we both wanted five grand for doing the shoot. When they asked me about it, I would say it's only fair that we get what everyone else received.

Marty called and told the office that we were upset about the payoff and were leaving the company. They didn't seem to care and didn't make us a counteroffer. I was hurt that they didn't care we were leaving and flew home to

Florida pretty bummed out. When I told Theresa what happened, she was not pleased. "What are we going to do? It's a shame you are more committed to Marty than to our marriage or your future."

"You're right," I said. "I'm going to call Marty and tell him that I am not leaving."

Before I could speak to Marty, Vince called. "Shawn, I had a talk with Marty, and I'm sorry to hear that you guys are leaving. I understand about the payoff. It's not right, but there's only so much money and I wanted to get you guys on the box. I figured it was better than nothing. I understand that you deserve more. You've done a lot for us, and I'm sorry to hear that you guys are moving on. I just want you to know, Shawn, I think you are an extremely talented man, and I think you have a bright future in this business. I think someday you are going to be a heck of a heel. I want you to know that whenever you and Marty finish doing the tag team thing, the door is always open. You have a heck of a future here."

"I don't want to go anywhere," I responded. "I just wanted to inform you that that was something we couldn't take. I don't want to leave. Can I call you back?" I hung up and called Marty. "What happened? What did you say to Vince?"

"I told him that the payoff wasn't right, and we are going to go somewhere else."

"What are we going to do? Where are we going to go?"

"We can go to WCW."

"Who have you talked to?"

He had talked to a guy named Joey Mags who was an underneath guy there. He hadn't even spoken to Magnum. Marty had thrown things out there that unbeknownst to me just weren't true. I guess it's strange that Marty and I were together for so many years and I still didn't have any real insight into him. He would open up sometimes, but other times he would be less than truthful, and in this case about a possible deal down in WCW. Now my career was in jeopardy. "Well you have to call Magnum. I want us to stay here, but if there is something guaranteed, I'll go."

Marty said that I should call Magnum, so I did. I told him that Marty and I were thinking of making a move and asked if there was anything down there for us. He said he'd love to have us. I told him we'd like to have a $200,000 guarantee.

"We don't have that kind of money," Magnum said. "We might be able to start you out at $70,000 and then if you guys get over you can always renegotiate."

It didn't take a genius to figure out that $70,000 meant taking a huge pay cut. I told Magnum I'd get back to him. I called Marty immediately and informed him of my conversation with Magnum. I said, "Marty, this is b.s. You never even talked to him before giving Vince the ultimatum. I'm not going. This is where I want to be. We've talked about one day this thing would run its course and we'd do an angle and go singles. I think it's time to do that. I'm going to call Vince back and tell him that I'm not leaving. Do you mind if I tell him that we want to do the angle against each other and go from there?"

"What's going to happen then?"

"I don't know what's going to happen. We'll do the angle. It will be cool and then we'll both be in control of our own destinies. We'll just have to see what happens."

"What's going to happen to me?"

"You're a great worker. I'll be a heel. You'll be a babyface. I'll go work with other babyfaces and you'll go work with other heels."

He wasn't happy about it, but I called Vince back and told him I didn't want to leave. I asked, "Do you really think I can do singles?"

"Yes," he replied.

"Well, I want to take you up on that. Marty and I can do an angle where I turn on him and we'll have to sink or swim."

"All right then. I'm glad you made that decision. We'll discuss it the next time at TV."

It's a shame that Marty and I ended our tag team on such a sour note. In the midst of three hundred days a year the little things started to add up and the Wheaties box incident pushed me past the breaking point.

When I became upset with Vince later in my career, I handled things differently. I yelled at him and we went back and forth, but I never said, "I am out of here." Randy Savage had taught me that the minute you leave, it's over. You have no chance for advancement. If you are still here, you still have a chance. "Don't take yourself out of the game," Savage said. Marty had nearly taken us out of the game.

I wanted to be in control of my own destiny. I didn't want to get punished anymore if Marty did something wrong. And to be fair, he shouldn't be punished if I did something wrong.

Marty was not happy about the split. He slanted the story of what happened so that I was the bad guy. He told people that I said that we would stick together on this. That was true, but he never told me that he was going to give Vince an ultimatum. I believe anyone in my position would have done the same thing I did. This was one of my first major decisions, and I was made to feel like crap for it. Most everyone believed I had dumped Marty and acted like a scumbag. It wasn't true, and it hurt to be labeled the bad guy.

Marty and I never officially won the Tag Team Championship, but I don't think that takes away from what we did in the ring. I don't want to sound cocky, but Marty and I were really good. If you never saw us wrestle, just ask all the guys that wanted to work with us. I believe we were as talented as any team that ever stepped into a WWE ring.

The Rockers had traveled many miles together over the years, and there's always a touch of sadness when relationships end. However, it was time to move on. I was eager to start a whole new chapter in my career.

15
making an impact

The first thing we had to do to get my singles career off the ground was break up the Rockers on television. Before everything with Marty went down, we were planning on doing an angle with the Nasty Boys. As part of that story line, I had suggested to Vince that the Nasty Boys throw Marty and me through the plate glass window on *Barber Shop*, Brutus Beefcake's interview segment. I loved the old cowboy movies where the guy gets thrown out of the bar and through the window. There's something about hearing glass break that makes you take notice, and that window on *Barber Shop* was an angle waiting to be done.

I suggested that Marty and I do the segment instead of us and the Nasty Boys. I also asked Vince if Marty could get a little bit of color.

"I don't know about that."

"Aw, just a little bit."

"Well, all right."

I described the idea to Vince the same way I describe ideas to him now. I became real excited. That's one of the things I think Vince always liked about me. I'm like a little kid when it comes to new ideas. I love creating angles, and I know Vince got a kick out of the fact that I came up with it, that I was creative.

To build to the segment, Marty and I started having problems in our matches beginning at *Survivor Series*. We did this for a couple of weeks and then at a television taping in San Antonio, we went on the *Barber Shop*. I superkicked him and tossed him through the window. Fans everywhere were shocked. The company didn't do things like that back then, and we got the impact we were looking for. I had serious heat now and started my singles career on a high note.

The plan was to run a program with Marty after the *Barber Shop* incident. Unfortunately, he was having some personal problems, and he was in and out of the company. We couldn't run the angle, and I didn't get the immediate push that I had been looking for. Instead, I wrestled random matches with guys like Jimmy Snuka and Jim Powers.

In early January, I did a couple of quick shots in Japan. When I returned to the States, I checked my phone messages. There was one from Pat Patterson telling me that while I was in Japan, Sherri Martel had done a great interview in which she had called me her boy toy. They wanted to put her with me. I was opposed to the idea. It wasn't anything personal, I just wanted to stand on my own.

Pat was persistent, though, and I'm glad he was. This was another situation where I found out how wrong I could be. Sherri was an awesome lady to work with. She was very excited to work with me and said she would do whatever I wanted.

When Sherri had managed Buddy Rose and Doug Sommers in the AWA, I had a schoolboy crush on her. Now, I remember thinking, "I ought to tell her all those things I thought about her." So I told her that I had always thought she was an attractive lady and asked her if she wouldn't mind dressing up in boots and leather instead of the evening gowns she was wearing. It fit my gimmick a whole lot better.

She said, "Great idea. I'll do it."

To be honest, I wasn't too hot on the boy toy name because I felt there was no longevity to it. But I liked the concept, and it did help me develop as a performer. I made it a point that in order for people to take me seriously, I had to be the one in control. Sherri couldn't be the dominant figure. She was completely cool with that, and just wanted to do well.

Now, I was portraying this young guy who has this older hot woman wanting him, and he's the one in control of the situation. It may sound strange, but by playing a confident character, I was getting more comfortable out in the ring and in front of the cameras.

Sherri's one of the few women I've known in this industry who understands how the business works. And she was tough. If Sherri saw that someone wasn't selling for me, she would yell, "Throw them out here, Shawn." I'd throw them out and she would kick them with her big old boots and scratch them on their back.

They would come rushing back to the ring to be with me where it was safe. I can't say enough good things about Sherri. We were only together for a couple of months, but she helped me so much. She encouraged me to be creative. I needed that at the time because I didn't know who I really was, I was just developing a persona and a style. Sherri's only agenda was helping me. She was always positive, and it was refreshing and comfortable to be around her.

| | |

One of my trademarks, and one of the primary reasons I finally got over big in this industry, is that I always sold for my opponents. That's why people wanted to work with me all the time. When I first started as a single, most guys didn't want to sell for me. They certainly didn't want to put me over. Guys would say, "You deserve a break, but I don't want to give it to you. It's just business."

I wasn't getting clean finishes, and you need a certain amount to be credible. The heat of the match, where I was beating people, was very short too. I was able to do a few things like my elbow off the top or the forearm shiver, but I wasn't getting a chance to establish things that were mine. Most of the guys didn't want to take a lot of bumps. The positive side of all this was that I was able to hone my selling skills, but I was floundering on the card because it didn't look like I could handle most of my opponents.

The master plan back in November was to build to a match with Marty at *WrestleMania VIII*, but he wasn't around, so they put me in a match with Tito Santana. Tito was a great guy, a solid professional who had been around for a long time and always did what was right for the business. I have a lot of respect for Tito, and he put me over. It wasn't the kind of win that springboards you to the next level, but we couldn't get the big blow off with Marty. The setup was great, but we didn't get to deliver on the main course, and that always hurts when you try to move up the card.

After *WrestleMania VIII*, I ended up losing to Bret Hart, who was Intercontinental Champion at the time, for about three straight months. We weren't close friends, but we got along fine and had good matches together. Like everyone else, he knew if he worked with me, he was going to look good.

One day in July, Bret came to me with a proposal. "Hey, I did this match years ago in Calgary with Dynamite Kid. It's a Ladder match where one of us had to climb the ladder and grab the belt to win. I haven't done it here because I didn't think anyone could do it, but I think we could do it. Do you mind if I mention it to Vince?"

"No, go ahead," I replied.

So on July 21, 1992, in Portland, Maine, Bret and I had the first Ladder match in the company's history. Bret won after drop-kicking the ladder and causing me to crotch myself on the top rope. This was the finish he and Dynamite used, and it would be the one Scott Hall and I would use at *WrestleMania X.*

▌ ▌

During the time I was working with Bret, I made a crucial decision. Working with Bret was fine, but we were just wrestling at house shows. We didn't have a program. I was going to work with Rick Martel at *Summer-Slam,* but that was a one- or two-time thing. It was good, don't get me wrong, but I wanted to do something that I could really sink my teeth into. I loved the business and really, really wanted to get into it.

Back then we would tape three or more television shows on the same day. Vince would set up an office so that anyone who wanted to talk to him could do so. There'd be a long line of wrestlers at every TV waiting to get their few minutes with Vince so that they could complain or suggest ideas.

Vince would listen, say your idea sounded good, and then somehow explain how it wouldn't work. But he did it in such a way that you'd come out of the meeting feeling good and being in complete agreement with him. Later it would hit you: "What just happened? How did he do that?" So you'd take the next couple of weeks to rethink your argument, and at the next taping you'd stand in line and the same thing would happen again. You weren't going to outwork the master of working.

One day I was standing in line. I really wanted to tell Vince about my passion for the business, how badly I wanted to succeed, and that I wanted to know what I had to do to succeed. There were a couple of people in line ahead of me, but I couldn't wait. I had seen Hogan and Savage ignore the line countless times and go up and knock on Vince's door and go in. I decided I would do the same thing. I walked past the people in front of me, knocked on his door, and asked for ten minutes of his time. He said, "Okay."

"What do I have to do to make it?" I asked. "I want to be one of your guys. I want to be one of those guys that's in everything. I believe I can do this. I'll do whatever I have to do to get better at it. Just tell me what it is I need to do and I'll do it. If you want me to work, I'll go work. If you want me to do something else, I'll do it. I'll never say no. I want to be on top. Tell me what I have to do and I will do it."

He sat there and nodded his head. "You just did it."

| | |

My encounter with Rick Martel at *SummerSlam* turned out to be a small but important step up the card. We were both heels, so it was different and challenging. We were fighting over Sherri's love. We were both so good-looking, she couldn't decide who she wanted to be with. We had a funny stipulation where Sherri wouldn't let either of us hit each other in the face lest we "mess up our perfect looks." At first, I wasn't too keen on that because I've always thought that to be a good heel you have to have some ruggedness to you, but it was a neat concept and a good place to be on a cool show. Any match where there's a stipulation is usually better than an ordinary match. We had a good build and a nice little contest that went to a double countout.

SummerSlam was held at Wembley Stadium in London, and wrestling in such a big and venerable stadium was a thrill. To the British, Wembley is *the* stadium. It's their Rose Bowl, Lambeau Field, and Yankee Stadium all rolled into one. There were 75,000 people there, mostly to see their countryman, Davey Boy Smith, beat Bret Hart for the Intercontinental Championship. While it's awesome to wrestle in front of a crowd that size, it can be a little disconcerting. In an outdoor stadium, you don't hear the roar of the crowd. The noise escapes upward, and that can throw you off if you are trying to read the audience. The electricity is not the same as it is in a packed indoor arena that holds 20,000 people. It's still awesome—however, when you are trying to feel the crowd, it's difficult to do.

‖ ‖

I had now been here long enough to realize that the really good workers, guys like Santana, Savage, Hennig, and Ricky Steamboat, got to be Intercontinental Champions, and I set a goal of winning the IC title. Sure I dreamed of becoming the World Wrestling Federation Champion, but 6'1", 215-pound guys like me with very little marketing savvy didn't win that title. This was a big man business, and I definitely wasn't a big man. I was a bumping heel that could make a babyface look great. I wasn't the marketing guy who was going to sell out arenas. So the IC title was the spot I was looking for, figuring that would define me as a great worker and a success.

I reached that goal on October 27, 1992, in Terre Haute, Indiana, when I beat Davey Boy Smith. I didn't know I was going to win ahead of time. I just walked in the building and Davey Boy came up to me and told me I was going over. I was very excited to hear the news, but I didn't want to show how I really felt because I didn't want to look like a mark. Pat Patterson had a little talk with me after I spoke with Davey Boy. He was always supportive and told me how I was different, that I was a heel who liked to bump for people and that I would do well with the belt. Davey and I ended up having a decent match. For the fin-ish we had him fail on a superplex attempt and I landed on top of him and got the 1-2-3. I had only been wrestling singles for about nine months and I had a real sense of accomplishment.

Shortly after I won the belt, I was wrestling at a TV taping and Curt Hennig, who was announcing at the time, called me the Heartbreak Kid. After the show, he told me about it and thought it would be a cool nickname for me. I wasn't so sure. I definitely liked it better than Boy Toy, but I didn't see myself as some tough guy. I was worried how that name would go with a young, smaller guy. I was afraid it might make me look like a wussy. I started to throw it into promos, and it took on a life of its own.

One thing I did ask the office to do was have the announcers come over the P.A. and announce after I had wrestled, "Ladies and Gentlemen, Shawn

Michaels has left the building." It was an obvious spoof of Elvis and I thought it would help me get heat from the fans who'd think, "Who the heck does this guy think he is?"

| | |

Marty came back after I beat Davey Boy and we were finally going to do our long-awaited program. First, though, I needed something to do for *Survivor Series*. Bret was now the World Wrestling Federation Champion, having beat Flair for the title in Saskatoon, Saskatchewan, just days before I won the IC title. Since there really wasn't any time to build something for either of us at *Survivor Series*, they put us together in a World Champion versus Intercontinental Champion match. We had a very good contest that he won with the Sharpshooter. It's funny when you look back and think how different things were and how much they would change over the next five years. No one could have ever guessed in a million years how different our next *Survivor Series* encounter would be.

I was riding pretty high and beginning to feel my oats. Even though I had lost to Bret, I had wrestled *the* champion at a Pay-Per-View. I still had my title, I had a new name, and I was on my own. And now, everyone wanted to work with me because I was having good matches. Professionally, I was becoming pretty cocky.

In order to generate a little extra heat, I began checking myself out in front of a full-length mirror before my matches. I was wrestling an extra named Steve May, and as I was doing my bit in front of the mirror, Marty ran out from the crowd to confront me. Marty grabbed my mirror and went to smash it over my head. Just as he was going to hit me, I pulled Sherri in front of me and Marty knocked her out. I took off backstage as he checked on Sherri.

Sherri stayed off television until the *Royal Rumble*. She stood in a neutral corner during Marty's and my match, acting like she didn't know who to side with. Towards the end of the match, Sherri turned on me. We weren't going to have her cost me the match, though, and I ended up going over after nailing Marty with the superkick. He got some heat back afterwards when he attacked me backstage as I was berating Sherri for betraying me in the ring. The angle played out well and left us the option to continue forward with it if we wanted to. Unfortunately, Marty still had his problems and ended up getting relieved of his duties shortly after the *Rumble.* Once again, we weren't able to conclude our feud with a definitive result.

The night before the *Rumble,* I stayed out too late. As I was walking back to my hotel, I tripped over a concrete parking divider and scuffed myself up pretty good. When I came to the building the next day, Vince was very angry with me. He was mad because I was out and not in good shape. I think he was thinking that he might really be able to do something with me, but all the partying I was doing wasn't good. If he was going to invest a lot of time and money in me, he wanted to make sure that I would be there. He was thrilled with me professionally, but I was certainly not endearing myself to him with my personal habits.

I apologized, but I really wasn't sorry. I was developing a chip on my shoulder. My attitude was, as long as I take care of business in the ring, whatever I do in my personal life is my business. Now I understand that I was wrong on several accounts, but at the time, I wouldn't hear any of it. I felt Vince had no right to tell me what to do in my free time.

I I I

With Marty now out of the picture for *WrestleMania IX,* I began working with a bunch of different people: Bob Backlund, Kamala, Crush, Owen Hart, Randy Savage, Tatanka (Chris Chavis), and the Nasty Boys. Wrestling Bob Backlund was neat. It was another time I was able to wrestle a guy who I had read about as a kid. Bob was a wrestler's wrestler, and I had an easy time working with him. I think he had fun working with me as well.

Working with Owen Hart was fantastic as well. He was great, and by far the most talented of all the Harts. With Owen you could call things on the fly, change things up, experiment, and basically do anything you wanted to do. He was a pure joy to work with. I lost most of these matches, but I'd always lose by DQ or countout, so I retained the title. What I was doing was making the guys I wrestled look good, and they appreciated that. I was a perfect heel Intercontinental Champion.

A month before *WrestleMania IX,* I separated my shoulder while teaming with the Beverly Brothers against Tatanka and the Nasty Boys. I had to take four weeks off, and that eliminated any chance of building something big with Tatanka, who I was going to fight at *'Mania.*

The injury occurred during an episode of *Monday Night Raw. Raw* was Vince's revolutionary idea to add excitement and intrigue to our product. He had a big meeting with all the guys and said that we were moving away from the Saturday morning novelty act image the general public had given us. Vince said we were sports entertainment and we were going to start going head-to-head with prime-time shows. He insisted that we were better than *Monday Night Football* and any block of sitcoms. To prove it, we were going to start *Monday Night Raw,* a weekly, live, prime-time show. Looking back, there's no question that Vince's decision to go live on Monday nights changed the way the public viewed us, and it is one of the primary reasons our business grew as it did. I beat Max Moon on the very first episode.

By the time my shoulder healed, we were fast approaching *WrestleMania IX.* Vince wanted me to have a few warm-up matches before the big show in Las Vegas on April 4. He sent me to Memphis, where I wrestled Jeff Jarrett on March 29, and Jerry Lawler on the thirtieth. It sounded simple enough.

Of course, nothing seemed to be simple with me anymore. After my match with Jerry, the referee went to hand me my belt and ended up smashing me in the mouth and knocking out my front tooth. I had to rush home to Dallas the next day to get a dentist to put a cap in my mouth. I was coming into *Wrestle-Mania* having just healed from a separated shoulder and a knocked-out tooth, and Chris Chavis and I had no storyline going into our match. We went twenty minutes before I was counted out. He was very big and thick and a little difficult to move. The match wasn't bad, it just wasn't anything special.

The big issue surrounding this *'Mania* was the return of Hulk Hogan. Bret was the champion coming into the show, and he was wrestling Yokozuna for the title in the main event. What was going to happen was that Mr. Fuji, Yoko's manager, was going to throw salt in Bret's eyes, which would allow Yoko to pin Bret. Hogan was then going to rush out and try to explain to referee Earl Hebner what had happened. Fuji would then challenge Hogan to get in the ring with Yokozuna and fight for the title right there. Only after Bret encouraged Hogan to "fight for what's right" would Hogan accept the challenge. Hogan would then beat Yoko and become the champion.

Bret told me he was upset with the situation, and I told him that his anger was justified. He had been out there pulling the wagon for nine months and now that it was big payoff time, here comes Hogan to snatch it. I recognized that that's business, but I agreed with him that it sucked.

As performers, we can only control ratings and houses so much. We are given characters and story lines—today we are even given words—and all we can do is put on the best performances we can. Now Hogan was going to come in, get a huge payday for *WrestleMania,* and then just work occasionally at big shows. Bret would once again be working his tail off two hundred and fifty days a year. From my perspective, he should have got the big payoff.

Bret and I used to talk frequently to each other. We weren't close, but I don't think he was close with anyone. We used to call him the Lone Wolf because he traveled by himself. At this time we shared a common bond, and that brought us together. We had our titles and were busting our humps every night. He also had a wonderful, dry sense of humor and was able to poke some fun at the situation. After Yoko pinned him and Hulk was running by him down the aisle to the ring, he very facetiously yelled, "Go Hulk! Go get him!" I guess that's all he could do about it at that point.

The Midnight Rockers.

Courtesy of *Pro Wrestling Illustrated*.

Me and Marty rewriting the book on tag team wrestling.

Copyright © 2005 World Wrestling Entertainment, Inc. All Rights Reserved.

Showing Jim Neidhart that Rocker style.

Copyright © 2005 World Wrestling Entertainment, Inc. All Rights Reserved.

Copyright © 2005 World Wrestling Entertainment, Inc. All Rights Reserved.

Working Pay-Per-Views like *Survivor Series 1996* with Sid Vicious was another step to a title win.

World Wrestling Federation Champion.

Copyright © 2005 World Wrestling Entertainment, Inc. All Rights Reserved.

My program with Undertaker was one of my favorites.

Copyright © 2005 World Wrestling Entertainment, Inc. All Rights Reserved.

It was great to share the spotlight with Jose.

Courtesy of Shawn Michaels.

Copyright © 2005 World Wrestling

16
nobody is going to beat you up

The post–*WrestleMania* plan for me called for me to work an angle with Curt Hennig. I was psyched. He was my friend and had helped me so much over the years both inside and outside of the ring. Curt had been the Intercontinental Champion before me, and I molded my reign after his. I saw how he worked as a heel and how he made everyone look good by flying all over the place. It's no coincidence that I was doing the same thing. At *WrestleMania* I had attacked him after his match against Lex Luger, and we picked up the feud with a street fight on *Monday Night Raw*.

These were the wild west days on *Raw* when we'd just

come up with an idea and do it. Lord Alfred Hayes was going to be interviewing me outside the Manhattan Center, and Curt was going to come out of nowhere and attack me. He was going to throw me through the windshield of Howard Finkel's (our longtime ring announcer) brand-new Cadillac, and then we were going to scuffle until the end of our segment. We didn't block off the street, nor did we ask any New York City authorities for permission to do this. Bruce Pritchard, who was producing the segment, told us that he didn't know what was going to happen after we started fighting. "When I tell you we have to go, we have to go."

So we got into the fight and Curt threw me into Howard's windshield. Then, all the police sirens started blaring. The cops pulled up and Bruce yelled, "Let's go!" Curt and I ran for the Manhattan Center. It may not have been the most organized of vignettes, but it certainly made for good television. Some poor guy from the production crew was left trying to explain to the police what happened and that they didn't have to file a report on the damaged car.

It was Vince's idea to smash Howard's new Cadillac. He liked to throw a few ribs in here and there and thought it would be funny to get Howard. He was going to fix or even buy Howard a new car. We shot the segment before the show. After we taped it, Vince brought Howard into his office to show him what had happened. "I'm sorry, Howard," he said. "We didn't know they were going to do all that."

We could all see that Howard was really bummed, but he tried to stay strong. "If it's for the company and best for business, I guess it's okay. I'm sure I can get it fixed."

Vince let him wallow in misery for a little while before breaking the news to him that he had been had. Everyone got a laugh out of it, and Howard ended up with a brand-new Cadillac.

The next week, I thought Curt and I would pick up where we left off. I was wrong. Marty was back again and I was now going to work a short program with him, and hopefully, once and for all, complete our unfinished business. Marty had come in and out quite a few times since we had split up and every time he came back, they put us together because we had never really gotten the total mileage out of the split. This time, I think they had every intention of

bringing him in, giving him a good kick start, and then using him as a middle to top babyface. Unfortunately, Marty's insecurities and lifestyle prevented this from happening. I don't want to sound too judgmental here because my lifestyle wasn't great, but his was always a little more extreme than mine. It's a shame that Marty couldn't pull it together then, that he never grasped how good he was and what a great career he could have had.

Marty and I were never the same after we broke up. There was an unspoken uncomfortableness between us, and I could feel that he and the guys he was now running with bore some resentment towards me. Remember, I was labeled the bad guy. Marty was telling people that I dumped him, I was only out for myself, and I was a pain in the backside. He was really into the locker room gossip, and I was really affected by it. On the outside I may have been brash and cocky but inside, the side I was afraid to show, I was hurting. I didn't like being branded a bad person and though I didn't show it, it hurt. The Nasty Boys and Davey Boy liked to stir things up and made jokes about how I dumped Marty. They laughed, I didn't.

In order to get Marty off to a good start, he was going to beat me on *Raw.* I was going to win the title back a couple of weeks later, so I didn't have any problems with this. I thought it would be good for Marty, and then I would move on with my angle with Curt. On the May 17, 1993, edition of *Monday Night Raw,* I issued an open challenge for my Intercontinental Championship. In disguise, Marty came to the ring and accepted my challenge. When he took his disguise off, the crowd popped big. I don't think they expected him to win, but they were definitely demonstrating that we still had some life in this on-again, off-again angle.

We put on a really good match that night. We had worked together so many times, we could have had a good match in our sleep. Our differences disappeared once we stepped in between the ropes. Marty won when Curt came to the ring and threw his towel in my face. The distraction allowed Marty to roll me up in a small package. The crowd went nuts. It couldn't have played out any better.

The next week we were up in Nova Scotia, and I went in to talk to Vince. I knew I was going to win the belt back from Marty, and I was concerned about my matches getting stale. Ever since I had won the Intercontinental title, I had been doing a lot of DQs and countouts. Every match ended in a similar manner. My opponent and I would put on an exciting show, but the endings were just brutal and took the wind out of our sails. He asked me what I wanted to do about it.

"What about giving me a bodyguard?"

"Who do you have in mind?"

Back in March after I had separated my shoulder in the match against the Nasty Boys, I was sitting at home one Saturday night and decided to turn on the WCW Saturday evening show. I was always working on the weekends, so I never had the chance to watch the competition. Now that I had some time, I figured I would check it out. So I'm watching, and I see this guy named Vinnie Vegas do an interview. He was really funny and entertaining, and I also couldn't help but notice that he was huge. I think they were billing him as seven feet and over three hundred pounds, which was pretty accurate. I remembered him and said, "I saw this guy on the WCW TV and he goes by Vinnie Vegas."

"I can't do that, Shawn. I don't want any WCW guys coming in. There are legal and contract issues I don't want to deal with."

"He's very funny."

"It's a contract issue and I don't want to get into it. We'll put this idea in the old computer and see what happens." He used to say that a lot.

I came out of our meeting and went looking for Rick and Scott Steiner. I knew they had been down in WCW and might know this guy's situation. I found Rick and asked him, "Have you ever seen this guy in WCW who goes by Vinnie Vegas?"

"Yeah, that's Kevin Nash. He's a good buddy of mine."

"Do you know what his deal is? I saw him on TV and I thought he was a riot."

"He's a great guy!"

"Well, I'd like to do a bodyguard gimmick with him. Do you know what his contract situation is?"

"I've got his number, I'll call him right now."

Rick ran down the hall and called him. "He'd love to do it," Rick told me. "He's going to go in tomorrow and see if he can get out of his contract."

The following day, Rick told me that Kevin said to have someone from the office give him a call. I told Vince, and the next thing I knew, Kevin was going to be at our TV the very next Monday. It was amazing how fast everything was happening.

Kevin was under contract to WCW, but he really wanted to come here. He went in to Ole Anderson, who was one of their bookers, and said, "I've tried the wrestling thing and it's not really working out. I gave it a certain amount of time and I'm just not doing great. I want to go back to being a bouncer. Can you let me out of my contract?"

Ole obviously didn't have any plans for him, so he let him out. Kevin took a copy of his now dissolved contract and faxed it to the WWE office. They looked it over and sent him a plane ticket to come to New York for next week's *Raw*.

Kevin and I hit it off immediately. I told him my story of seeing him and trying to get him here and he was very thankful and gracious. I didn't think it was that big a deal. It wasn't until later on when people would look at me like I had two heads and say, "So you didn't even know who he was?" did I think I might have done something unusual. Throughout my career, if I saw someone who I thought was good, I would say something to someone. Yet, I was known as one of the biggest s.o.b.s in the business.

Part of the reason that I think I had such a bad reputation was that I wouldn't answer every bad comment that was said about me, nor would I go running to the dirt sheets with my own dirt. Because I didn't respond, challenges to my character went unanswered and I paid the price. People would anonymously claim that I wouldn't do jobs and this would get printed in the gossip sheets and be treated as the gospel truth. The truth is, there is no "no" in this business. You can't refuse to do a job. Vince says it's going to be a certain way, and that's the way it is. He has ultimate power in this business. If you don't believe me, just ask Bret Hart.

The fact is, I lost to and bumped for everyone I was asked to. Why do you think so many people wanted to work with me? It wasn't because they liked me personally, it was because they knew I could bring out their best.

You might be asking why I didn't respond to all the allegations. The answer is I didn't want to get caught up in all the gossip. I thought it was stupid, and it was already driving me crazy. I figured if I responded it would turn into a never-ending cycle that would make things even worse. I wasn't going to do it. So I suffered with the bad reputation and let it eat away at me.

Kevin and I struck up an immediate friendship and I asked him what made him want to come work here. His answer contained some of the nicest words anyone has ever said to me. "Shawn," he said. "I was watching you and I said that's a guy who is a rising star. I had the opportunity to hook up my wagon to that rising star and I was all over it. I knew you were going to make it in this business, and if I had a chance to go with you I was going to go." Kevin was very open about his feelings, and I found that to be really comforting. He was the first guy who I met in the business who I could talk to and trust. I also kind of looked up to him. From a wrestling standpoint, there was no doubt that I was the leader, but in life, he was the leader. He might not have had a great formal education, but he was sharp and had a lot of street smarts.

I was not a very deep thinker and was pretty naïve about how and why other people acted certain ways. Kevin would point stuff out to me. He didn't try to stir things up like other guys, he simply looked out for me. It was the first time that I had a real ally.

I told him about my situation in the locker room, how a lot of people didn't like me. "It doesn't matter," he said. "I like you."

"Well, a lot of people want to beat me up."

"Nobody is going to beat you up. Don't worry."

Now we had to figure out what we were going to do with him. The first thing we had to do was figure out a name. Shane McMahon came up with Diesel, and the more we heard it, the better it sounded. Our next step was coming up with his personality. We all figured that a guy with me should have a cool character. I had played with the idea of having a Secret Service type bodyguard, but Kev didn't really fit that role. The "cool" idea was much better, so Kevin was going to come out with a jean jacket and shades. We also decided that he wouldn't be very active. With his size, all he needed to do was hit my opponent with one punch or kick. Any more at this point would be overkill and would take away from his mystique. Kevin agreed to everything. He didn't have any inhibitions, and he wasn't afraid to laugh at himself.

We were now spending Tuesdays up at the company's TV studio doing interviews called *Face to Face*. The very first time Kevin and I went there, Sgt. Slaughter, who was working as an agent, walked up to Kevin and said, "You are with Shawn. Here's your schedule. Kiss your wife good-bye." Kev got a big chuckle out of that.

Kevin and I were very quick and natural together. We have the same sense of humor and were destroying people on these interviews. It didn't take me long to figure out that I was better if I had someone to work off. And with Kevin, it all came so naturally.

He ended up making his debut on June 6 at a house show in Albany. This was the night I was going to win the IC title back from Marty. Kevin walked out in the middle of the match. No one knew who he was, and a big gasp emanated from the crowd when this giant made his way toward the ring. Marty turned to see what was going on, and I superkicked him for the win. They showed the footage of this on the next *Raw* so everyone would know what had happened.

I'd work one more televised match with Marty that summer, but for all intents and purposes, we had finally concluded our story. I was now resuming my angle with Curt Hennig and heading into *SummerSlam*. On paper, Curt and I should have had a great match. We were both great workers, and we liked

wrestling each other. The only problem was, our styles didn't mesh. What we both did best was bring out the best in our opponents. Being dominant was something neither of us felt comfortable doing. My best offense was getting beat up all the time. His was getting backdropped or thrown into the turnbuckle. It's strange, but two great wrestlers don't always equal a great match. We only went ten minutes. I won via countout after Kevin threw him into the ring post.

17
a different light

I was twenty-eight years old now and in many ways the complete opposite of that boy who was enthralled by the treasure hunt and who sat nervously in class, dreading the moment the teacher would call his name during roll call. In other ways, I hadn't changed at all. If you remember back when I was in third grade and my mother wanted to give me the "switch" for something that did not warrant it, I ran from her. I could not accept being punished unfairly. Twenty years later, Vince McMahon was about to find out what my mother had learned those many years ago.

About two weeks after *SummerSlam,* Vince called

and told me I had tested positive for steroids. "What?" I asked incredulously.

"You tested positive for steroids."

"I'm not taking steroids."

"The test came back positive. You have to take six weeks off."

"I'm not taking six weeks. I didn't do anything!"

At the time I weighed almost 240 pounds. I was fat and couldn't believe he thought that I was taking steroids no matter what the test results were. "Look at me, I'm out of shape. I'm drinking a case of beer every night with Nash and matching him meal for meal. I would tell you if I took steroids. Why would I of all people take steroids?"

Every Tuesday night after the *Face to Face* interviews, a whole bunch of us would meet up at the Holiday Inn at Newark Airport and we would go to the bar. I told Vince, maybe someone put something in one of my drinks. I told him that I might be a pain in the rear sometimes, but one thing he could always count on was my honesty. I would always tell him the truth. And I was, I didn't take steroids. I took a lot of other things which I told him about. But I did not take steroids. If I had done this, I would admit to it.

"I have no choice. You have to take the six weeks," Vince said.

"Fine!"

"Well, you have to give the belt back to us."

"I'm not giving the belt back to you."

Vince was angry, but I wasn't going to budge. I didn't do what they said I did. If I was being punished for something I did wrong, no problem. But I didn't do it. I told him about the things I did do and said, "If you want to punish me for that, that's fine, but I'm not giving your belt back."

"Fine. We'll talk in six weeks."

And that's how we left it. To explain my absence on television, they had "President" Jack Tunney announce that I had been suspended for "insubordination." They held a battle royal to pick the two guys who would then fight for the IC championship. Scott Hall and Rick Martel won, and then Scott beat Rick to become the IC champ. They gave him another championship belt.

I didn't do anything special during my six weeks off. I hung out at home and went to the gym. I had to get in better shape. I was really heavy. Scott was calling me tiny Elvis—he meant the fat Elvis, of course.

I still talked to the guys on a regular basis, and about four or five weeks into the suspension, we came up with the idea that when I came back I would claim that no one ever beat me for the IC title and I had the belt to prove it. We thought we could do a belt versus belt angle with Scott.

At this point in Vince's and my relationship, I would go off on Vince periodically and then call him back and say I was sorry, and that I had lost it. He was always patient and forgiving. I think he put up with me because he really admired my desire to be good and, for lack of better words, my love for the business. Vince also knew that I would do just about anything for him. I didn't apologize for the steroids, because I hadn't taken them. After a few weeks, we had both cooled down and everything was fine between us. "How about me coming back and saying that no one ever beat me for the belt." Vince liked the idea. He was always saying, "Let's turn a negative into a positive," and that's what we did. Scott and I were soon off on a program that would end in what many people call the greatest match of all time. I don't know if it was or it wasn't, but I do know that it was the match that catapulted me from being a great worker and Intercontinental Champion, into a real star with World Wrestling Federation Championship potential.

When Scott and I started our program, we knew we were going to build to a match at *WrestleMania X,* but we had no idea we were going to do a Ladder match there, not even after doing a few at house shows in January 1995. I don't know who actually came up with the idea. My guess is that Pat Patterson, who always came up with great ideas, pushed for it. It made perfect sense to do a Ladder match because both of us had legitimate claims to the IC title, and both of our belts could hang from the rafters above the ladder. There were two belts and there could only be one champion. Why not make one of us climb that ladder and grab to see who really deserved to be called the Intercontinental Champion? We didn't have to force anything. It wasn't like the ladder was thrown out there to be interesting or exciting. It fit within the story, and that's why I think the Ladder matches they've had since can't compare to this one. A lot of them were really good—they just seemed a little forced.

We wanted to make sure that we came into the match with a lot of steam. At the *Royal Rumble,* I interfered in Scott's match against Irwin R. Schyster. I hit Scott with my belt, and IRS scored the pinfall, but another referee disallowed the pin and Scott won a short time later.

I was in the *Royal Rumble* match and was able to stay in for a decent amount of time and get over. I pulled a "Curt Hennig special." I remember watching him in the *Rumble* one year, and he was bouncing around all over the place. He was almost knocked out a million times but always saved himself at the last minute. He didn't win the *Rumble,* but he got over like a million bucks because the camera was always on him. I thought, "That's what I am going to do," and the spotlight stayed on me and helped me get over.

| | |

WrestleMania X took place at Madison Square Garden on March 20, 1994. Scott and I were rushing around most of the day doing interviews and autograph sessions, and we didn't have a lot of time to prepare for the match. About the only thing we did do was climb the ladder so the production crew could determine what height to hang the belts.

There was a real buzz in the Garden when we came out for the match. The belts were hanging from the ceiling, the ladder was standing in the entrance, and the anticipation of the unknown was palpable. I could almost feel that something special was going to happen.

We started the match with basic Wrestling 101 moves, and then I threw Scott out of the ring. Kevin—as my bodyguard, he always came to the ring with me—clotheslined Scott and was sent to the dressing room by referee Earl Hebner. Scott then took control. He threw me into the turnbuckle, and I flew out onto the floor. Scott came after me and lifted up the padding that covered the concrete floor around the ring. The crowd oohed and aahed in anticipation of me being dumped on the hard ground, but I poked Scott in the eye and tossed him back in the ring. I sent him into the ropes, but he reversed it and nailed me with a real stiff clothesline. He followed it up by going for his finisher, the Razor's Edge, but I flipped him over the ropes and onto the concrete floor that he had exposed.

With Scott down for a bit, I grabbed the ladder and brought it to the ring. He stopped me with a punch before I could bring it in and tossed me in the ring. Then as Scott attempted to slide the ladder under the ropes, I took a running start and baseball slid the ladder right into his stomach. For the next ten minutes we went back and forth, using the ladder as a weapon, and every time we did, the crowd yelled louder and louder. I jammed it into his midsection, I smashed it on his back. I tried to climb for the belts and he grabbed my tights and exposed my fanny for all the world to see.

I climbed up the ladder and splashed him all the way from the second rung, before going for the belts again. Scott recovered in time and knocked me and the ladder over. I went flying off into the ropes and bounced high in the air. He then whipped me into the ladder, which I had earlier propped in the corner. The force of the collision sent me out of the ring. The crowd was deafening now. Scott beat on me with the ladder outside the ring, eventually slingshotting me into the ladder and causing it to fall on me as I fell backward. I was beat like a rag doll, but Scott wasn't done. He threw me back in the ring and smashed me in the face with the ladder. I was sent out once again, and he started to climb for the belts.

Every time one of us climbed for the belts, the crowd went crazier and crazier. The energy they produced was soaring through me. I struggled back up and climbed the ropes from the outside and flew at Scott, who fell off the ladder. We both lay there for a bit, trying to recover. Eventually, we struggled to our feet and started to climb the ladder at the same time. We threw a few blows at each other before he bodyslammed me over the top of the ladder. By now, I could barely hear myself think.

Scott climbed the ladder again. This time I drop-kicked it, knocking him off it.

I took control now, sending him into the ropes and nailing him with the superkick and then a piledriver. It was now time for something really special. I brought the ladder to the corner, climbed up to the top turnbuckle, and splashed Scott ladder first. The crowd went nuts as I straddled the ladder over Scott, who was lying prone on the canvas, and began climbing. It looked like I was going to win.

Scott struggled up, though, ran off the ropes, and smashed into the ladder. I flew off it and landed on the ropes, or I should say the ropes landed between my legs and I rolled headfirst towards the mat. I tried to regain my bearings as Scott started to climb the ladder, but I hooked my foot in the ropes and was unable to stop Scott from climbing the ladder, snatching the belts, and winning the match.

When we made it to the back, we knew we had stolen the show. We didn't know that we had set a new standard. We just knew we had a great match. Soon, everyone else started putting the match over, and that really gave us the sense that we had done something out of the ordinary. The icing on the cake was when Gorilla Monsoon told us, "I think that may have been the greatest match I've ever seen." Gorilla Monsoon, of all people! He had been with the company since its inception in 1960. He wrestled for over twenty years and then went on to become a great announcer and front office person. He garnered more respect than just about anyone else in the business, and he was very old-school. He appreciated ring psychology and wasn't into gimmicks like ladders. His was the compliment of compliments because he didn't give out many.

My mentors had always told me that it didn't matter if you won or lost, only that you put on a great match. I'm sure they were proud of their student. I lost the match, but I made my career. People began to look at me in a different light.

18
new beginnings

Any time you come off a loss at a Pay-Per-View, what you do the next night is very important—more important than the loss the night before. I thought I could make a big impact with a brand-new interview segment and had thrown out the idea of doing one sometime before *WrestleMania X*. I figured it would elevate my status in the public's eye, because if I didn't wrestle all the time, the times I did wrestle would seem more special. Roddy Piper was the master of this. When he was doing Piper's Pit, you almost never saw Roddy wrestle on TV. He only wrestled on major occasions. That's exactly what I wanted to do. The Ladder match changed a lot of people's perspective of me, and I was now trying to become a star and special commodity.

It was my idea to call the segment *The Heartbreak Hotel.* I was a big Elvis fan and I was, after all, the Heartbreak Kid. It was the perfect name. Kevin and I were quick on the stick and I knew we could do a good job, which we did. We really enjoyed doing it as well. We didn't script things, so we were able to use our wits to stir everyone up.

Along with doing *The Heartbreak Hotel,* I became Kevin's accomplice. It was almost a reversal of what he had done for me. It made no sense for him to have me for his bodyguard, but I'd come to the ring for all his matches and cause trouble. I was very active on the outside and still bumping all over the place.

Away from the arena, Kevin, Scott, Sean Waltman—the 1-2-3 Kid—and I were really becoming a tight-knit group. We traveled together, partied together, and discussed wrestling all the time. We were a rarity in this business: we were friends.

I had known Scott since '85, and Kevin and I had been close since the previous May. Kid arrived right before Kevin. He actually made his first appearance the night I had that street fight with Curt Hennig. He beat Scott in a huge upset, and those two started a little program. Scott took Kid under his wing. Scott had been broken in by Curt and believed in the "take the young boy in under your wing and school him" mentality. We knew that Kid was young and didn't know anybody here, so we just asked him to jump in the car his first night. He sat in the back, we tossed him a beer, and he rode with us until he left for WCW three years later.

The four of us liked to have fun, but we also were very much into our jobs. We talked business all the time, trying to come up with angles, matches, and character changes. Kevin and I did most of the talking. Kid, once he became more comfortable, spoke up, while Scott was pretty quiet for the most part. Every once in a blue moon, though, he would come out with bits of brilliance.

When I was just beginning my singles career, I thought about what finisher I would use. Several people mentioned the superkick, which I had taken from Chris Adams in WCCW, but I didn't believe I could use that because I'd already been using it in my matches as just another move. I hadn't been beating anyone with it. I thought I needed something new.

After I started using the Fisherman's Suplex as my finisher, Scott came up to me and said, "You know, you ought to use the kick for your finisher. It's the best move you've got." He was right.

You could see Kevin and I were having a good time.

Another time, shortly after Kevin came in, we were riding in the car and talking about moves Kevin was doing in the ring. I thought it was impressive that a man his size could leapfrog, so I had him do it a couple of times. Scott blurted out to Kevin, "You're the biggest guy in the company. Why are you avoiding contact? I think it's stupid." Kevin and I looked at each other and admitted that was true. "Good call," we said.

Scott, with his self-deprecating personality, replied, "I'm just a dummy. I don't know what I'm saying," and we spent the next two hours trying to convince him that it was a good idea. Scott always had lots of good ideas and was very wise. We were always trying to convince him that he wasn't a dummy.

Kevin, Scott, Kid, and I could crack jokes on each other or occasionally get mad at one another, but it wouldn't dent our friendship. Right before *Wrestle-Mania X*, we went on a European tour. Scott and I were wrestling and Kevin was going to be down at ringside with me. Chief Jay Strongbow was the agent there. He loved Kevin and by this time had warmed up to me as well. Before we went out there, and unbeknownst to Scott and me, he asked Kevin, "Do you think you can shake the ring, big man?"

"I don't know."

"Thinking of a spot here."

Chief Jay had nicknames for everyone, and he always called me Teaspoon. Scott had given me that name because I was small compared to most of the guys.

"Teaspoon and Chico [his name for Scott] do a double knockout. While they are down, you shake the ring."

"Okay, I'll try it."

We did the double knockout and the crowd started rumbling to try and get us energized and to our feet. All of the sudden we heard this really loud noise of metal against metal. Kevin was banging a chair against the ring post!

Europe was what we called a virgin market. We didn't go there very often, and you didn't have to do much to get the crowd going. All you had to do was take a tackle and the fans would come out of their seats. Well, here's this seven-foot monster banging this chair against the ring post. They had no idea what to make of it, and they went dead silent. I yelled to the referee, "Tell him to put that chair down!"

He did, but by this time the match was a debacle. The crowd couldn't get back into it, and we finished it quickly, Scott won, and then we came to the back.

"Chief," I screamed. "I know you love Kevin and I love him too, but tell him to get over in his own match!"

I then asked Kevin what he was doing out there. "I went over there to shake the ring but it didn't budge. So I figured I would just pick up the chair and start banging it or something."

After a while I calmed down and realized that it was funny because it was so stupid. It made no sense. It killed the match. I was very much a ring general then, and when people made mistakes, I would get pretty upset and yell at them. No one ever said anything to me about yelling at them. I think that's because they respected my ability. I don't think it endeared me to them anymore, but I could live with that. I know Scott and Kevin didn't mind, they were my buddies. Sometimes I still wonder what in the world Kevin was thinking banging that chair against the ring post.

| | |

I often say that I've traveled the world and seen nothing. And for the most part, that's true. My career has taken me all over the globe, from Japan to Kuwait to Singapore to Dayton, Ohio. I must have logged more than a million miles through the years, and until very recently, I never had much interest in the places I went. To be fair, it wasn't like we had a lot of time to sightsee. We'd come into a town, wrestle, and move on to the next town. Every once in while, we had opportunities to see sights, but I never took advantage of them. I was too interested in partying.

In April of 1994, we did a quick tour of Israel. Now that I am a Christian, I wish that I would have taken some time to see the sights. I could have walked where Christ walked, and that would have been amazing. Unfortunately, in '94 I had no interest in that. I remember a lot of guys went to check out the Dead Sea, but I didn't even go there.

I did have a ball wrestling Owen Hart, though. We were in a Tag match against Bret Hart and Scott in Huron. I worked as Ric Flair the entire match. I did the strut, the knife-edge chops to the chest. I crashed into the turnbuckle like he does and even did his fall. The crowd had no idea that I was imitating my hero, but they ate it up and we just had a ton of fun.

When we came back to the States, Kevin beat Scott for the Intercontinental Championship. It was his first title and we were all happy for him. I couldn't celebrate for long, however. I had some personal business that I had to take care of.

| | |

Theresa and I were hanging on by the barest of threads. We had a very strange marriage, and it wasn't fulfilling for either of us. I had my career and totally separate wrestling life. We didn't spend much time together and had grown apart.

I had a personal appearance to do in the Poconos, and she came with me. We thought maybe a few days alone in a nice place might help repair our relationship. One day into our trip, I was called down to Tampa to testify in a court case. This was serious business and everything I had worked for over the years might be taken away. I told her I had to leave. Theresa said she understood, but I could tell she was not happy. While I was in Tampa, she called and said she wanted a divorce. She told me she was absolutely sure about it, and we started arguing. Then she said, "I'm allowed to have half."

I became very angry. Theresa wanted to leave and take half of everything I owned. I felt like the whole world was crashing down on me at once. I had finally made some money in this business, and now it might all be gone. I realize that was selfish, but that's what I was thinking. The idea of getting divorced didn't bother me as much as losing half my money did. I told her I couldn't deal with this right now and asked her if we could talk about this when I got home. She said, "Sure."

We had moved to Dallas from the Tampa area a few years earlier because neither of us liked it in Florida. By the time I had returned home, she had already moved out of the house. Being alone and having a few moments to sit and think made me realize that Theresa was right: We had no future. We barely had a past. I called her that night and we discussed our situation in a very rational manner. We both agreed that getting a divorce was the way to go.

Theresa and I settled everything in a reasonable and amicable manner. We even used the same lawyer, which is almost unheard-of in divorce cases, and she didn't even want the fifty percent that Texas law provided for her. All she wanted was our car, a few belongings, and enough money so that she would be comfortable while beginning her new life. When the divorce became final, I wasn't heartbroken. I definitely cared for her, but I wasn't in love with her. All I cared about was wrestling.

I I I

I enjoyed being Kevin's sidekick, but after a few months I starting thinking about what I might do upon returning to the ring. He was doing well as the IC champ, and I figured we could do well as Tag Team Champions. It would be good for both of us. He would have two titles and I would have one. If he had to lose the IC belt, he could always drop it to Scott.

Some people think we were these big manipulators looking to keep others down. We weren't. Putting the tag titles on Kevin and me made good business sense. It was a way of doing something we hadn't done, and it was a way of keeping ourselves on or near the top of the card. Kevin and I were over. If we weren't, Vince would not have given us the titles. There's no manipulating Vince, and we weren't bad-mouthing other people to get the titles. It's my understanding that some of the boys made a big to-do over this. It was Vince's decision to make us Tag Team Champions. Scott, Kevin, and myself made the Intercontinental title white-hot. We wanted to see if we could do that to the tag team titles.

Kevin and I beat the Headshrinkers in Indianapolis to win the championship. It was the third time I had ever won a title here, and the second time it actually counted (remember the fiasco in Fort Wayne). I don't know if there's any significance to this, but I won all three championships in Indiana.

The following day, at *SummerSlam* in Chicago, Kevin dropped the IC title to Scott. This was a really fun match because Walter Payton was in Scott's corner. Walter was a very neat guy and very into the show. I remember going to Vince and saying, "Let me do a spot where he chases me. I guarantee he won't catch me." That's right, I, the guy who ran a 5.1 forty in high school, thought that the great Walter Payton wasn't fast enough to catch me. What a piece of work I was!

What we did instead was have me accidentally superkick Kevin. Then Walter pulled me out of the ring so I couldn't stop Scott from covering Kevin.

Any time we did something with athletes, it usually went pretty well. They were huge fans and appreciated our athleticism. Lawrence Taylor, the NFL Hall of Famer who wrestled Bam Bam Bigelow at *WrestleMania XI,* came to the back after his match and said, "There's no way I could do this more than once. How many times a year do you do this?" When I told him about two hundred, he exclaimed, "That's like a football game every night with no off season!"

After defending our titles for a month, we found out Vince had bigger plans for Kevin: he was going to win the World Wrestling Federation Championship. It was somewhat ironic that we had just won the tag team titles and were going to try and get them over and now we had to split up, but it was great that Kevin was going to get *the* championship. Vince wanted to turn Kevin babyface, so we teased problems in our team. At a television taping in White Plains, New York, I accidentally superkicked Kevin during a match against Scott and Kid. This is one of my favorite matches. It was so fun and relaxing to be working with friends. I didn't have to worry about anything. There were no trust issues. We all just went out and had a good time. It may have been the most enjoyable match I've ever had.

| | |

At *Survivor Series* we did the full turn. Kevin and I were on the same team with Jeff Jarrett, Owen Hart, and Jim Neidhart. We were wrestling Scott, Kid, Davey Boy Smith, and The New Headshrinkers. During the contest, I "accidentally" superkicked Kevin again. We lost the match and he came after me backstage. I verbally assaulted him and took off. He was now a babyface and I his chief rival heel.

Three days later at Madison Square Garden, Kevin beat Bob Backlund in less than ten seconds to become the World Wrestling Federation Champion. It was a great moment for Kevin, Scott, Kid, and myself. I was happy for Kevin. Yes, I had brought him in. And yes, I had been wrestling longer than he had, but I wasn't jealous or bitter. He was my friend.

After he won the title, he pulled me in the shower and said, "I have you to thank for all this. When I came here, I told you I saw you being a rising star, and

I wanted to hook myself to you. I have you to thank for everything. I never thought I could be a World Wrestling Federation Champion, and I learned so much from you." He said the best thing that ever happened to him during his career was standing ringside and watching me work. Kevin told me he learned more from watching me than from anything he'd ever done in the ring. And then he said, "We are friends, and that happens very rarely in this business. That's why nobody likes us."

I told him how happy I was for him. "Let's make sure we'll always talk and that we won't let anybody stir up a lot of stuff to ruin our friendship. That means more to me than anyone." That night Vince took us out to Smith & Wollensky for a steak dinner.

After Kevin won the title, we really started to feel the heat in the locker room. Kevin's the champ, I'm one of the top heels, and it looks like we are pretty influential. No one said anything to us. They didn't have the guts to do that. But we could feel it. There was a lot of gossip about why Kevin and I never dropped the tag team titles. People claimed that we didn't want to lose to anyone, that we wouldn't put anyone else over. That's not true. We were never asked to do so, and it wouldn't have made sense for us to lose. Who wants their champion to lose in a tag team match right before he wins the championship? That's not going to make him look very strong. But if we had been asked to lose, we would have. It's a shame that people felt compelled to spread rumors. We didn't get a chip on our shoulders when someone else had their run. Why were they giving us a bunch of heat?

| | |

Vince let us know pretty early on that I would be facing Kevin at *WrestleMania XI* in Hartford. My job was to make Kevin look as good as I could. In order to do this, it made sense to make me as strong as possible going into our match. Kevin had worked a couple times as champion, but folks weren't working with him that well. He needed a decent win. So the bigger they built me up, the better Kevin would look after his win. Most of the time before *WrestleMania* we push the guy we are going to go with afterwards. This time it was different because I was getting the big push at the *Royal Rumble.*

In order to build up my steam, I came up with an idea for the *Royal Rumble*. I told Pat Patterson, "If you want to get me over, put me in first and let me last the whole time and win it." Pat always liked my ideas, and he wanted to do something different too. I was the type of character that you wanted to hate, but you had to admit, "He's good." And that's good heat. My heat derived from the fact that everyone thought they could take me, but they weren't completely sure. And I was cocky. I wasn't a cool heel like Ric Flair, or a big strong one like Undertaker. I was hateable through and through. If I won the *Rumble* from the first position, it would really make the fans angry. They'd be dying to see Kevin knock the snot out of me. However, there'd be that doubt. Maybe this guy can beat the seven-foot monster?

Pat and I discussed having a finish where Davey Boy, who would be the last

That's Davey Boy twisted up in the ropes with me.

one in there with me, would clothesline me over the top, but only one of my feet would hit the floor. Davey would think I had been eliminated and while he was celebrating, I would toss him over the top and win the match.

Vince was hesitant. The year before he had Bret and Lex Luger do something similar and it didn't work. "Don't worry," I said. "I can do it."

"No."

"I can do that. I'm an athlete."

"Okay. But I know how you are. Just hit the one foot and come right back up. Don't worry about dangling and all the melodramatics. You don't have to go all the way with it. If he hits you too hard and you can't control yourself . . ."

"I can control myself."

During the *Rumble,* I hung a little longer than maybe Vince would have liked me to before I pulled myself back in the ring. I knew they were going to play it back on replay, and I wanted to make sure they got it and it looked good. The *Rumble* worked out exactly as planned. I entered number one and Davey Boy entered number two. It was Pat's idea to have Davey come in at the beginning as well. It made the ending exciting because the crowd knew that one of us was going to make history. We battled through the other twenty-eight competitors, and then Davey hit me with the clothesline. I scraped my foot and hung from the ropes just as we had talked about and pulled myself back into the ring. Davey Boy was celebrating his "win" standing on the turnbuckle when I came up from behind and tossed him onto the floor. I was going to *WrestleMania* to face Kevin.

Despite our good show at the *Rumble,* Vince had two big worries going into *WrestleMania XI.* The first was whether our fans would buy the possibility of me beating a guy as big as Kevin, and the second was the overall health of the company. To alleviate his first worry, he decided to bring in Sycho Sid as my bodyguard. Sid was very big, 6'8" and over 300 pounds, and very intimidating. He had a different character than Kevin. He wasn't funny and loose and always wore a scowl when the cameras were on. Sid looked like a real tough guy. You knew Kevin was tough, but that wasn't the first thing you noticed about him. He would sort of lull you into a sense of comfort and then beat you up. This was more than just a subtle little difference between the two, and Sid's edge gave me the equalizer that Vince was looking for. With Sid by my side, Kevin's title was in real jeopardy. Sid, for his part, was very into playing my bodyguard.

As for Vince's financial concerns, he decided to bring in Lawrence Taylor and have him wrestle Bam Bam Bigelow in the main event. Business was down. We hadn't sold out a nontelevised event at Madison Square Garden since 1989, and the company was going through a relatively long transition period. Vince never sold our problems too seriously, but we could see the numbers falling off at shows.

I never panicked about this situation because as a performer, all I could do was go out and put on the best performance I could. Everything else was out of my hands. I likened it to an actor playing a part in a movie. All I can do is make the best out of the script. If nobody goes to see it, I don't know what to tell you.

Bam Bam Bigelow, a wrestler who was below Kevin and me on the card, and LT, a football player, were in the main event, but these kinds of things happen at *WrestleMania*. Folks that aren't a part of the wrestling business sometimes grab the spotlight and big payday at *WrestleMania*. We work hard all year and then somebody else comes in and gets the biggest piece of the pie and leaves. Vince explained it to me this way: if we could use these guys to get more eyes watching our product, then we would all win in the long run because if we put on a good show, these new eyes were going to continue to follow us. His logic made sense, and LT's coming in didn't stick in my craw.

Working as a heel against a big guy like Kevin was an easy thing for me. In the worst-case scenario, all I had to do was bump all over the place, but wrestling Kevin was far from a worst-case scenario. Now, I couldn't go out there and beat him up, nobody would buy that. Instead, I chopped him down, and *then* I beat him up. It worked, and a lot of people say it was one of his best matches. I take that as a huge compliment.

I always want to do something special at *WrestleMania,* and this year I decided to do a moonsault off of the top rope for the first time in my career. I had done plenty of backflips, but I had never moonsaulted from the top onto my opponent on the floor. Before the match, Kevin and I were talking, and I brought it up. "What do you mean?" he asked. "Onto the floor?"

"Yeah."

"Are you going to do it tonight?"

"I don't know."

"I'd sort of like to know. I'm gonna have to catch you. Whatever I have to do, I'll get my body in the way."

"You're so big, if you can just break my fall."

"I usually do the cross body with you, are you going to do that?"

"No, I'd like to try the moonsault. I've never done it. If I get up on the ropes, I'm doing it. I can't chicken out in front of the people."

"I'll be there."

He was, and it worked out fine.

Unfortunately, not everything worked out as well as the moonsault. Vince was hooking his wagon to Kevin. He thought that the more powerful Kevin looked, the more people would be attracted to him. We were going over the match and we came to the point where I was going to kick Kevin with my superkick and attempt to cover him. Vince said, "I want a strong kickout."

Kevin didn't like it. "That's Shawn's finish. I've got to barely come out of that."

"I want you to be strong."

"That's not going to make me look strong. That's Shawn's move. The people are not going to like that. They are going to think you are pushing me too hard."

The fans knew that my superkick was a strong move, that it should hurt everyone, even Kevin. Within the context of the match, they would expect the kick to hurt him. If Kevin popped up after a count of one, we would destroy the fans' suspension of disbelief and ruin their experience. They would be taken out of the moment and feel cheated. They'd be angry and boo, mostly at Kevin. I might even garner some sympathy because they'd think that I was getting the shaft.

It made more sense to have Kevin struggle out. Fans always like babyfaces who struggle. It gives them someone to get behind. "Vince," I pointed out. "You want the fans to get behind him. He's my buddy, and I want the fans to get behind him. It needs to be a one-two-barely up. That will get him over. If he powers out on one, they are not going to like it."

We had seen it the year before. Vince tried to force Lex Luger down the

We could feel the Garden crowd turning.

people's throats, and it didn't work. You can't say I am pushing this guy, and I don't care. The people have to want to buy into the person. They have to see something in him that they can identify with. We understood that Vince was looking for the next big thing, but we knew we couldn't force it. Vince has that "I can do anything" attitude, which is why he has been so successful.

We told him that we thought the people weren't going to like it, but Vince wanted it, so that was what we did. When the time came for the kick, I hit Kevin with it and he popped up at one. The boos came raining down. "I knew it!" Kevin grumbled.

I quickly called for a belly-to-back suplex. I crawled over to him and said, "Barely kick out." We got a two count as he just got his shoulder up. The crowd, wanting to get back into it, screamed, "Ahhhhhhh."

"I think we got them back," I told him, and we finished the match without further incident. When we came backstage, we went to Vince, shaking our heads. "Yep, bad call," he admitted frankly.

The next day, we had a television taping in Poughkeepsie. When I arrived at the building, Vince told me he wanted to talk. "Shawn, we are going to switch you babyface."

"What! It's because of the kickout, isn't it?"

"It was a bad call on my part. I admit it."

"Why is it affecting me? I'm the only heel that you have."

"They like you, the people like you, Shawn."

"They like me, but they like to hate me. Now is not the time. You make the mistake and it costs me in my career!" I was not happy.

"We're going to have Sid drop you—injure you—tonight, and you'll go home for six weeks."

I was so frustrated, so bummed. We had told him that the people were going to boo. "Vince," I said, "I would never tell you how to run your entire business, but please, leave the wrestling to me."

Then I went and told Kevin what was happening. "They're taking me off for six weeks."

"What for?"

"They are turning me babyface."

"It's because of the kickout, isn't it!"

What could we do? Sid turned on me that night. He attacked me from behind and powerbombed me three times before Kevin rushed to the ring and chased him off. I was now injured and off on a six-week paid vacation.

19
the kliq

Kevin and I were sitting in the back at *WrestleMania XI*
when an unfamiliar face walked up to us. "I don't want to
interfere," he said, "but my name is Paul Levesque. I talked
to Terry Taylor [down in WCW] and he said you are the guys
to hang out with. So if you don't mind, I'd like to hang out
and travel with you."

That is how I met one of my best friends, Triple H, or
Hunter, as most people call him. I thought it took guts to
introduce yourself to the two guys who were in the main
event at *WrestleMania*. He was very nice about it. I can
remember years before when the Nasty Boys introduced

themselves to Marty and me. They took a little different approach. "We hear you guys like to party. We like to party too. We are going to hang out with you," and they did and we had fun.

Hunter was much more respectful. He was flattering us in a way. I think he was saying, "You guys are where the industry is going and I'd like to be with you."

We said, "Sure," and Hunter jumped in the car with us the following day. For the next year and a half, he, Kevin, Scott, Kid, and I were almost inseparable. We spent so much time together, Lex Luger gave us the name the Kliq. We thought that was cool.

I was very close to Vince now, and so was Kevin. Hunter, through Kevin and me, was beginning to establish a relationship there. Because we had Vince's ear, most of the other wrestlers began to resent us. They didn't like me already. Kevin is such a friendly person that he was tough to dislike, but he still got heat for being in the Kliq. Many thought we were using our relationship with Vince to stay on top and keep them down.

Were we bad-mouthing others and "trying to keep them down"? No. We could get on people if they didn't want to do business, but we told them to their face. We had this pirate guy, Jean Pierre Lafitte, and he didn't want to put Kevin over. Kevin was *the* champion and Lafitte was fairly low on the card. The champion beat all of us. So we buried him, *but* we did it to his face. We let him know everything we were doing. We called Vince up and told him that "the pirate needs to go." Vince told us to lighten up, he would talk to Lafitte. Vince didn't fire him. He didn't think our suggested punishment fit the crime.

Were we using our political clout to keep each other on top? Absolutely. What we did was no different from what Hogan, Savage, Piper, and Bob Orton Jr. had done before. If you are on top, you want to make sure you keep working with people on top. That's how you stay up there. The only difference between us and Hogan's and Savage's crew was that we actually liked each other. That's another reason why we had heat. We didn't resent each other's success. We weren't bitter. There were five of us, and it didn't matter which one was on top. We could always work with, and trust, each other. In addition, we were also smart enough to want to wrestle other top guys like Undertaker and Bret Hart. It would have been stupid of us to not want to wrestle people who were that good.

We got close to Vince by design and wanted to be close to him. We liked and admired him. It was the smart thing to do. Pat Patterson was always telling me, "The office is not your enemy. We are here to help you. We hired you to work here. You think we are actually out to get you?" We understood Pat was right and tried to work with Vince and the rest of the office. Vince, for his part, could see that we cared. We cared about our careers and the company's well-being. When I received my six-week "vacation" after *WrestleMania XI,* I spent most of it up in Stamford at the company's television studio. I wanted to learn how they put together a show. I wanted to learn as much as I could about the business. I was legitimately interested. Vince liked my passion and curiosity.

Vince also appreciated that we were honest with him. When he asked us a question, we gave him an honest answer. I think Vince respected us for that. Most people would tell him whatever they thought he wanted to hear. They were afraid of him. If he asked us about something and we thought it was bad, we told him. We did not, however, go to him and bury people.

Not too long after Hunter started with the company, we were sitting in a restaurant in Indianapolis talking business like we always did. We knew we had a lot of talent in the company, but something we were doing wasn't working. The world was changing. We thought we needed to take an edgier approach.

At this time, the company was giving guys jobs as gimmicks. We had a garbage man, a dentist, and the pirate. Those aren't gimmicks. They are occupations. Also, we weren't doing any cool storylines. We had great talent like the Gunns, Bart and Billy, but we would just have them win the titles, lose them, and then win them back. There were no stories. It was as if we were still stuck in that era where the Rockers and the Rougeaus could get a six-month program out of me being hit once with the megaphone. That wasn't going to work in 1995. The perfect example is this angle Bret Hart was doing with the pirate Lafitte. The pirate stole Bret's jacket. That was the angle! Bret was like, "Oh my God! What am I supposed to do? I'm really angry now. He has my leather jacket. I want to kill him!" That stuff just wasn't cutting it.

What we needed was to have programs where each week we added to the story and threw more gasoline on the fire. WCW was coming on now. They were just about to go head-to-head with us on Monday nights. We needed to be better and more with the times.

We were talking about all these things and decided that we ought to call Vince. He had once told me, "You guys always think that I know everything. You think I am aware of everything that is going on. I don't know unless you tell me. You guys talk all the time, but you can talk in the locker room, you can talk to the agents, you can talk to Pat, but a lot of stuff doesn't get to me. If you have something important to say, you should tell me."

So I called him. I told him how everything we were doing sucked, and how we had to change everything. I gave him a few suggestions, and he asked, "Do you want me to fly there? We can discuss this if you have some ideas." I figured, why not? We can't do any worse than we are already doing.

Vince flew in to Indianapolis and rented a conference room in a hotel. Hunter, who was still fairly new, wasn't sure if he should be there. "I haven't been here that long, I probably shouldn't weigh in on this."

"You're in this room. You have an opinion and you are going to weigh in," said Vince.

So Hunter stayed, and Vince took out a list of all his performers. He asked us who we thought could go, and who we thought was deadweight. There weren't that many that were deadweight. There were plenty of guys we didn't like, but if we thought they could work, we told Vince, "They can work." We weren't buddies with Chris Candido, but we thought he had ability, and we told Vince that. We couldn't stand the pirate, but we said he could wrestle.

We also discussed our concerns with the angles we were doing and the types of characters we had. Vince listened to everything we had to say. He didn't tell us that anything was going to change right away. Nobody got fired either. He just thanked us for our input and our honesty. We felt better because we were able to get a lot of things off our chest and tell the one person that mattered.

Vince came to the show that night. It was very unusual for him to be at a house show in Indianapolis. When word leaked out that we had a meeting with Vince, there was some serious heat sent our way. All sorts of rumors came out from the guys who talked to the dirt sheets. Some accounts had us threatening Vince with a walkout, others had us drawing up a list of all the people we wanted fired. None of that was true.

| | |

At *King of the Ring* with Kama.

When I came back from the "injury," Vince didn't have a specific plan for me. I wrestled Sid a few times, and then wrestled Kama—Bear, as we liked to call him—at *King of the Ring.* I like wrestling Bear. He was big, but he could move and he knew karate so he could do things that other guys couldn't. I liked being in there with versatile athletes. It kept me fresh and challenged me. I have to admit, though, I wasn't that happy with my role. I said to Vince, "You turned me babyface for this?" What I didn't realize at the time was there are periods when it is okay to catch a breather, survey the landscape, and then see where the best place to go is. Essentially, I was impatient. After all, Vince had a whole roster to deal with.

At *In Your House 2,* I beat Jeff Jarrett for the Intercontinental Championship. Jeff was doing well with Road Dogg at the time, but I think he was having some professional squabbles with the company. He left right after I beat him. Not many people mention this one when they talk about my greatest matches, but I was real proud of it. Jeff and I did a real good job here, nothing fancy, no crazy moves. I won with the superkick after Road Dogg accidentally tripped him.

It was my third time winning the Intercontinental Championship, but it wasn't old. I didn't feel like it was a step sideways in my career. I always believed that you made the title, the title didn't make you. That's one of the problems with the business now. We put titles on guys, hoping that it's going to get them over. You need to get over first, then you get a title.

The only thing I wondered about was giving both titles to babyfaces (Kevin was still World Wrestling Federation Champion). I believed that with two babyface champions the fans would be satisfied and wouldn't have anyone to come out and root for. I believe business is best when you have a heel champ and the fans are clamoring for their babyface to beat him. Vince thought differently. He usually liked having a babyface champion and having people coming after him. I guess that's just a difference of opinion we have.

| | |

SummerSlam was now upon us, and the creative team decided that Scott and I should do another Ladder match. They asked me how I felt about it. "I know we can put on a good show, but as for how I feel about it, I don't like it."

Scott and I both believed it was a no-win situation. We had already done a Ladder match, and we knew we couldn't top it. To me, it was, "I want him to kick out strong on one," all over again. We didn't make a huge deal about it, though. It was one of those things, if you want it, I'll give it to you and I'll make it the best I can. This is your show. I don't like it, but it's up to you.

This time everyone wanted to get their two cents into the match. Normally getting more heads together is good. You can get more ideas. But there's always one or two people suggesting such stupid ideas that you just want to yell, "Get out!" The night before the match we were scrambling for ideas. Plenty of people were offering ideas, and it got to be too much. Then right before the match, Vince came to us and told us that we couldn't use the ladder as a weapon.

"What?"

"You can't use the ladder. We have a new violence code. Some people are starting to come down on us."

"It's a Ladder match. I have to hit him with it."

"Can't do it." So we didn't.

A record-setting 18,062 people crammed themselves into the Pittsburgh Civic Arena to see if Scott and I could top, or at least match, what we had done at *WrestleMania X.* The odds were against us; however, I don't think there was a disappointed fan in the entire arena.

The new restrictions made it a lot tougher for us, but we made up for it by doing a few more moves off the ladders. (We used two ladders in this match.) I suplexed Scott and hit a moonsault off the ladder, and Scott hit his Razor's Edge on me while I was climbing the ladder.

We thought we had a finish that would leave the fans gasping. I would hit my superkick while standing on my ladder, knocking Scott off his ladder. Then I'd go up and grab the belt. I kicked Scott, but when I went to snag the belt, it didn't release and I fell off my ladder. Recovering quickly, I backdropped Scott over the ropes onto some exposed concrete. This allowed me time to climb the ladder again. I grabbed the belt and had to tug on it, but it finally released.

I have to say that even though I felt like there was no way we could pull the match off, it was a wonderful challenge. We did as good a job as possible. Was it the first Ladder match? No, but it couldn't have been. The important thing was that we had stolen the show once again.

| | |

I held the title until mid-October, when an incident outside the ring forced me to abdicate it. Kevin, Scott, and Hunter were on a European tour and I was traveling with Kid and Davey Boy Smith through a run in western New York. We did a show in Binghamton on the thirteenth and decided to stay overnight in Syracuse en route to a show in Utica on the fifteenth. Upon arriving in Syracuse, we checked into our hotel and told some folks in the lobby that we were looking for a good place to go out. They said, "Follow us," and we did. This was back in the time when we did stupid stuff like that.

They led us to a small club. Everyone in the club knew who we were. It was one of those places where I felt like Fonzie. The women were all over us, and I'm sure this didn't endear us to any of the other guys there. I don't want it to sound like I was God's gift to women or anything like that. I received attention because I was on television. In our culture the vast majority of people think that if you are on television you are someone, and that's what was going on.

I wish I could tell you more about what happened that night, but the next thing I remember is waking up in the hospital the following morning with a big cut under my eye and a concussion.

Apparently, someone in the bar told me that I was out of it. So I left to go out and sit in the car until Kid and Davey were done. As I went out, a bunch of guys followed me, and as I was getting in the car, they attacked me and beat me up pretty good. How many guys came after me? I couldn't say. Somehow I made it back to the hotel and was placed in front of Sunny (Tammy Sytch) and Chris Candido's door. They saw that I was in bad shape, called an ambulance, and came with me to the hospital. When I woke up, Sunny was sleeping next to me on a gurney. That's all I know.

Later that day, I asked Kid and Davey Boy what happened. I wasn't angry, I just wanted to know what went down. Anybody who's gone through life and never lost a fight hasn't been in many. I figured we had all been in a fight. I was just like, "This sucks." Then, I noticed that they didn't have a scratch on them. They had a bunch of different stories and after a bit, I knew I wasn't going to get a straight answer out of them. Were they MIA? Or were they so wasted that they honestly couldn't remember what happened? If they had been MIA, I wouldn't have been surprised. I accept my friends for who they are, and they were in no shape to do anything anyways.

When Kevin and Scott came back from Europe, they tore into Kid and Davey. They sort of had a big brother complex when it came to me, and they were very angry with those guys. Everyone knows this wouldn't have happened if Kevin and Scott would have been there.

Vince wasn't happy when he saw me. He was first and foremost concerned about my well-being, but he also gave me the "you shouldn't be out doing that stuff" lecture. I must have looked pretty bad, because a lot of people besides Vince were making a big deal about my injuries. It's funny, but because I had no recollection of what happened, I wasn't traumatized or troubled by the incident. It was like it hadn't happened to me. I was sore and groggy, but I've been beaten up and sore for twenty years, so feeling physical pain was nothing new for me. I didn't think it was that serious. Vince, however, thought it was serious, and he wasn't going to let me wrestle.

We had an *In Your House* Pay-Per-View the next week in Winnipeg, where I was supposed to wrestle Dean (Shane) Douglas. The decision was made that I would forfeit the title to Douglas in Winnipeg. Gorilla Monsoon, the World Wrestling Federation president, would announce that I was unable to wrestle. Douglas, now the Intercontinental Champion, would have to defend his title against Scott. Scott beat Douglas and once again became the IC champion. It was the office who decided Scott would win the title. There was no great conspiracy on our part to keep the belt within the Kliq. And with all due respect to Shane, he wasn't getting over. They had already given up on him.

Shane came in with a big reputation from ECW. He was a dirt sheet hero. He talked to the sheet guys, and they built him up like he was the second coming, but he had little talent. He wrestled Kid when he first came in, and Kid came to the back and said, "Isn't going to happen." If you can't work with Kid, you can't work period. Kid was the wrestling barometer. Everyone that came in the door worked with him so that they could be evaluated. The fact is, Douglas was no good. We tried to help him. Hunter tried to come up with some material and angles with the guy, but he was worthless.

I've heard that Douglas claimed that we were sandbagging him, but that makes no sense at all. Who goes out and says, "I'll show you and the fans, I'll have a bad match"? Neither Kid nor Scott was going to go out there and stink the joint out. That's a reflection on them.

Douglas got over in ECW because he could cuss and knock other people. He bad-mouthed Ric Flair to no end. He'd say, "Ric Flair couldn't lace my boots." Who did he think he was? I don't mean to disrespect the guys who were in ECW, but they did things simply for shock value, and there's no art to that.

When I was in D-Generation X, in 1997 and 1998, we mocked the status quo and a lot of people, but we did it in a very sophomoric way. We played on words and hinted at things. If one of the women wrestlers had a boob job, we would say something like, "Did you get the mumps last week?" We were very over-the-top, and there was a lot of satire in what we did. As Vince always says, "eyebrows up." We weren't crude just to be crude.

As Kevin, Scott, Kid, Hunter, and I left Winnipeg and headed off for Brandon, Manitoba, where the following night's *Raw* was going to be held, we were faced with the challenge of figuring out what I was going to do next. Whenever something bad happened, Vince would always say, "Let's turn a negative into a positive," and that's exactly what we did. By the time we arrived at our hotel two and a half hours later, we had come up with a revolutionary angle that I would soon play out with Owen Hart.

That Monday night, I did an interview with Jim "J.R." Ross. I spoke about the incident in Syracuse, about having to give up the belt, and about the precariousness of my health. This was one of the first times we ever used a real-life incident and integrated it into an angle.

We had planted the seed that I had suffered a serious injury. A couple of weeks later in Richmond, I wrestled Owen. He gave me an enziguri—a kick to the back of the head—and I collapsed. No one besides Owen, myself, Vince, and Jim Ross and Jerry "the King" Lawler—who were announcing—knew that I was going to do this.

We really wanted it to look real and had convinced Vince that we should go to dead air when this happened. If J.R. and King kept talking, people would know it was a work. Vince didn't like the idea of going to dead air, but he finally agreed. As I lay prone on the mat, J.R. and King dropped their headsets and made it look like this was not part of a story line. The last five minutes of the show was all dead air with pictures of me laying in the ring and the EMTs trying to revive me.

I was taken to the hospital, where I worked the doctors. I acted like I was all groggy. Hunter came with me and played his part of concerned friend perfectly. I even had to sign a release to leave the hospital. Officials there told me that they had been flooded with inquiries about my condition. We pretty much fooled everybody.

On the following week's *Raw,* they announced that I was suffering from post-concussion syndrome, and on the one after that, they had a doctor say it was too risky for me to wrestle anymore. They even put together a video package narrated by Vince, in which he stated that even though Superstars appear to be superhuman, we are just mortal men.

Todd Pettingill interviewed me from San Antonio the following week, where he noted that I had never won the World Wrestling Federation Championship and now my career looked like it was over. He asked me how I could deal with coming so close but never being world champion. I was so upset with the question, I ended the interview and walked off.

As 1995 drew to a close, most fans had a lot of empathy for me. I felt great, though. I knew I was going to get the opportunity to become World Wrestling Federation champion. Vince McMahon had told me a few weeks before.

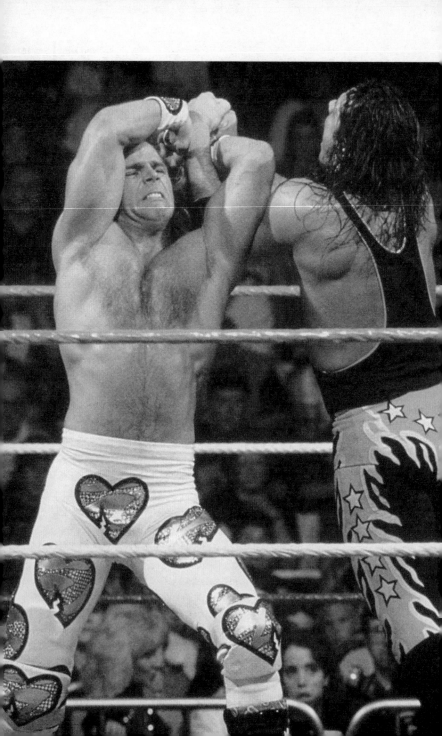

20
dreams and
nightmares

Sometime in the fall of 1995, Vince decided to change

course, and Bret Hart beat Kevin for the World Wrestling

Federation Championship at *Survivor Series.* I don't know

why this happened. Business wasn't great, but it had picked

up a little bit during Kevin's run. Maybe it was because

WCW was coming on strong and Vince felt he needed to

shake things up. They had Hogan and Savage, plus all their

mainstays, like Ric Flair. Eric Bischoff was running WCW

and he decided to put on WCW's *Nitro* opposite *Raw.* For

the first time, we had direct competition in our time slot. I'm

sure Vince sensed that he needed to do something.

I know Vince didn't plan on keeping the title on Bret for long because it was about that time that Vince told me he wanted me to beat Bret at *WrestleMania XII.* Vince thought we were both great wrestlers and that we could put on a heck of a show. He commented on how hard I worked, how I earned and deserved the title. He also told me to keep it quiet. He still had to talk to Bret about it. He said, "Bret will be fine, he'll do business. Bret's good about that."

It felt great to know Vince thought so highly of me, that I could be "the man" the company was going to go with. I wasn't going to do any celebrating yet, however. I had been around long enough to know that anything can happen and that things could change in a blink of an eyelash.

After Owen knocked me out, I took two months off from the ring and came back at the *Royal Rumble.* Any time you take time off from TV, you come back fresh in the fans' minds. This was important because I was now a babyface, my "heroic" comeback from post-concussion syndrome insured that, and I needed the fans behind me.

It was essential that I build as much momentum as I could as quickly as I could. I wasn't going to top last year's wire-to-wire win in the *Rumble,* but I had to win. I entered thirty-two minutes into the match and won twenty-five minutes later after superkicking Kevin out. With the win, I earned a title shot against Bret Hart.

We couldn't go right into my program with Bret because we still had an *In Your House* Pay-Per-View to do before *WrestleMania.* Vince definitely wanted to keep me front and center, so the next night on *Raw,* Owen Hart challenged me for the right to fight Bret at *WrestleMania.* I accepted and met Owen in the ring in Louisville on February 15.

Since Owen had nearly ended my career a few months back, we had unfinished business to take care of. It was a smart thing to put us together, not only because of that, but also because my title shot was now in jeopardy. If I didn't win, not only would I lose my shot at the championship, but I might lose my dream. Nobody wants to see a guy they like have his dreams crushed. I was putting everything on the line. People like folks who risk everything in chasing a dream. The fans wanted me to win, but the thought of Owen winning and having two brothers face off at *WrestleMania* for the World Wrestling Federation Championship was enticing. It left the result unpredictable.

During the match, we wanted to make sure we played off Owen's nearly ending my career. I think we did a good job. He hit me with his enziguri, the same kick that had rendered me unconscious in November, and then went for the pin. I managed to kick out after a long 2-count, and the crowd ate it up. They were really behind me now because I had showed them I was a fighter. The end came when I avoided another enziguri and nailed him with the superkick.

| | |

It was Vince who came up with the idea to go with the "boyhood dream" story-line for *WrestleMania*. He brought me in one day and said, "I want to tell your whole story. How you wanted to be a wrestler since you were twelve, your dream to be a champion and all the ups and downs of your career to get to this point. There's nothing better than that. It's true, it's real."

Jose Lothario was a big part of my story, and we decided to bring him in and have him train me for the match. It was a feel-good moment for our show, and in real life as well. Who isn't going to empathize with the kind old trainer helping his protégé win the World Wrestling Federation Championship?

A lot of people didn't like having Jose there. They thought having him there was corny, that it brought down the coolness of my character. I'm not going to say they didn't have a point. The world had changed, and this was not the time to be a white-meat babyface, but I didn't care. Jose was a big part of my story. My family was a big part of my story. I wanted them to be a part of it. I didn't care if some people thought it wasn't cool.

I haven't always been the best at choosing what's right for business over what's right from a personal standpoint, and this is something I'm perfectly willing to be knocked for. This was a situation where the wise business decision may not have been to have Jose there, but I wanted to. I didn't want to leave out that part of the whole story we were telling because it might not be "cool" to have a sixty-year-old man on television. Besides, business had picked up since I came back. With a main event of Kevin and I versus Undertaker and Bret Hart, we sold out Madison Square Garden for a nontelevised show for the first time since 1989. That was big. MSG was, and is, WWE's business barometer. Business looked like it was really turning around.

Jose was glad to be with me. He had never been involved in anything this big. He was thankful and appreciative. Our relationship was different now. I was a full-grown man and I had been in the business for ten years at this point. Jose knew that and didn't address me as a boy anymore. We shot the vignettes of him working me out in San Antonio and had fun reminiscing about old times. I saw Jean and his kids. She was very happy for me. She told me, "I always told people you would be world champion!" I think Jose was very proud of me too. He's a very reserved guy, and he would never tell me that to my face, but my mom used to say that he was proud of me.

It was Pat Patterson's idea to have Bret and me work a one-hour, most-falls-wins Iron Man match. Whenever he thought of or heard a good idea, he would get so excited. He told me, "The people will go crazy! They will love it! You two guys will tear the house down!"

I was psyched because I would finally have the chance to go an hour in a singles match, and because it would be a real challenge to keep the fans interested for the entire time. Most matches were pretty short, with lots of high-risk maneuvers. To pull this one off, Bret and I were going to have a great *wrestling* match. The challenge was huge, but I was up for it. When I won the title, I wanted people to say, "He's the champion because he is the best." I wanted to be the Ric Flair of this age. I knew I would probably never be the huge marketing draw like Hulk Hogan, but that was fine. I wanted to be respected by my peers and the fans as the best worker. When guys wrestled me, whether they liked me or not, they were going to have to admit, "He's the best." And no one was ever going to blow me up—tire me out. I remembered years ago when I met Ric Flair in a bar. He was throwing them down like they were going out of style, but by the time I got to the gym the next morning, he was already there, probably halfway done with his workout. No one ever tired him out. My girlfriend at this time, Themis, was a personal trainer and she was getting me into the best shape of my life. Did I want to go an hour with Bret? I would have gone two if Vince wanted.

At this point, Bret and I got along fine. I don't ever recall having a bad time with him until *after* I won the World Wrestling Federation Championship. When we first talked about the match, Bret said, "Vince spoke with me and I'm on board. I'm more than happy to do it for you. I don't have a problem putting you over. I just want the match to be good." He then made it very clear that he was doing me a favor, and he reminded me that he had told me a few years ago that he thought I would be the guy to take his spot.

I understood that Bret wasn't thrilled to be losing the title. Nobody ever wants to lose it. No one ever wants to step down from being the top guy. But that's business, so you do what the boss asks you to do. Our conversation was a little uncomfortable, but that was normal.

With that out of the way, we now had to discuss what we were going to do. Bret was a bit worried about going for an hour. His first concern was fitness. Wrestling for an hour is not like strolling through the park. You have to be in great shape to be able to do it. He told me that he would let me know how he was feeling during the match by giving me numbers between one and ten. If he said anything below five, it meant he was feeling good. If he said "eight," we needed to slow down. If he said "ten," we would grab a hold. I was very cool with this system. We wanted to know how the other was feeling so we could make the match as good as possible.

Bret was also worried about how we would fill the time. I know this is going to sound offensive coming from me, but Bret was not a great wrestler. He was good—very, very good—but not great. He wasn't that versatile in the ring. The things he did, he did well, but he didn't do a lot of exciting stuff. With Bret, you couldn't put a twist on the Russian leg sweep, the backbreaker, the drop of the elbow from the second rope and then the Sharpshooter. Once Bret went into his routine, he wouldn't change it up.

In my mind, once you have something established, like he had with those moves, that's when you begin to play with it. You don't ever play with it when you are establishing it, but once it gets over, you can mess with it and get the fans to go up and down.

His inflexibility—his selfishness—is one of the reasons he had trouble working with Kevin. Kevin may not have been great physically, but he had a great, creative mind. He liked, and needed, to do different things. When I worked with him, we did lots of different things. That's why we were able to have some really good matches. Bret didn't want to mix it up when they worked. He had to have everything his way. True, they had a personality clash as well, but when Kevin was going to drop the title to Bret at *Survivor Series* in '95, Bret needed to cater

With Gorilla and Jose. Earl Hebner lays out the rules for Bret and me.

to Kevin, the guy who was doing him the favor. Bret didn't—it had to be done his way.

With me, he was a little better. When we discussed the match, he said, "We need to first start thinking about different moves. We know all of our basic stuff that we do, that we want to get in, but we're in an hour match. We are going to have to do moves that we haven't done before. How do you feel about you coming up with the first thirty minutes, and I come up with the last thirty?"

"That's great," I answered.

Wrestling an hour was special, but I thought we could make it even more exciting if we kept it to one fall and ended up going to overtime tied 0–0. I didn't think Bret and I should be beating each other a bunch. If we were that easy to beat, we shouldn't be there wrestling for the World Wrestling Federation Championship. We built this match up as a contest between the two best wrestlers in the world, and at the end of an hour we weren't going to have a fall. What do you do then? You *have to* go to sudden death. I didn't think Bret would make a big deal about going to overtime after the match and use it as an out that I didn't really beat him.

I wanted to make the end of regulation as thrilling as possible too, so I came up with the idea where he would have me in the Sharpshooter and I'd be hanging on for dear life as regulation time ran down. Some people had a problem with this, saying that it would look like the clock saved me from tapping out and would make me look weak. I just thought it was good drama. I've always worked for excitement, and I believed the fans would be yelling and screaming as the clocked ticked down to zero.

At the end of regulation, we had Gorilla Monsoon come down to the ring and order the match to continue until there was a fall. Two minutes later, I nailed Bret with a superkick out of the blue. I went for the cover, but couldn't get to him because I had been in the Sharpshooter for so long. Slowly, he managed to struggle to his feet. I too had recovered a bit, and I ripped him with another superkick and this time made the cover.

As I knelt in the ring clutching the belt to my chest, reality started to set in. Winning the World Wrestling Federation Championship did not fulfill my boyhood dream. It had far, far exceeded any dream I ever had as a boy. I tried to capture what winning the title meant to me during my post-match celebration, but it was so soon and everything was happening so fast. It would take a little time for everything to sink in completely.

When I made my way back to the dressing room, most of the guys came by and congratulated me. Whether they liked me or not, they knew about my desire to be a wrestler and to be the best. Everyone knew it was a huge moment for me. Wrestling was all I had in my life, and this was my moment.

Pat Patterson, the man who supported me from the first minute Marty and I came in, and had supported me ever since, hugged me. Vince hugged me. Kevin hugged me. It was very emotional, and I was completely spent both physically and mentally. I broke down crying.

About the only person I didn't see was Bret Hart. Usually, you shake hands with your opponent after the match and thank each other. I never saw Bret after the match, and he never said a word to me. Bret took off immediately, and I wouldn't see him for another seven or eight months.

After I left the arena, I had a few moments to myself in my hotel room before I headed over for the post–*WrestleMania* party that Vince throws every year. Alone in my room, I was finally able to take a minute and digest what had happened. I waited a long time for this to happen—twelve years. I always believed I could be the best wrestler in the world, but I didn't know if I would ever get to be champion and be recognized as such. And then there was the constant struggle of being unpopular within the industry. I loved to wrestle, but the politics, the gossip, the "it's all a work, brother" drove me nuts, and I never felt at peace.

Now, I felt at peace. I felt relief and joy. It's the kind of joy that I have every day now. It comes from within. I had plenty of happy moments in my career, but those were different. Those were fleeting moments caused by an external event. Sitting on my bed, staring at the belt and remembering my drive to Louisiana so many years ago, I felt complete. I thought to myself, if it's all over tomorrow, it doesn't matter. I've gone to the top. Those few minutes in my room were nice and quiet. It was the best quiet I ever heard.

I understand winning the World Wrestling Federation Championship in sports entertainment is not the equivalent of winning the Super Bowl. But in this line of work, I don't know what else there is besides the world title that can signify that you deserve to be called the best in the business. If it isn't, at what point in our business do you get to say, "Damn good job, you did it!"

Was I the best? Only time will tell, but I believe my body of work certainly put me up there. There are only two guys who get that title. The first is the guy who is considered to be the best wrestler, and the other is the guy who may not be the best wrestler, but will draw the most money. Both are flattering gigs. Steve Austin and Hulk Hogan weren't the best wrestlers, but they draw the most money. As for Ric Flair and myself, there's an argument to be made that we were the best wrestlers of our time.

I I I

When Vince hugged me in the locker room after I won the title he said, "I want you to enjoy this." I did for about a month. Then everything began to fall apart.

Right around the time of the *Royal Rumble,* Kevin told me that he and Scott were offered a lot of money to go to WCW. They were giving Vince their notice and would be leaving in ninety days. I was bummed. I had four friends that I could count on, and two were leaving. (Kid would end up leaving before Kevin and Scott, so I was really only going to be left with one friend, Hunter.)

Kevin tried to soften the blow. "I wouldn't leave if I didn't know you could handle it," he said. "Things are going to be secure here. They are going with you. I've got to go and make some money. You have to look at it this way. We are not leaving, we are expanding. Scott and I are going down there, and we are going to be on top. You and Hunter are going to be on top up here. We'll control the business."

We joked about that. But there was no conspiracy. What was he going to say? We'll go down there and work underneath? You want to be on top. Let's put it this way: we're not the mob. It's not as though people were dying in phone booths in WCW. They went there, did a lot of the things we had talked about with Vince at the meeting in Indianapolis, and sure enough they got over huge.

I've always had a pure friendship with Kevin, and I never felt any resentment for his success. He's probably made more money than I have, and I'm the one who got him in the big time. Good for him.

Kevin and Scott were due to leave in May. In April, right after I had won the championship, we went on another post–'*Mania* European tour. We were there for two weeks, having a whale of a time, as we always seemed to do in Europe. One night in Hamburg, Germany, we were having dinner at a restaurant and the subject of our last show together, which was going to be at MSG on May 19, came up. Someone threw out the idea of all of us coming out together and saying good-bye to the fans. We didn't make a big deal about it. We didn't come up with a name for it. It was a one-time conversation that I soon forgot about.

A week after our European trip, Kevin and I squared off at the *Good Friends, Better Enemies* Pay-Per-View in Omaha. It turned out to be our best match, and maybe the best match of Kevin's career. Kevin had turned heel, and we wanted to make it a No Holds Barred match. We asked Vince whether Kevin could throw me through a table. We weren't doing any "hard-core" spots like that at this point in time. "No, I don't think we need that," Vince said.

"Please. We have to do a little something. We are not talking about doing something crazy like they do in ECW. It's No Holds Barred."

"I just don't want to go there."

"Please, we'll keep it special."

Vince finally agreed. Then Pat chimed in with an idea. "Mad Dog" Vachon, an old-time wrestler who had made his name in the AWA, was going to be at the match. He had a prosthetic leg, and Pat wanted one us of to pull it off and hit the other guy with it. He thought that would be hilarious and knew Mad Dog would go along with it. I turned to Kevin and said, "I'm not touching that! You're doing it!"

The entire match came off perfectly. Kevin attacked Mad Dog, who was sitting in the stands, and ripped his leg off. He whacked me with it and then powerbombed me through the announcer's table. The crowd went nuts. I eventually recovered and made my comeback, spraying him with a fire extinguisher before nailing him with the superkick. Kevin and I had pulled off the company's first "hard-core" match. It's a shame that this style of wrestling would become so commonplace. When used sparingly it's very effective, but like many things in this business, they saw something that worked and ran it into the ground.

This match was one of the first times I "loaded up"—banged my foot against the mat—to cue the audience that the superkick was coming. Like many things in my career, this wasn't planned. I just did it and noticed that the crowd took to it. It's a great anticipation builder, and I used it from there on out.

Six weeks had passed since I won the World Wrestling Federation Championship, and things were going very well. It was now time for Kevin and Scott's final show at the Garden. Kevin and I were main-eventing in a steel cage, and we had sold the place out for the second time in a row. The subject of saying good-bye to the fans had not come up since that one night in Hamburg.

Kevin and I were standing at the curtain getting ready to go out for our match when Hunter came running up to us. "Are we going to do the thing?" he asked.

"What thing? What are you talking about?"

"The thing we talked about in Europe where we go out and say good-bye to the fans." Hunter never drank. He remembered everything.

"We don't know. We have a Cage match. Go ask Vince if we can do it. If he says yes, come on out, we'll be there and we can do it."

"All right."

We had our match. I hit Kevin with the kick to win, and started celebrating. Kevin was still lying on his back when the next thing I know, here come Scott and Hunter to the ring. I thought, "I guess we're doing it." So I walked over to Kevin and gave him a big kiss. He rose up and I said, "They are coming down."

Scott and Hunter came to the ring, and we all hugged and bowed to the fans. In wrestling terms, we broke kayfabe. We weren't playing heel and baby-face. Our actions, our admission that we were friends, told the fans, the vast majority who already knew, that what we did for a profession was a work. The fans, for their part, loved it. About a third of the sellout crowd was still there, and they were cheering their tails off.

When we came to the back, Vince asked me, "Was that important to you?"

"Yes, it was. I appreciate that. Thanks."

We hugged, and he said, "Then it's important to me." That's how we left it that night.

One week later, we were in Florence, South Carolina, for the *Beware of Dog* Pay-Per-View. Vince called Hunter and me into his office and said that he had received a lot of heat for letting us do the good-bye. "All the old-timers were offended," he said. "I didn't know it was going to go that far."

"But you told Hunter it was okay."

"Not to do all that, I didn't."

"How was I supposed to know? I was in the ring."

"Shawn, you are the champion. I can't punish you, but I want you to apologize to everyone. Hunter I can punish, and I have to. If I don't punish you and show everyone that I am serious, I'll lose credibility. You are going to have to eat this."

Hunter had been scheduled to win the upcoming *King of the Ring* tournament, but Vince told him that that wasn't going to happen. For the next year, all Hunter did was put other people over.

Steve Austin ended up winning *King of the Ring,* beating Jake "The Snake" in the finals. I didn't pay much attention to other people's programs, so I didn't know it at the time, but the night he beat Jake was the first night he uttered the phrase, "Austin 3:16 says I just whipped your a——!" This was the beginning of Steve's ascent to the top. Steve was great and deserves all the credit in the world for becoming the star he did. But it's strange how things work out in this business. Hunter gets in trouble, Steve gets plugged in, and the rest is history.

Before Hunter and I went around to apologize to everyone, we talked. "You asked him, didn't you?" I asked.

"Yeah, he said it was fine. He said it was okay."

I felt bad for Hunter. He hadn't done anything wrong. Vince turned on us because he was getting a lot of heat, and now Hunter was going to pay the price. "I'm sorry," I said, "but he's the boss and there's not much we can do."

So we went around and apologized to everyone. I didn't care too much about the boys, because right or wrong, they were going to find some reason to be mad at me. I did feel bad for upsetting the agents, and they were still hot. They felt like it was a knock on them and the business they had created. I understood and explained that wasn't our intention. It was just four guys saying good-bye to each other in a special place, Madison Square Garden. We had some of our greatest moments there, and now we were back to selling it out. We felt like we were a big part of that. It was an honest-to-goodness heartfelt moment for us and that's all we wanted to convey. We didn't mean to offend anyone. Obviously, we didn't take the agents' feelings into consideration, and that was wrong.

Every agent wanted to discuss what we did and tell us why they were offended. We listened to them and apologized again. I have a great deal of respect for our agents. Whether they liked me or not, they respected me, were patient with me, and helped me with my career.

| | |

Kevin and Scott had left, the boys already hated me, and now the agents did. What else could go wrong? How about having perhaps the worst match of my career the very same day.

There was a horrendous storm blowing through Florence. It was pouring rain, and the wind was blowing a hundred miles an hour. The production crew was worried about the power going out. I was scheduled to wrestle Davey Boy Smith, and every five minutes someone would come up to us and give us a new finish. If the power goes out, we'll do this. If it doesn't, we'll do this. Wait, if it does, we won't do that, we'll do this. Back and forth and back and forth. It was mayhem.

The power went off, and no one knew what to do. We were doing a live Pay-Per-View, and this had never happened before. The technicians went to work and managed to turn the power back on, but by now the night was a disaster. We got all our matches in, but were only able to show two of them because of time constraints. We actually did another *Beware of Dog* two days later to make up for the big cluster. My match went on the first airing, and it was the worst of my career.

Davey and I were stumbling along when a lady in the crowd started screaming with one of those voices that just grates on your nerves. Her voice was ruining the match. I yelled at her to shut up, which you could actually hear if you were watching on TV.

Much to the displeasure of the fans, we wrestled to a draw. Everything had gone wrong that day, and I was frustrated and angry. I was the champion and had to deliver, especially at Pay-Per-Views. Normally I considered the day after the Pay-Per-View to be just as if not more important than the Pay-Per-View itself, but as champion that didn't hold as much water, especially when you had a stinker like we had.

It also didn't help that Kevin wasn't around. If nothing else, Kevin could always see the lighter side of things. He wasn't Yoda, but he had a way of making me not worry. If he were there, he probably would have said something like, "Okay, so you are 100–1. Try being me! I'm 10–100, and apparently the only good matches I've had are with you!"

Unfortunately, Kevin wasn't there, and Hunter had his own problems to worry about. I was a perfectionist in the ring and I hadn't delivered. For the first time, I was feeling the pressure of being champion.

Davey and I had a rematch at *King of the Ring,* and the following month I wrestled Vader—Leon White—at *SummerSlam.* Both were good matches. In between the Pay-Per-Views, I was tearing down the house every night wrestling

Goldust—Dustin Runnels. I was busting my rear, getting every ounce out of my body, and every night I was having the best match on the card. I should have been on cloud nine, but I wasn't. All the work I was doing didn't matter. Business was down. It was all about ratings and Pay-Per-View buys now. I may have been delivering in the ring, but as champion I was not delivering the bottom line.

There were several reasons why I think the company was not doing well financially. The first had to do with our overall presentation. We had gotten rid of the dentists and the pirates, but we weren't yet cutting edge. We weren't quite up with the times, so our storylines didn't resonate. We also didn't have many bona fide stars on the roster. WCW had taken many of them. We had great talent, but most of it hadn't yet been established. Austin was still on the rise. Hunter was being buried for the "Curtain Call" incident. Mick Foley had just arrived and hadn't made a name for himself. Glenn Jacobs—Kane—was a year away from becoming a star. As far as established WWE main eventers went, it was Undertaker and myself.

Meanwhile, WCW was on fire. Kevin and Scott had come in as the Outsiders there and had gotten over huge. Hulk Hogan joined them in July and rechristened their group the nWo. This was the age of the rebel. Hulk Hogan saying "Say your prayers and eat your vitamins" wasn't getting you over. Thumbing your nose or showing the finger to authority figures was the thing. That's what people wanted to see.

And there I was, good old white-meat babyface Shawn, traveling around with my elderly trainer searching for feel-good moments. It wasn't going to work. I was too "cute" for the times. I was a good heel. People liked to hate me. They didn't like to like me.

Our head television writer, Vince Russo, even wanted me to start calling the fans "my Kliq," as Hogan had called his fans his *Hulkamaniacs.* Hulk had his *Hulkamaniacs,* and that worked for him, but I thought it wasn't going to work for me. I felt it would take me even further away from the rebellious character that the fans had originally rallied behind, and I also didn't want to come across as pandering to our audience. I questioned the idea, but the creative team wanted it, and I started calling fans "my Kliq." It was not a huge hit.

With all these factors converging at the same time, it didn't seem to matter how hard I worked or how good my matches were. We were doing well at live events, but television ratings and Pay-Per-View buys were down. Since I was champion and the company standard bearer, it was all falling on my shoulders. None of the guys would say it to my face, but through all the gossip, they were letting me know that I wasn't getting the job done. I think a lot of them wanted me to fail and relished seeing me getting blamed for the bad business. Wrestling was my life, and the idea of failing began to eat me up.

It wasn't like I sat back and analyzed everything and came up with solutions to present to Vince. Instead, I lashed out and let everybody have it. Wrestlers, agents, Vince, everyone was fair game as far as I was concerned. How could it be my fault we weren't doing well? I was our best wrestler, having our best matches, and I worked as hard as humanly possible. I had to headline every Pay-Per-View, and that was a lot to put on my shoulders. It was very frustrating!

I'd go out have a great match and come to the back and yell, "Now follow that!" I'd see some guy who had just stunk out the joint giving advice to some youngster, and I'd go up to him and say, "Yeah, you're the one to be giving advice!" I'd come to the arena and tell everyone I was going to tear the house down, which only put more pressure on me. I was plenty confident on the outside, but inside, I was insecure and confused.

In the middle of our *SummerSlam* match, I snapped at Vader. I wanted to do something special, something I had never done before. I was going to go for my elbow off the top, but have him move out of the way. I would catch myself at the last minute, land on my feet, and then drop the elbow on him. I jumped off the ropes and shifted my body to land on my feet, but he never moved. He was just lying there and there I was standing up like an idiot. I yelled, "Move!" and kicked him. I shouldn't have yelled at Leon. I liked him and he was good. Leon was like a big old bear. He was mean to everyone else, but he was nice to me. What I did was unprofessional. I was snapping under the pressure.

There was some gossip going around that I was asked to lose to Vader and refused. That's simply not true. I was never even asked to put him over. He came in with this reputation of being a bully. Apparently, Vince had a stern talk with him and whipped him into shape in no time. When Leon was here, he just couldn't do enough for me and everyone else. He was letting me slam him at house shows. The idea behind me fighting him was simply to give me a big guy to beat. Vince never said, "I want you to put Vader over at *SummerSlam*." If he

had, I would have done it. Leon pinned me twice on television. If we were going to give him the title, wouldn't you make me look stronger going into the match, and then let him beat me?

By September, I was completely stressed out and going into the *Mind Games* Pay-Per-View against Mankind—Mick Foley. This was a one-shot deal and my only real professional experience with him. Mick had a different and unique style with the deranged madman character he was portraying, and I liked it. Mick's character allowed my character to get a little aggressive, and I needed that as much as possible. Mick was very pleasant to work with and very good. I won via disqualification. With all the brawling, it certainly wasn't a traditional Shawn Michaels match, but it is one of my all-time favorites. In Mick's book, *Have a Nice Day,* he wrote, "I don't think I've ever been that good again. This match is also on the short list of the three best things I've done in wrestling."

| | |

Away from the ring, I traveled with Hunter. He was good to talk to, but he didn't do anything, he didn't party. I also traveled with Jose and a young lady for a while, but that wasn't the same as being with the guys. At a show in Tampa, I returned a call from Vince. He didn't want me riding with Hunter anymore. "He's a heel, and you're a babyface," Vince said. "The guys don't like you riding together. You have too much heat."

Hunter did all the driving for us, so I asked him, "Who am I supposed to ride with, myself? You are working me every day. I sleep in the car."

Referee Timmy White ended up driving me and helping me out with my schedule. Timmy was a great guy, but I made his life miserable. He was one of the first people I apologized to when I came back in 2002.

On the lighter side, there was one funny episode during these troubled times that deserves mentioning. Some genius in the office thought that having me pose in *Playgirl* would be good publicity for the company and help me get over. Since I wasn't going to pose naked, I agreed to do it. I thought, "Well, it's a magazine that women read, so why not?" I figured if *Playboy* was for men, *Playgirl* was for women.

When the magazine came out, I went to do an autograph session. At the session, it was about a 60-40 mix of guys and girls, which was normal for one of my autograph sessions. The only thing was, the men there were not your usual wrestling fans. There were a lot of bald guys wearing leather. I even received a "love note" from one of them. I was shocked. I had no idea. Hunter came up to me and said, "It's a magazine for gays, you know." That was the first time I had seen the magazine and the last time I did an autograph session for it.

| | |

On November 16, 1996, at *Survivor Series* in Madison Square Garden, Sycho Sid beat me, and my eight-month run as World Wrestling Federation Champion was over. Vince told me well in advance that he wanted the title on Sid. Vince also let me know that I was still going to be the guy he was going to go with and that he wanted me to win back the championship at the *Royal Rumble,* which was going to be held in my hometown of San Antonio. The big issue in this match was that the fans turned against me.

I was a white-meat babyface, and the MSG crowd hated that kind of character. When I was a heel, they loved me. When Kevin and the rest of us broke kayfabe and did the curtain call, they ate it up. After *WrestleMania X* and the Ladder match with Scott, I was their man. I was the guy they all said belonged on top. Once I made it there and my character changed into a good guy, the same fans turned on me. I couldn't do anything right. The New York crowd is a very smart one. They knew I was struggling and they smelled the blood in the water. In the middle of our match they started to cheer for Sid.

Now Sid was a good guy. He was huge and had a tremendous body, but he

couldn't work a lick. I think one of the nicest things anyone ever said about me is that I got a nice match out of him. It's hard to do. Bill Goldberg and Sid are the two most difficult guys I've ever been in the ring with. They are big, hard to move, and pretty mechanical. They're just very tense, and they are so big and powerful that they can really hurt you.

As poor a worker as Sid was, the fans wanted me out of the spotlight. I didn't know this at the time, but a fair portion of our fans get behind you on the way up, and then, when you get there, they turn on you. They did the same thing with Hunter a few years later. When he was chasing the title they loved him, said he was the greatest thing in the world. Once he got on top, they tried to destroy him. All of a sudden he couldn't work anymore, and the only reason he was champion and main-eventing Pay-Per-Views was because he married Stephanie McMahon. That's b.s.

The fans' reaction surprised me. During the match, I played off the crowd noise and started working as a heel would. I love working heel, and it's a lot easier. But that wasn't my role, and I shouldn't have. As a professional, I shouldn't have reacted to the live crowd. I should have played to the television audience, but I hadn't grasped that yet. When I go to Canada now as a babyface, I know I am going to get booed, but I have to work like a babyface and play to the television audience. I know our announcers will cover for me and somehow make it look like I am the good guy despite the crowd's boos.

Everyone in the locker room who didn't want me to be on top heard the crowd. Vince heard them, and he had to address the situation. Was I not the person to go with now? After all, the Garden is the Garden and the company gauges things on the Garden. This was not good. So how did I deal with the situation? Pretty much the same way I dealt with all my troubles during my title reign. I became angry and went out and got wasted.

| | |

My title reign had started with such promise. There was the win over Bret, the fun trip to Europe, the great match with Kevin at *Good Friends, Better Enemies.* Everything was going well. Then came the "Curtain Call" and the *Beware of Dog* debacle. Business turned down, the competition ramped it up. The pressure got to me, and the locker room became a nightmare. The ring became my sanctuary. For twenty or thirty minutes a day I was at peace.

Vince didn't have a great year either. WCW was coming on so strong, and it was stressing him out. It stressed the whole company out. You could see it and feel it. I knew if it didn't go well, changes had to be made. As champion, I was going to be blamed despite my performance in the ring. I don't want to sound cocky, but I put on so many good shows with everyone I worked with. From purely a match perspective, I believe I performed as well as any WWE Champion ever had in a similar time frame, and that more than anything else was what bothered me.

The truth was that the fans didn't like me as a babyface. They liked me as a heel. There is nothing harder in this business than being a white-meat babyface. On top of that, to be the champion, to be the guy, I daresay I had an impossible job. The only reason the fans stuck by me for as long as they did was because of my in-ring performances.

I could have dealt with it in one of two ways. I could have lobbied to change my character, or danced with the lady that brought me. I chose the second option. I couldn't give in. If I gave in, the fans might have really eaten me alive. I was going to keep doing what I do, and one day, I believed the fans would say, "I have to like him because he is better than everyone else."

the truth is not always popular

Despite what happened at Madison Square Garden, Vince stuck with his plan to give me the title at the *Royal Rumble.* Since it was taking place in San Antonio, the theme behind my victory was going to be "the hometown boy makes good." We did a lot of publicity for the show, all of which centered around me. They put my picture on buses, I gave lots interviews for the local press, and I was all over local television.

This was incredibly exciting and elevated my spirits a little. I wasn't just walking through Windsor Park Mall, I was headlining a show that was going to be putting

60,000 people in the Alamodome. The match itself wasn't very good. I had the flu and was up all night in the bathroom the night before. I spent the whole day of the show sprawled out in Vince's office's trying to get some sleep.

Sid and I only went about fifteen minutes. It was one of those things that I wished could have been better. I could usually work around people, but the combination of my physical condition and Sid was too much for me to over-come. The match didn't stink, but it was a bit of a letdown considering the buildup and the sixty thousand plus that were in the Alamodome. I hit him twice with the same video camera that he had hit Jose and me with during my loss at the Garden, and then connected with some Sweet Chin Music for the victory.

I started to refer to my superkick as Sweet Chin Music during my first title reign. I was watching Roger Clemens pitch. He knocked a batter down with a high fastball and the announcer exclaimed that Clemens had delivered some "sweet chin music." I liked the sound of that and started to call my superkick that. Like the stomping of the boot and the name Heartbreak Kid, it wasn't planned, it just happened and caught on.

Winning the title this time was quite different from the first time. It was similar to the first and second Ladder matches. There can be only one first time when it's completely special. I don't mean to imply that it didn't feel great to have the title back. It did. But this time, being part of the event was bigger than winning the championship. It was so cool to be doing all the publicity events in my hometown and wrestling in front of 60,000 people, even if I wasn't feel-ing well.

| | |

Two weeks after the *Rumble* I was having a three-way match with Sid and Bret Hart when I tweaked my bad knee. It swelled up and was sore, but at the time I didn't think it was too serious. It had happened before. Just to be sure, though, I called Vince and told him I wanted to get it checked out. He mentioned Dr. James Andrews, who's worked on countless top-caliber athletes, but I said I'll just go home and get it checked there. I went to see my doctor. He took an MRI, looked at the results, and then said to me, "You will never wrestle again."

"What?"

"You have no ACL in there."

"I know. I've been wrestling for years with no ACL."

"You are not going to wrestle on it anymore. Your knee has deteriorated. You need a knee replacement."

I was devastated. He was a doctor, and I thought his word was final. I thought my career was over. At the next TV, which was a special Thursday edition of *Raw*, I told Vince what my doctor said. I broke down and started crying.

There have been two times in my life that I've been really scared: here with the knee, and then a year later when doctors told me my back was shot. I reacted negatively both times. I didn't do anything but wrestle, and the idea of not being able to wrestle was a tough pill to swallow.

Vince felt for me. He knew how much wrestling meant to me. He told me no matter what happens, I'd always have a job here. Then he said, "We have to get the championship belt off you. We will make an announcement tonight."

That night I went to the ring and told the world that I was retiring. I told them I had lost my smile, that I just didn't have it in me to wrestle anymore. Vince and Gorilla Monsoon were in the ring with me. It was very emotional. It wasn't a work.

The reason I was retiring was because of my knee, but the truth was, my fight wasn't what it once was. I wasn't Superman anymore. I was burnt physically and emotionally. A month earlier, my mom noticed that I wasn't looking too good and she said, "Honey, they are running you to death. You don't look so good."

"I'm working a lot."

"Yeah, all the time. You don't even smile anymore. You always had such a sweet smile. You've lost your smile."

I had lost my smile. I was exhausted. Nobody ran harder than me when I had that title, but I can't blame my woes on the business. I wasn't living a healthy lifestyle. When I had time off, I wasn't taking care of myself. My mom wasn't aware that I was running myself so hard.

So the speech I gave about losing my smile was real. The emotion I showed out there was authentic. I broke down on national TV because I was emotionally spent. I think most of the fans that care for me know I've been open with them over the years. I was that night.

| | |

As soon as I gave that speech, the rumors started flying. Everyone wanted to know, what really happened? Why did Shawn give up the title and retire? The most prevalent rumor was that I quit in protest at having to drop the title to Bret Hart at *WrestleMania 13*. That is not true. This was not a scheme I concocted to avoid losing the title to Bret. Had I been asked to? Yes. Did I want to? No. I've said it before and I'll say it again: there is no refusing to do a job. Ask Bret Hart. Ask the people in Montreal. It only happens if Vince allows it. I'm not going to say that I would have been fine working with Bret. I won't say my unwillingness to work with him didn't cause a problem from a creative standpoint. That's fair. But again, I'm sure I'm not the first guy who's ever done that.

I retired because a doctor told me I could never wrestle again and I took his words at face value. Some people may not believe me, but these are probably the same people who think I faked my back injury that made me retire in 1998. I have a four-inch scar, a metal plate, and four screws in my back to prove it. You've got two choices when it comes to me and injuries. I am either the toughest guy you ever met, or you believe in the miracles of Jesus Christ and that he heals. Take your pick.

| | |

My problems with Bret began shortly after *WrestleMania XII*. When he found out that we were going to be working together, he came to me and said that people would really believe we were feuding if he made derogatory comments about me in public. He told me it was going to be a complete work.

He ended up writing some newspaper columns in which he not only buried me, but he attacked my family. He said something to the effect that my character was gay and he couldn't understand what kind of parents I had since they let me portray this image on TV. I didn't read the actual articles he wrote, but I know he wrote them because he later apologized to me for writing them. I was not happy that he went after my parents. He apologized again and said he had gone too far.

Bret believed he was some kind of great role model, but he wasn't. He was just full of it. No sooner had he apologized than he went right back to bad-mouthing me. This was a pattern with him that drove me nuts. He would say things about me, apologize, and then go right out and say more bad things about me.

Sometime during the fall of '96, Bret signed the biggest contract in the company's history, reportedly $1.5 million for twenty years. During his time off, Bret threatened to go to WCW. Vince believed he couldn't let this happen and signed him to the huge contract.

I was making $750,000 a year. When Vince had signed me to that contract in early 1996, he told me, "Shawn, I'm signing you to the biggest contract we have." The money was great, and it wasn't the actual dollars that I was concerned with. I knew the strain WCW was putting us under, and Vince and I handled my contract in the most amicable manner. All I said was, "I'm just asking that you don't pay anyone, except Undertaker, any more than you pay me. That would be an insult. 'Taker is separate. What he gets he deserves, but I don't think anyone else deserves more than me."

"Don't worry, it won't happen."

When I found out about Bret's deal, I was livid. Vince and I discussed it at the same meeting where he asked me about working with Bret at *WrestleMania*.

"You are paying Bret all that money and that is b.s.," I said. "I'm slaving up and down the road, and you are paying him twice as much as me. You think he is twice as good as me?"

"No."

"Then why are you paying him twice as much as me?"

"I had to give him the big contract, Shawn. He had my back up against the wall. He was going to go to WCW, and now I have to get the money out of him. Do you want to have a match with him at *WrestleMania*?

"I don't want to work with him, he's been nothing but mean to me. He treated this company like dirt. I don't want to do it."

"Well, I wish you'd think about it."

"I don't need to think about it. I don't want to wrestle him, he's been a jerk."

"You don't think you can put all that aside?"

"I don't want to. He's done nothing but be a jerk."

Then I hurt my knee and the whole issue of me working with him at *'Mania* disappeared. If Vince would have pressed me to put Bret over, I would have. I'm sure I would have made life miserable for a lot of people, but I would have done it. When push came to shove, I always did what Vince wanted.

| | |

I went home the day after I gave my retirement speech and tried to figure out what I was going to do. As it happened, Steve Austin had blown out his knee and had gone to see Dr. James Andrews in Birmingham. Vince called me and asked me to see Dr. Andrews as well. I acquiesced this time and went to Birmingham.

Dr. Andrews, unlike a lot of other doctors, understands athletes and knows that they can do things ordinary people can't or won't. He told me that my knee was terrible, but if I wore a brace, trained my legs, and did some rehab, I would be able to wrestle again. He said I might as well try because if I got the replacement, my career would be over, no questions asked. I had nothing to lose by trying to come back.

I ended up rehabbing with Steve at HealthSouth in San Antonio. Steve was in pretty bad shape, but he really wanted to make *WrestleMania*. He was now going to fight Bret Hart in an I Quit match and was looking forward to the payday. I like Steve and I'm glad he made it back. He had a great match with Bret, and even though he lost, he made himself that night. Bret bloodied Steve up pretty good and put him in the Sharpshooter. Steve, however, refused to give up. He eventually passed out from the pain, but his "never say die" attitude struck a chord with the fans. They started cheering for him and showing animosity towards Bret.

My rehab went well, and I returned to the ring on May 25, wrestling in a Tag Team Championship match with Steve against the title holders, Owen Hart & Davey Boy Smith. I couldn't wait to get back in the ring. I flew around all over the place and put on one of my best performances. Early on in the match, I did my backflip off the top, and I did it for a very specific reason. I knew that everyone, including Bret, was saying that I faked my knee injury to get out of putting him over at *WrestleMania*. I wanted to rub it in their face. Every time I heard rumors about me, I made sure I did something to stick it to the guys who were spreading them.

Someone started spreading rumors that I was refusing to lose to people. So I started walking around the locker room bragging that I wouldn't do jobs. I was teasing and egging them on. It was my method of getting back at them. Of course it was then reported that I was going around bragging about not doing jobs. It seemed so pathetic to me that grown men would go running to dirt sheets and spreading gossip rather than confronting me with any problems they might have had. As my problems with Bret wore on, I told him, "If you have a problem with me, say it to my face. Don't go around talking behind my back."

People can accuse me of being a lot of things, but they can't accuse me of not being a man. I was always honest, sometimes maybe too honest, and that's why I think a lot of guys didn't like me. The truth is not always popular, and neither was I.

By the time I wrestled in the tag match, Bret and I had nearly reached the breaking point. He had said bad things about my folks and apologized, but now he had gone on to stir things up by telling the dirt sheets and others that I faked my injury and retired before *WrestleMania 13* in order to avoid putting him over. He also had been lambasting me in his promos on television.

Once again, he came to me and apologized for stirring things up. We were at a TV taping and we were talking in the back. He said things had gotten out of hand. I told him, "You've done nothing but bury me, and I don't say anything." I looked him right in the eye and said, "Bret, I've got nothing to lose. Look at me, I have no life. If you do it again, then I'm taking the gloves off. You can't do anything to me. You can't hurt me. You can say whatever you want about me, and I'll say it's true. The difference between you and me is that I'll admit to all the stuff that I do wrong. I don't hide it. But if you keep screwing with me, that's it."

I had heard enough of the "I'm sorry's." I was tired of him trying to work me and talk about me to other people. I don't like getting caught up in all that gossip and dirt. I think it's cruel. I get no jollies out of telling somebody he sucks, he's only worth one star, or this or that, and I don't like people who don't know me telling me how to do my job.

Bret was such a hypocrite. He said it was over. We shook hands and I thought we had finally put it all behind us. Bret and I were scheduled to do an interview segment. It was supposed to be a wrestling promo. He talks bad about me and then I talk bad about him. That's how it works. Well, he went on this tirade and just didn't stop. It was a while before I got my rebuttal in. As I made my way backstage, someone told me that he had gone so long they had to go off the air before I spoke. So the whole time, viewers saw me standing there looking like an idiot.

I was furious. He had done it to me for the last time. I was now going to take the gloves off. He had pushed and pushed and pushed me some more. It was like the kids teasing me about my name when I was in elementary school. If you keep pushing me, I'm going to eventually fight back.

Kevin and I used to needle folks, but we weren't malicious. I didn't want to work with Bret Hart, but there was no cruelty there. The whole time he was on top, I did nothing but support him and do what I could to make business better. When I had my opportunity, he did nothing but try and tear me down and hurt me, and no matter how many times he apologized, it never ended. He was insensitive, selfish, spoiled, and cruel. All the things that he claimed I was, he was in spades.

The next week, I cut a televised promo on him and made the comment that he had been seeing "sunny days," exposing what I believed was his secret relationship with Tammy Sytch. Many in the locker room found it to be very amusing, but Bret didn't speak to me for a couple of weeks.

During that time, you could feel the tension in the dressing room. Occasionally we would be in there together, but we never talked. I wasn't very good at handling it, and being the lightning rod that I was, I openly mocked the mood. "Feel the tension in here," I would yell. "You can cut the tension with a knife!"

On June 9, we had a television taping in Hartford. I was in the dressing room when he came up to me and said, "I just want to say . . ." I cut him off before he could finish. "Don't talk to me. You haven't said a word to me for three weeks. If you can't talk to me for three weeks, I don't want to talk to you now." I don't think Bret was used to people talking like that to him. About five minutes later, I was turning around to get some gear out of my bag and I felt somebody push me from behind. I turned around and Bret asked, "What's your f—— problem?"

"You!" I yelled.

He tried to punch me, but I peeled back and he missed. He pushed me again, and this time I stood up. He swung again and missed. The next thing I knew, he went for a double leg dive. I caught him around the upper body and we went straight back through a piece of paneling. We had each other in front face locks when Pat Patterson and Davey Boy came over and grabbed us. Pat was yelling, "Come on, you guys!" I let go and Bret yanked a handful of my hair off my head. That hurt like heck, but I didn't retaliate. The fight was over.

I went storming into Vince's office and told him, "I'm out of here, this is b.s.!" I saw Aldo Montoya—who later wrestled here as Justin Credible—and asked him if he'd give me a ride back to my hotel. He wasn't working that night, so he took me. I missed the show and flew home the next day.

Vince sent my lawyer, Skip McCormick, who I had hired when I found out about Bret's contract, a letter stating that I had violated my contract. Skip responded by writing a letter claiming that WWE had failed to provide a safe working environment. Skip told me that they were trying to blame everything on me, but once he wrote the letter, it would be back in their lap and they would ask me to come back. That's exactly what happened. In a few weeks we had settled everything and I was back. As far as I know, nothing happened to Bret as a result of the fight.

|||

Steve Austin and I were still Tag Team Champions when Bret and I fought. Vince didn't know what was going to happen with me after the fight, so while the lawyers went back and forth, he and Jim Ross announced on television that I had been suspended for four to six weeks and that a tag team tournament would be held, with the winner getting a shot at Steve and a partner of his choice, who turned out to be Dude Love—Mick Foley. The four to six weeks announcement gave them the necessary cover to figure out what was going to happen with me.

While I was off, I told Vince that I wanted to leave. I asked him to let me out of my contract and let me go to WCW and be with my buddies. I was miserable. Vince wanted to talk with me in person, so he flew down to San Antonio and we met at the Embassy Suites Hotel near the San Antonio airport. My dad was concerned about me and wanted to come to the meeting, so he came to the meeting too. Before we could even talk about me wanting to leave, Vince looked right at me and said, "I think you have a problem with prescription pills."

"My son doesn't have a drug problem," my dad responded. I told my parents that I didn't have a problem, and they took me at my word. The truth was, though, I was escaping through the pills whenever they were available. In retrospect, I realize I did have a problem, but at the time I didn't think so and wasn't going to admit it.

After the uncomfortable exchange, I asked for my release. "Just let me go, Vince. I'm miserable, I am making everyone else miserable."

"You don't want to go there. They don't know how to use a guy like you. It will drive you nuts. I know you are going through a tough time now, but it will be worse for you down there."

"I miss my friends, and you won't let me travel with Hunter. It's just not fun anymore. I don't want to do this if I can't have fun."

"We need to make it fun again then."

I told him Bret's contract was still bothering me. It's always been important to me to be recognized by my industry that I am one of the best, and at that point, I felt I was the best performer in the industry. I didn't understand how you could be better than someone at something but only get half of what he got.

Vince knew that I was frustrated with the situation and explained how WCW had taken so many of his top guys that his back was against the wall and he had no choice but to sign Bret to the big deal. He told me the same thing he told me when I went through the steroid debacle: sometimes you have to learn to eat crap and like the taste of it. But he also made it clear that he didn't think Bret would see the end of the contract. The company couldn't afford to pay him that much for such a long time. Vince said, "We'll make this work. We'll get you back to enjoying wrestling and continue to build on it."

"Tell me how." I knew enough that the way I was going was no way to live.

He just said, "We'll work through it."

By the end of our conversation, I think we were drawn closer to each other. I felt better, and now I didn't want to leave. I knew things were going to change. I trusted Vince.

| | |

When I came back in the middle of July and Vince asked me if I could work with Bret, I said, "Yes." He sat both of us down and asked us if we could work together at *SummerSlam*. We wouldn't be wrestling each other. Vince wanted me to be the special guest referee in a match between Bret and the World Wrestling

Federation Champion, Undertaker. It was a good idea. Bret and I had a well-publicized history. Who knew what could happen with us two in the ring, and if I messed with 'Taker in the ring, it could set something up between us.

Both Bret and I claimed that we could do business with each other, but that the other one was the problem. After a little hemming and hawing, we agreed to work together. The truth of the matter was, I was no longer that angry. After my meeting with Vince, I knew I was going to be moving beyond Bret. I was going to do my best not to let him bring me down.

The stakes couldn't have been any higher for the Hart-'Taker matchup. The stipulation was that if Undertaker won, Bret would never be able to wrestle in the United States again. If Bret won, he would become the cham-

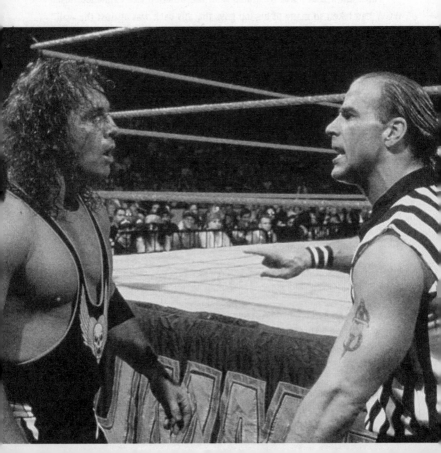

pion. Towards the end of the match, Bret spit on me. I then went to hit him with a steel chair, but accidentally nailed Undertaker instead. Bret went for the cover, and I reluctantly had to count the 1-2-3. After the match, Undertaker stalked me to the back. We had started what was going to become, for me, the most professionally satisfying program of my career.

22
cool hand luke
and the funny guy

Mark Callaway, Undertaker, first came to the World

Wrestling Federation in 1991. He showed up at *Survivor*

Series, and had been working on top ever since. Though we

had been in the same locker room for six years, we never

wrestled each other. Vince didn't believe anyone would buy

me working with a guy with his presence and size.

We weren't close away from the ring either. We were

cordial and professional to each other, but that was about it.

When we went on European trips we would occasionally

hang out, but we never became friends. I could never read

'Taker. He was always calm, collected, and smooth. I was

the complete opposite, obnoxious and running around all the time. I knew he didn't really like me, but he was such a pro, he wasn't going to let his personal feelings get in the way of business. As long as I didn't offend him, which I didn't, he was going to leave me alone. He always told me, "You always delivered in the ring, Shawn. That was good enough for me."

Mark was different from everyone. It was as if there was Mark, and then there was everyone else. He was untouchable. His gimmick was so over, his work was unparalleled. He was so secure in himself and his character. To me, he was Cool Hand Luke, an entity unto himself. I was thrilled to have the opportunity to work with him.

Vince allowed me to work with Mark because I wasn't going to be doing it alone. Hunter and a relatively new female Superstar, Chyna—Joanie Laurer— were going to be at my side. We weren't calling ourselves D-Generation X yet, but the seed had been planted.

Hunter and I had met Joanie a year before at a hotel in Springfield, Massa-

Me, Chyna, and Hunter.

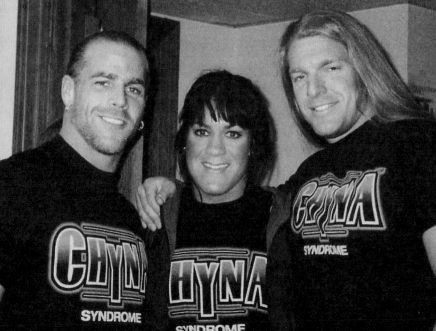

chusetts. She was a big, strong girl, and from the moment we saw her, we wanted to bring her in as a bodyguard. We pitched the idea to Vince, but he didn't like it. "Nobody is going to buy a woman beating all these guys up."

Several months later, we were in Tampa and we heard that Kevin and Scott wanted to bring her to WCW. We went to an IHOP with Shane McMahon and told him all about her. "She's big enough that guys can sell for her," we said. "If they have a problem with her, tell them to grow up. She can do all the old-school stuff."

Shane was into it. He and Hunter went back and eventually sold Vince on the idea. Chyna debuted in February 1997, and aligned herself with Hunter not too long afterwards.

During the month off after my fight with Bret, Hunter, Chyna, and I went on a cruise called the Wrestle Vessel. It was a promotional deal the company had with a cruise line where fans could cruise and meet their favorite Superstars. We were having a late dinner and talking business. We thought it would be fun to work together as an alliance. Hunter was a heel, I was going to turn heel after *SummerSlam*, and I knew we would have a great time working together. We were getting excited and having a good time and I said, "You know what? I think you need to ditch that snobby Hunter Hearst Helmsley gimmick. You are a very funny guy. You need to be more like you are. That whole Greenwich snob isn't you." He agreed, and DX was one step closer to happening.

| | |

I turned heel right after *SummerSlam*, cutting a promo in which I said that I could not be held accountable for hitting Undertaker with the chair and costing him the championship. The fans loved to hate me, and now they had an excuse. I was a heel and happy again. I started referring to myself as the Showstopper and the Main Event. I had always wanted to use the name Showstopper. Yokozuna used to call himself that among the boys, in a funny, not cocky sort of way. I blatantly stole it from him, and it caught fire and never went away.

At one of the next TVs I was going to do an interview with Jim Ross where I would call Undertaker out. 'Taker and Vince were at a trade show and weren't there, so what was going to happen was that I would call him out and he would come up on the TitanTron, threaten me, and I would act all scared. I was walking around the back in these skin-tight biker shorts that I used to wear because I knew it annoyed a lot of people. As a joke, I stuffed a roll of gauze down my pants and started goofing around. Right before I was set to go out and do my interview with J.R., Brian Adams—Crush—double-dog-dared me to go out in the arena and on television with the gauze in my shorts.

I was never one to turn down a double-dog-dare, so I gathered everyone at a television monitor and went out there fully loaded with my gauze. J.R. was trying to do a serious interview, but I was acting up and being obnoxious. I was jumping around, bumping and grinding, the gauze was pretty evident, and I cut the most over-the-top promo. I was having a blast and I knew all the boys in the back were loving it. I finally called Undertaker out and he came up on the screen and threatened me. That part worked fine. J.R., though, was understandably angry over my making a mockery of his interview. He left the ring to go back to his announcing position, and I decided to have a little fun.

I grabbed the mike, knowing full well that Undertaker wasn't there, and yelled, "You know what, if the Undertaker is so tough, why doesn't he come out and fight me right now?"

The crowd exploded, hoping to see us go at it right there.

"Undertaker," I continued, "let's do it right here, right now. If you don't come out here by the count of ten, that means you are afraid of me." I counted to ten. "See, he's afraid of me!" I came to the back, and the boys thought it was the funniest thing they had ever heard.

The next day, Vince called me. "I'm fining you $10,000 for that incident last night."

"What for?"

"You humiliated the company and Undertaker." He went on this long tirade about how I was unprofessional and rude to J.R.

"I have to tell you something. I thought it was funny. Everyone thought it was funny. Ross was hot? That's funny stuff. Don't you think it's funny? People do that all the time. I wasn't the first guy to stick gauze down my pants."

"Well, you offended some woman in the production truck."

"Are you sure?"

"Yes."

"I don't think that's true." Hunter had been on the headset while I was out there and he told me that some women were laughing about it. "That's not what I heard, Vince. I heard she thought it was pretty funny too."

"That's not the point."

"That is the point. It is funny. We are getting our backsides kicked in the ratings. We have to start doing better stuff. Our girls get boob jobs all the time. One week they come out they are flat and the next week they have huge breasts and nobody notices. The fans all see it. How come no one comments, 'Sable, did you get the mumps last week?' Gauze in the shorts, that's funny. You can't tell me that's not funny."

"It's just unprofessional and has nothing to do with our business."

"We need to start kicking it up."

Two months later Vince called everyone into a meeting and announced that we were going to go with a much racier, edgier production. This was the beginning of The Attitude Era. Vince came up with the new scratch logo and said, "We are now going 'there.'" I know I wasn't solely responsible for the "attitude" revolution, but Hunter and I definitely played a big role in convincing Vince it was the way to go.

Vince decided not to fine me, though I did apologize to J.R. 'Taker didn't have a problem with what I did. Crush was a good friend of his, and when he told Mark that it was funny, 'Taker said, "Crush is my boy, and when he told me it was funny, I knew it was okay. I love a good joke too."

The last thing I wanted to do was offend 'Taker and I told him, "I waited until we were off air, I knew it would be edited. I was one hundred percent entertaining the boys. I would never do anything like that to you."

"I know. I sort of wish I was there to see it."

Undertaker and I squared off for the first time on September 7 in Louisville at the *Ground Zero* Pay-Per-View. The match went to a no-contest when Hunter and Chyna interfered on my behalf. This was the perfect setup for the match that many believe is both his and my finest.

I I I

We were really starting to heat up as a company. We had become edgier and were getting bigger and more raucous crowds. We hadn't yet caught WCW, but we were on our way. Vince was fully behind the DX concept for Hunter, Chyna, and me, and he wanted to really push us. He could sense that we had something special going on with our irreverent attitude and sophomoric actions.

Before we could get to my rematch with Undertaker at *Badd Blood* in October, we had to get through a special Pay-Per-View that was being held in Birmingham, England, on September 20. Davey Boy Smith was the European Champion, and he was from Birmingham. I told the creative team, "If you want to get me some heat, have me screw him for the title in his hometown." They loved the idea. Davey Boy was so over in England and he never lost there. Screwing him out of the title in front of his hometown fans was a good business decision because I would generate a ton of heat.

Davey never once expressed to us that he was upset with our plans. But he wasn't the kind of guy who would say anything to your face. He would do it in the back. He wasn't mean, that's just the way he was brought up in the business: you bury guys behind their back. It's my understanding that Bret really got him wound up about losing in his hometown. For Bret, the important thing was not about what was right for business, but about looking like the good guy in the eyes of the wrestling industry.

I had Hunter, Chyna, and Rick Rude, who was with us for a brief time, assist me in applying a figure-four hold on Davey Boy, and the referee stopped the bout. The crowd went nuts. They were throwing beer, food, just about anything they could get their hands on, at us. It was honest real heat in Birmingham.

Even though I had already been World Wrestling Federation Champion, I had no problem becoming the European champ. I didn't look at it as a step down. On the contrary, I felt I could make something of the title. Before the show, we were discussing what was going to happen with the agents and producers at the day's production meeting. Someone spoke up and said, "If we do this, Shawn, wouldn't you be the first person to have held every belt here [World Wrestling Federation, Intercontinental, Tag Team, and European]?"

"That's right," Vince said. "We need to have a name for that. That's monumental. That's huge."

The show's director, Kerwin Sifes, suggested "Grand Slam."

"Sounds good," Vince replied. And that's how I became the first Grand Slam Champion.

| | |

Since my first match with Undertaker ended in a no-contest when Hunter and Chyna interfered, the logical thing to do for the rematch was surround the ring with a cage so that they couldn't interfere again. I suggested the idea to Vince and he liked it. At the time we were using these big blue metal cages that hurt like heck when you hit them and looked pretty stupid. So when Vince approved the cage idea, I asked him if we could go back to using the regular chain-link cage.

"Well, I always used the other ones 'cause the big guys couldn't climb it."

"'Taker's an athlete. He can climb it." And then, all of a sudden I remembered a Cage match I had seen years ago between Buzz Sawyer and Tommy Rich where they had a top on the cage. I asked if we could put a top on the cage.

"Why would you want that?"

"I don't know, it's just a cool different look. Plus, who knows, maybe we can do something up top."

"I'll call creative and see what we can get done." A week or two before the match, Vince told me that they could build the structure and had even suggested putting it outside the ring so we would have the area around the ring to work with too. Cage matches are good, but when the cages are right up against the ring and you have less space, you can only do so much. The more it can be like a regular match the better.

Badd Blood was being held at the Keil Center in St. Louis. They took 'Taker and me out into the arena on the day of the show and had us check out what they had built. They also told us, "It's not a cage, it's a cell." It was awesome: a chain-link cage with a top twenty feet above the ring. The first thing I thought when I saw it was, "We have to get on top of it." 'Taker said I was crazy.

"Come on, we can do it." I climbed up and 'Taker followed. We could get

up there. Our only problem was that the cell was going to be locked so no one could interfere in our match. How would we get outside the cell so we could climb it? Pat Patterson came up with the answer. He suggested we knock out a cameraman during the match. The medics would come down and open the cell to get him out. When the door was open, I could run out and start climbing. 'Taker would follow.

Later that day, we received word that Brian Pillman had passed away. It was sad, another wrestler dying before he should have. I wasn't that close to Brian, but I still felt awful. I knew he had a wife and kids and my heart went out to them. This wasn't the first time a fellow wrestler had died when I was working a show. It happened in 1993 when I was in Milwaukee and heard that Kerry Von Erich passed away. It's very strange. You are in mourning, but then you have to go out and perform. It's just very weird. Everybody was down when they heard the news.

Our plan involving the cameraman worked just as we had planned. 'Taker back-body-dropped me over the top rope and onto the cameraman. I attacked him then to make sure the people knew he was hurt and give reason for the EMTs to come down and open the cell. They did, and I ran outside. 'Taker followed and shot me into the cell. I started bleeding like a stuck pig and began climbing. When 'Taker followed me up the cell, the sold-out crowd of 21,151 went bonkers. When he press-slammed me on top of the cell, I thought the roof was going to come off the place.

I recovered and made my way to the side of the cell by the announcers' tables. I went to climb down, but 'Taker was in pursuit. As I hung off the side with my fingers on the top of the cell, 'Taker kicked them. Off I went into the Spanish announcer's table. It was easily the biggest bump I had ever taken. It hurt, but my adrenaline was pumping so hard, I didn't care. 'Taker eventually made his way down and brought me back inside the ring and gave me a chokeslam. Then, for good measure, he nailed me with a chair. I had whacked 'Taker pretty good to start our program, and this was his professional receipt. I had never been hit so hard in my life. My eyes felt like they were going to pop out, and my entire head started bulging. I felt like one of those cartoon characters that gets hit with an object and his whole body starts reverberating with pain.

Just when it looked like 'Taker could pin me for a hundred count if he wanted, Kane came out with Paul Bearer. Kane was Undertaker's half-brother, and they had been teasing his arrival for weeks. He walked down to the cell, ripped it open, and hit a Tombstone Piledriver on Undertaker. I rolled over on 'Taker and got the cheap cover.

My body ached like I had been run over by a truck, and I had to get twenty-nine stitches after the match, but I felt like a million bucks. I gave a huge "Follow that!" when I made it to the back—of course, we were on last!

'Taker has said this is his favorite match, and that's the greatest compliment I could ever receive. Working with him was unbelievably satisfying. 'Taker is so good and so smooth. I know he didn't care for the way I handled myself, but when we got in the ring he trusted me. He respected my ability and could see through all the crap. Mark is a very smart guy. He would go on to work a great program with Kane. I had earned a title shot with my victory and went on to a match you might have heard about.

montreal

I was sky-high the night after *Badd Blood.* I just had

perhaps the best match of my career, and Hunter, Chyna, and

I were going to christen ourselves D-Generation X (which

was Vince Russo's idea) on this evening's *Raw.* Even the

thought of having to work with Bret in the coming weeks

and at *Survivor Series* couldn't bring me down. I wasn't

going to let him get to me.

From my perspective, I had won the battle with Bret. I

was main-eventing Pay-Per-Views while he, as champion,

was working Tag Team matches. My confidence was back.

There wasn't anything that he was going to do or say that

I worried about. People had turned on me because they had heard a lot of un-true stories, many of which were made up by Bret. I never once gave my side, because it seemed so transparent to me, and I was taught the guy who is talking the loudest and defending himself the most must be hiding something.

Working with Hunter and Chyna was so much fun and I didn't want to ruin that. I also have to give Vince Russo a lot of credit. He came up with some great ideas for us. He helped create a real awesome gimmick where we were doing and saying all the things you want to in real life, but can't because it isn't nice and you'd get in a lot of trouble. And we were very popular. As Hunter has said, in the fall of '97, DX was the hottest thing in sports entertainment not named Steve Austin.

We were in Kansas City—another sellout, by the way—and Hunter and I were doing an in-ring promo. I asked to see footage of my victory from *Badd Blood.* Instead, video from the "curtain call" came on. This was done to rein-force the insubordinate image of DX. Bret came out and confronted me, calling me a homo and a degenerate. (I believe he meant it.) I responded by saying that the only reason Bret was in the main event of *Survivor Series* was because he was wrestling me. Bret and I were at it again, only this time, our personal ani-mosity towards each other blended perfectly within the storyline we were con-ducting.

Later that night Hunter beat Bret via countout after I superkicked him while Chyna distracted him. During the match, I started picking my nose with Bret's Canadian flag. I really didn't mean to offend anyone. I just figured it would get me extra heat, which it did.

| | |

At this point, I really didn't know what the situation with Bret was. My feeling was that Vince wanted to get the title off him. His contract was taxing the com-pany way too much if he wasn't going to be *the* man. I didn't know where Steve Austin was in his talks with Vince. I'm sure they already had an idea of where they were going long-range. The ideal situation for Steve was to win the title from a white-hot heel. Bret certainly wasn't one. I, on the other hand, was there.

It made sense to me that Vince would want to put the title on me and then have Steve beat me.

All I knew for certain is what I talked about with Vince. I was back into performing and uninterested in the inner workings of what was happening with other guys. I talked to Vince often, but all our discussions concerned creative ideas. I was not talking about other guys' business.

A week before *Survivor Series* I found out Bret was going to WCW. I know Vince suggested Bret go and talk to WCW again. Vince said he would help Bret get a great deal there. Vince was going to give WCW the impression that he was willing to pay Bret even more money, so WCW would up their offer to him. WCW did, and Bret signed with them.

For the last several months, Hunter and I had been speaking to Vince on the phone every Wednesday to go over any creative ideas or concerns we might have. Vince valued our opinions and set aside some time to talk to us. The Wednesday before *Survivor Series,* we were on our weekly conference call. "Shawn, barring some miraculous change this weekend, we are going to work a DQ. The next night Bret has promised me that he will come out and give up the title. He will go off to WCW, and we can work some sort of tournament or something like that. I'm not comfortable with that, but Bret has given me his word. I feel I can take him at his word. Regardless of the relationship that you and he have, I've always asked him to do business, but he's just not willing to do it for *you.* I can't change the match with someone else."

I asked Vince why he didn't just have Bret drop the title to someone else the following night on *Raw.* I recall Vince then saying Bret had creative control over his last thirty days.

"So it's not really just me, is it? He doesn't want to drop the belt before he leaves?"

"No, he doesn't. It would be one thing if it were in the States, but especially in Canada. He just doesn't want to do it."

"All of Canada is his? We're not in Calgary. What if I didn't want to do any jobs in the United States?"

"I know, I know, but that's the situation. He has creative control."

There were a few seconds of silence.

"I know I'm not supposed to be talking here," it was Hunter. "Maybe I'm out of line here, but what kind of business is that? Who in the world says, 'I don't want to drop the belt'? You helped him to get a better deal there and he is leaving. That isn't right. That's b.s. How in the world can you trust him? This is the same guy who while he was off, after dropping the title to Shawn, went behind your back and negotiated a deal with WCW only to come back and renegotiate a twenty-year way-out-of-bounds contract with you. He has not done good business since, and now he is leaving to get even more money, by you giving them the impression that you wanted to keep him. We have people leaving in the middle of the night and taking their belts and dropping them in trash cans on WCW. [This was in reference to former women's champion Alundra Blayze, who had done that.] We can't afford for that to happen with the World Wrestling Federation Championship!"

"There's nothing we can do about that. My hands are tied. What can we do about that?"

It was my turn to chime in. "I'll do whatever you want. We'll just take it off him. I'll just swerve him or whatever I have to. You tell me what needs to get done. You and this company have put up with so much from me. My loyalty is here with you. I will do whatever you want."

"What are we talking about, Shawn?"

"Whatever it takes. If we have to do a fast count or get him in a hold and tell someone to ring the bell, I'll do whatever you want me to do."

"That's pretty serious. That has to be a last resort. I still have until Saturday to talk to Bret. That may have to be a real option. This cannot be discussed with anyone. Pat can't know, nobody can know about this but the three of us right now. It's something we will have to talk about."

Hunter and I talked when Vince hung up. We both felt that Vince was already thinking about a possible swerve, but he couldn't ask me to do that. I needed to volunteer.

The day before *Survivor Series,* Saturday, November 8, Hunter and I arrived in Montreal. The standard operating procedure at a Pay-Per-View was to hold the production meeting the night before at the hotel. We had the meeting, and as everyone was leaving, Vince asked me, Hunter, and Jerry Brisco, a longtime agent and close confidant of Vince's, to stay. We sat down and talked. "He's not willing to bend," Vince said. "Are you willing to do what we discussed?"

"Yeah, I'm willing to do what it takes."

"This is serious."

I knew it was. I could hear it in Vince's voice. I had heard urban legends of swerves in the past, but nothing of this magnitude.

"I don't know what's going to happen, but he is going to flip. Jerry can show you some holds."

"I'm not worried about that. We can run Hunter down to the ring if anything happens."

We couldn't discuss how it was going to happen because we didn't know how Bret and I were going to set up the match. Once Bret and I figured out what we were going to do, then, and only then, could Vince and I decide how it would go down.

"I don't want you telling anyone about this," Vince continued. "And when it happens, you deny you knew anything about it until the end. This is my decision, but I can't physically do it. I don't want the heat going on you. Some is going to go on you inevitably because of your history with Bret and because you are the guy doing it, but this is my decision. I don't want you telling anyone. If anyone asks you, you didn't know anything about it.

"But when it's over with, it's over with. Bret's going to be hot. You have to put the heat on me. He needs to be mad at me. He's going to be mad at me, and he is going to want to hit me. I'm going to let him. I owe Bret that much."

Vince also said that Earl Hebner was going to be the referee, and he didn't know anything yet. "I'll talk to him," I said. "I'll clue him in."

Hunter, Jerry, and I went back to my room. Jerry and I had a fine working relationship, but now we had shared something and were brought closer together. "Shawn," he said. "I'll be in the Gorilla position if anything goes down. I'll get down there, but I'm not as fast as I used to be. Is there anything I can do for you?"

"No, Jerry. If it happens, it happens. I'm not worried about it." I was in the mind-set that we just needed to get it done. Jerry felt the same way and was angry with Bret for not doing business and forcing our hand.

"You've been a bear to deal with, Shawn, but this is different. You've never done anything like this. This is wrong, what Bret is doing. I'll be there."

"I'll be there too," Hunter chimed in.

It really was a strange moment. We couldn't even tell Pat. He was Vince's right-hand man, but we all knew he didn't have the mettle for this. He would have gone to Bret and tried to work things out. Pat liked Bret and didn't like confrontation. It was very telling that Jerry was in on it. He was old-school and would be there. We had to take the title from Bret. He left us no choice. To my knowledge, only the four of us knew what was going on.

Sunday felt very strange from the moment I woke up. It was completely different from the other two days I won the championship. Becoming the champion was such a non-issue. I can't help but to liken what was going on to a Mafia hit, and I was going to be Jack Ruby. Everyone knew it was going to be me.

Our hotel was right across the street from the arena, and I arrived there at the normal time, 2:00 P.M. The tension in the building was palpable. A lot of people knew that Bret didn't want to drop the title. He had been filming a documentary, *Wrestling with Shadows,* and had talked openly about not wanting to lose. No one knew what we had planned. However, because of Bret's and my history, most people thought that a fight between the two of us might break out. Everyone probably thought that Bret not wanting to put me over must have been burning me up.

Brian Lee and Ron and Don Harris were three guys who didn't like me. I had a falling out with the Harris Twins back when the Kliq had their heat. We were in the Garden, and Kevin, Scott, and Hunter were in Europe. They came into the locker room and told me, "If you ever mess with us, we will beat the hell out of you." I had no idea why they said that to me, but I was bona fide scared. Those two guys were big, and they were bad. As far as I was concerned, they could have torn me up.

The Harris Twins had left and come back and were now working as the Disciples of Apocalypse—DOA. When they came back, they apologized for that incident, and I was fine with them. We weren't friends by any means, but we didn't interact much so we didn't have any problems either.

I was walking in the back and they came up to me and said completely out of the blue, "We know that Bret isn't doing right by the company. We've got your back no matter what happens. If anything goes down, we will tear him limb from limb." It was so bizarre. They did not know we were going to swerve Bret. They were basing this solely on the gossip from *Wrestling with Shadows,* and Bret's and my history. But they backed up what they said. Those guys did not leave my side all day unless I was in a private meeting.

It was only mid-afternoon, but it felt like this was a powder keg getting ready to explode. I saw Vince. "Have you thought about it? Do you have any ideas?"

"Yeah. I know it isn't glamorous, but usually when I wrestle Bret, I throw the figure-four on, and maybe we can ring the bell real quick and say he gave up. Or, maybe we can work a spot where I hit him with the kick and when I cover him, I'll just hold him as hard as I can and quick count."

"Have you discussed it with Earl?"

"No, not yet. I can't talk about anything until Bret gets here. We don't know where we are going yet."

"As soon as you know, you have to tell me and then we need to get Earl on board."

Pat Patterson started coming to me now. He was the agent for the match, and he kept asking me what I thought we should do. I didn't really say anything because Bret hadn't arrived at the building. Normally I'd discuss it first with Bret and then the three of us would sit down. But Bret wasn't there. I was just sitting with the DOA guys most of the time.

It really started to become fascinating in a weird, nerve-wracking sort of way. A lot of things get talked about and are never done, but we were actually going to do this, and the moment was at hand. I was excited and scared, and my adrenaline was pumping. There were a lot of guys who hated me and took Bret's side in our issues. They believed Bret had won the day and wasn't going to lose to me. I'm sure he had told them we were going to do a DQ. But these guys didn't know that I was holding all the cards. I would look at his friends and think, "You don't know, but this game is already over." Still, I was very nervous.

Bret didn't arrive at the building until sometime near five o'clock. This was unusual for him, but everything was unusual that day. I saw him and he had his camera crew that was filming his movie. I mean it is so crazy. I can understand how some people think that the whole deal was one giant work. What are the odds that he's filming a documentary on the biggest, most controversial day in the history of the business? What can you say? It was a strange day, and I guess this was par for the course.

He wanted to talk in private, so we ducked into a room and started up again with our past and how sorry he was, and how he didn't mean to be this way, and that he has so much respect for me as a worker. He said that we had our differences, and we both went over the line. I agreed. Then he said, "Part of me feels that this is a big work on the part of the office. They made it worse. They knew we didn't want to work together and kept putting us together and they kept adding fuel to the fire." That may have been true. With all due respect to Bret Hart, though, that's so his style: blame everybody else but yourself. I'm man enough to admit it: we *both* acted unprofessionally. Even if Vince and everyone else did take advantage of the situation, who can blame them? It was good for business.

We had our hundredth conversation about putting things in the past, and he said. "It's not about you. I can't do it [put you over] here in Canada. I am a hero here. They don't understand how Canada is. It's different here. It's not like the States. Don't take it personally. It's no reflection on you. Everyone will make it out to be because of you, but that's not why. And I didn't want to leave, but I'll tell you, Vince is sort of forcing me out. Yeah, I got a good deal in WCW, but I'd rather stay here. Vince just made it clear to me that if I stay here I am not going to have the title."

I was thinking, "You take yourself pretty seriously, don't you?" He's dropping a title, but it's the same title someone else let him win. I know that first time you win it it's real, but it remained always real for him. It was just a conversation that I couldn't believe I was having with a guy who had been in the business for twenty years and was forty-plus years old.

Bret kept going on about how the office didn't understand what his losing would mean in Canada. It required a mentality that I can't grasp. I don't know what he was thinking, but it was beyond anything I had ever heard before. I just sat there and listened. I started feeling a little sorry for the guy, because he was going on and on about being a hero. I was thinking, "You poor s.o.b."

At the end of our conversation, it got a little warm. We had done this several times before, but it felt sort of genuine this time because Bret was getting shown the door. There was a trace of humility on his part. Vince was pushing him, not

me, out. Bret didn't say that, but it was true and he knew it. "Can I trust you?" he asked. I said, "Yes," and immediately felt guilty. Despite all our problems, I really felt bad for him because I knew this was the end and he had no idea what was coming. When he was done talking, we shook hands and agreed, "We are going to go out there and tear it up."

After our meeting, I went and found Hunter. "Oh, my God!"

"What?"

I told him about the conversation I just had with Bret and I said, "I am going to look like the biggest heel in the world!"

Vince wanted all the heat on him, and Vince was going to do everything he could to make it so. The fact was, though, he was Vince McMahon, and what were people going to do to him? He knew that I was going to take the brunt of it, and because I was willing to endure that, we bonded like never before. We didn't say anything to each other about it. We didn't have to.

| | |

A little while after I spoke with Hunter, Bret and I started to go over the match. Pat was coming in and out of the room every now and then, to check on us and throw in some ideas. We were talking things through, and Bret came up with this spot where I get him in the Sharpshooter and then he reverses it by pulling on my leg.

Ding! The bell went off in my head. I can't remember the rest of our conversation and how we laid out the match because I knew it was never going to happen.

I guess Bret trusted me after our previous conversation, because unbeknownst to me at the time, he had talked about a swerve happening and had been told by some people not to let me have any false finishes or let me get him in any holds lest we had plans to swerve him. Maybe he just forgot in the moment. I don't know. He came up with the Sharpshooter and I knew right away, that was it.

What normally happens after you discuss a match with your opponent is you break off, absorb what plans you have made, and then get back together and go over it one more time. So we went our separate ways.

Shane McMahon was not at the meeting the night before, but by this point I knew that he knew. His dad must have told him. I went into Vince's office to tell Vince about the Sharpshooter scenario, but he wasn't there. Shane was.

"Where's your dad?"

"Do we need him?"

"Yeah."

Shane took off to find Vince. Normally I'd be hanging out in Vince's office a lot, but not today. When I left the meeting with Bret, I couldn't go straight to Vince's office. I stopped, talked with Hunter, and took a circuitous route to Vince's office. I've walked into his office plenty of times in front of everybody. This time, I looked to see who was around. I had to be careful.

They came back to the office, and I told them, "You are not going to believe this, but he came up with a spot where I get the Sharpshooter on him and then he's supposed to reverse it by pulling my leg. When I put him in it, when I turn him over, we can ring the bell right there."

"That's it. That's the one. Have you told Earl yet?"

"No, I wanted to tell you first. I wanted to make sure it was okay."

It was about seven o'clock when I walked into the locker room. There were only a few people in there and none were close to Earl. He was putting on his referee garb, and I started to put my boots on.

"Earl, I need you to listen to me very carefully." I was speaking very softly. "We are doing a big swerve tonight. I am going to get Bret in the Sharpshooter, and I need you to ring the bell."

He was a bit confused and in a normal tone of voice said, "Wait a minute."

"Earl, be very quiet. I need you to listen. This is very serious. Earl, we are screwing Bret tonight. We are going to be having the match, and you have to ring the bell. We are taking the title off him tonight. He doesn't know. Can you do it?"

"What are we doing?"

"I am going to get him in the Sharpshooter, and I need you to ring that bell. I need you to ring that bell and just get out of there."

"Are you serious?"

"Yes."

"Okay. I'll do whatever I have to do. Does Vince know about this?"

"Yes, of course. You can confirm that with Vince. I'll let you know if anything changes, but for now, that's what we are doing, no matter what you hear."

Earl left and talked to his brother Dave, who was an agent, and they went and saw Vince. I saw Dave later and he was visibly different, so I knew that he knew. Dave and Jack Lanza, another agent, are very close. I looked at Jack and I knew that he knew as well.

So Bret and I got together and went over the match again. Pat was in the room with us, and he had no idea what was going to happen. He had a strong relationship with Bret. He wouldn't have done it, and Vince knew that. That's why he didn't tell Pat. It was a big issue, not telling Pat. Vince knew it was big for me because he knew I believed in Pat and that I respected him. Pat was hurt by the whole situation between Bret and me. Pat always wanted work to be enjoyable. He liked both of us and was way too close to both of us to be in on this.

As we were going over the match, Bret asked, "Do you want to do something with the flag again? When you stuck the flag up your nose in that one match, you got a ton of heat up in Canada. I'm telling you they were just livid. You want to do it?"

"Sure, I'll do whatever you want."

After the deal went down, everyone made a big deal about me jerking around the Canadian flag, but like the Sharpshooter, it was his idea. This was beyond the *Twilight Zone.*

I was nervous and having a hard time staying still. It's one thing to talk about it, but it was another to actually do it, and it was go time. I was going to a place I could not come back from. I was already unpopular with the fans who read all the stuff Bret put out there. I swallowed that. In the locker room there were a couple of the boys on my side, more on his, and then there were a few that thought the whole thing was stupid. I only knew that what happened this night was going to have repercussions, none that were good. This was a situation where I was made out to be the bad guy, and now I was playing the bad guy, and doing it with a smile. This was not one of those times when Vince said, "I want you to enjoy this."

I walked up to the gorilla position. Hunter was there, so was Brisco. Vince started drifting to us and Pat was there as well. Then Davey Boy, Jim Neidhart, and Owen Hart came up next to us. The finish, as far as everyone else knew, was that Hunter was going to come down and interfere, and then those guys would come down, and there would be a big fight and a DQ. But when guys are going to do a run-in, they don't stand at gorilla before the match starts. It was very unusual for them to be there, and since I knew what was happening, I was thinking they were there in case something happens. After all, they didn't need to be there for another twenty minutes.

The Molson Centre was sold out, and when I came from behind the curtain and into the arena I heard the people's screams. I got in the ring, looked at Earl, and screamed, "Are you ready to do this? Are you ready?"

"I'm ready."

"You have to do it, Earl, you got to do this, don't worry. Just do it and get out of here." I could see the nervousness on his face. Who knows what the crowd was going to do? Poor Earl, I think he aged twenty years that night.

This was different from any other match *ever.* This business is filled with talking about doing stuff. Ninety-nine-point-nine-nine percent is talking. I was excited, but in a perverse way. There was so much adrenaline pumping through my body. I felt insane.

I did my bit with the flag, which riled up the crowd even more, and then we started. We structured the beginning of the match where we would do a lot of fighting on the outside of the ring to take advantage of the fact that the people knew our history and would buy us turning this into a brawl. We also agreed that we work snug tonight. So we brawled on the outside before taking it into the ring. We had been in the ring for just a little bit when Vince started walking down to ringside with Sgt. Slaughter. I had no idea Vince was going to come down to the ring.

Bret didn't say anything. I whispered, "Why is Vince coming down?" We continued on with the match and a few minutes later reached the point where Bret was going to start his comeback. I would stop him and then clamp on the Sharpshooter. It was a good little transitional spot.

I remember looking at Earl and saying, "Here we go." Wrestlers say that all the time in the ring, so if Bret heard it he wouldn't have thought anything of it. I

called for the move, snatched him up, and put him in the Sharpshooter. I locked eyes with Earl as I spun Bret over and put the hold on. I yelled, "Ring it, ring it now!" As soon as Bret started pulling my leg, the bell rang. I let him pull my leg and did the best I could to carry through with our plans and have him start to reverse the move. I did not know Vince had called for the bell as well. I believe he came down to try and make it as clear as possible that it was his decision to do this and not mine. It was an attempt to deflect heat from me and put it on him, but I did tell Earl to ring the bell. After it rang, I acted like I was mad and didn't know what was going on. I heard Vince yell, "Give him the belt!" I rolled out of the ring and grabbed the championship belt. Jerry and Hunter had run down to the ring and Jerry started walking me back to the curtain. Hunter was right behind. The crowd was in a complete uproar. Then, right before I ducked behind the curtain, I raised the belt high up in the air as a heel would do to incite the crowd. Part of me was thinking, "Just get out of there!" My business side thought, "Something is going on here, but I've got to act like whatever happened was supposed to happen."

When I got behind the curtain, it was complete chaos. Davey Boy yelled, "What happened?"

"I don't know. They rang the bell." Jerry and Hunter kept moving me. Earl was gone. He left the ring and ran to the back, where his brother had the car running for him. He jumped in and was out of the building in no time at all.

They shuttled me into the locker room. There was this stunned look on a lot of people's faces. I saw the DOA guys and I went and sat next to them. Hunter was pacing. Then he left to go check out the situation. Everyone was rushing around in the back, and out in the arena, Bret was tearing up the television monitors and spitting in Vince's face. 'Taker was sitting in the locker room, not far from me. He looked over and asked, "Did you know that was going to happen?"

"No, I didn't."

"All right."

By this time Bret had made his way back, and he was beyond furious. He asked me if I knew anything about it. "As God is my witness, I didn't know anything about it, Bret." I lied, plain and simple. As a Christian now, I wouldn't say that. But I'm not going to pretend that I didn't. That's what I told Bret. I wasn't afraid of him. I was sitting with the DOA. If we got into a fight, we got into a fight. I had people around me.

Davey Boy was yelling.

I didn't say a word. I just sat there in between the DOA.

All of a sudden, Vince, Brisco, and Shane walked into the locker room. Vince told Bret, "You left me no choice. I'm sorry that this had to happen, but it's a decision that I made."

Bret walked up to Vince and punched him in the face. Vince took what looked like to me the worst dive ever. He crumbled down to the floor, and Shane and the others helped him up. After he was back on his feet, Vince looked at Bret and said, "I owed you that." He then left the room. I heard a little while later that Bret was so full of pride because of the punch. I don't think he was aware that Vince knew that he was going to do it and took a dive. Once Vince left the room, Bret took his boots off, put his shoes on, grabbed his bag, and left. While all this was going on, Hunter was out in the hallway getting cussed out by Bret's wife. They captured that in Bret's film.

I stayed in the locker room with Hunter and Chyna for a long time. I didn't even shower or change clothes. After everyone else had left the building, we headed out and began walking back to our hotel. As we approached the street, we saw a large crowd gathered in front of the hotel. We put our heads down and ran through the mob. They were yelling obscenities at us, and one woman punched Hunter in the face. The lobby was jammed with angry people as well, so we sprinted all the way to the elevator. We were safe now, and we went to my room to try and settle down. I looked at Hunter, he looked at me, and then I said, "We did it, didn't we?"

"You did what you had to do, Shawn."

Now my thoughts turned to the future. I was worried about what would happen at tomorrow's *Raw* in Ottawa. Vince could say that he wanted all the heat on him, but I knew that ninety percent of the people were going to think it was my fault, that I was the bad guy.

Hunter did the best he could to alleviate my worries. "Bret put us in a bad position as a company. He wasn't thinking about anybody but himself. It may take time, but people are going to realize that you didn't have any choice and you did the right thing. You have to know you did the right thing."

It was all sinking in now, and I paced back and forth for a long time. It was weird. I had been wrestling for thirteen years and now I wondered if it would ever be the same again. Would I ever be able to goof around in the dressing room? Am I ever going to be able to go in the ring and just have fun again?

I couldn't stop wondering what the boys would do. I knew they were talking about it now and would be on the drive to Ottawa. There are few things more dangerous than giving a bunch of wrestlers time to talk about something. Whatever the story was, it was going to be one hundred times worse by the time everyone made it to Ottawa.

I believed in my heart that I did the right thing, but I still felt a little dirty. I knew that I wasn't well liked, and even though I said it didn't bother me, there was always a part of me that wished people would like me. As petty or as juvenile as that sounds, that was how I felt. Was I going to be hated forever now? It had been a long year, starting with my knee injury, the controversy surrounding my not wrestling at *WrestleMania 13,* and then the whole Bret Hart situation over the spring and summer. I had finally started having fun again with DX, and now this had happened.

Hunter—and Joanie, who was there too—could see the troubled look on my face. They asked if I was going to be all right. I told them I'd be fine, and they left, saying, "Call if you need anything."

I was alone for the first time all day. I was still in my gear, sitting there on the bed. I had worked so hard to become a good wrestler. Once I got to that point, I worked even harder because I wanted to be the greatest. Now I had been involved in the biggest scandal in wrestling history. People might forget how good I was and just remember me for this. I always told people, "You can say what you want about me, but I am no liar." Now I had lied. I had done what people had always accused me of doing, which was swerving behind people's backs.

All I ever wanted to do was be a wrestler, but through my own shortcomings and circumstance, I kept getting caught up in all this other junk. Every time I thought it couldn't get any bigger or worse, it did. I knew I was the cause of most of my problems, but I still believed I was a decent guy. I was tired, frustrated, and worried.

| | |

When I arrived at the building in Ottawa, I immediately sought out 'Taker. I cared what he thought. Mark and I weren't buddies. However, we had just come through our program and had become closer. There isn't anybody in this business that I respect more than him. I respected him before we worked together because I felt he deserved it, I respected him after we worked together because he had earned it.

He was in a meeting with Vince and when he came out he said, "I had a long talk with Vince and he explained things to me. Everything's cool."

"Is it?"

"Yeah, everything is cool."

"I need it to be that way with us."

"It is. Don't worry."

Vince told me that he explained everything to 'Taker. I didn't ask him what he said. I didn't want to know. I had learned not to seek answers to questions that I might later on have to lie about. I never wanted to have to perjure myself. If I didn't know the answers, I wouldn't have to lie.

Vince also called a meeting that day to explain the situation to all the boys. He said it was his call and if anyone didn't like it, they could leave. Mick Foley had walked out in protest, but was back the next day. I guess his job was more important to him than his principles.

Owen Hart walked out too, but his situation was much different. Owen was such a good guy. He felt he should show loyalty to his brother, and that's understandable. Vince knew that and told Owen he was welcome to come back. When Owen came back, he talked with me. "I know all the stuff that went on between you and Bret, but I am not my brother. You and I have always gotten along."

"We have. Your brother always brought out the worst in me. I don't know what to tell you. I'm sorry. He just pushed my buttons. I don't know if we are too competitive, but we just don't mix." Owen told me that Bret was putting pressure on him to leave and that he didn't want to leave. All Owen ever wanted to do was take care of his family. Everyone knew that.

Owen died in a tragic accident at the *Over the Edge* Pay-Per-View in 1999. When he passed away, the world didn't just lose a great wrestler, it lost a wonderful human being. The night following *Over the Edge,* a special *Raw* was aired in his honor. It's been said, and it's true, he's the only guy in the business that you could have an entire two-hour show about and not have one person say one negative thing about him. Owen was a great man.

| | |

Bret had asked me not to bury him after he left the company. He told me he wouldn't bury me in WCW. Considering his track record, I didn't believe him. I told him I wouldn't, but I did—within the context of a story line. I was doing the DX gimmick and it was part of our new attitude. A week after Montreal, Vince went on television and spoke about how "Bret screwed Bret." Everyone knew about the swerve, and we were going to try and capitalize on it. We mocked him for thinking he could pull a fast one on us. As a heel, it was natural for me to go out there and gloat. So that's what I did. On the November 24 edition of *Raw,* I brought out "Midget Bret," put him in the Sharpshooter, and ridiculed him, as any heel would. Reality and TV came together, and our ratings jumped. Stone Cold was coming on like gangbusters and the company would ultimately bury WCW. It started the night after Montreal. It ended with Vince taking over WCW in 2001.

lost 24

It didn't take long for the heat in the locker room to cool down. The company was charging forward and DX was flying. We didn't just ridicule Bret, we made fun of everyone and everything from President Clinton to the European Championship.

Commissioner Slaughter thought he could destroy DX by forcing Hunter and me to fight for the European Championship, so we decided to make a mockery of our match. Hunter ran the ropes like a big goon, we pretended to fight, and he pinned me after a grueling one minute and seventeen seconds. We were so over-the-top. The fans loved us.

We were supposed to be heels, but we were so funny and politically incorrect that they couldn't help cheering us.

Life had become such a roller-coaster ride. The seriousness of Montreal had brought me down, but I was right back up with getting to do the DX gimmick. When Vince told me that he was going to go with Steve at *WrestleMania XIV,* I wasn't bothered at all. Steve deserved it. Also, I was having so much fun now, the championship didn't matter that much to me. Maybe I was manic, up one month, down the next, but that was how I felt.

| | |

Physically, however, I was hurting. I had wrestled Ken Shamrock early in December at the *D-Generation X* Pay-Per-View, and my back had been killing me ever since. Every morning I had to gobble down a bunch of pain pills just to get out of bed. My back had bothered me at times for many years, but it was something I could always work through.

I wrestled Undertaker in a Casket match at the *Royal Rumble* and took a back body drop right on the casket. I didn't feel anything unusual and didn't think too much of it. Two days later, we were shooting a vignette in Davis, California, and I felt stabbing pain in my lower back. I flew home that Wednesday. When I woke up Thursday morning, I couldn't move. It felt like there was a hot searing knife tearing through my back. I had never felt that much pain in my entire life. I couldn't stand up, so I rolled out of bed. My phone was a few feet away from the bed, but I couldn't get to it. I could reach the cord, though, so I grabbed it and pulled the phone to me. I dialed up my parents and I said, "I can't move. I need somebody to come get me to the hospital."

They called an ambulance and came right over to my house. With my arms and legs dragging lifelessly behind me, I started crawling towards the front door. It was probably ten yards from my room to the door, and my folks lived twenty-five minutes away. They beat me to the door. The ambulance came soon afterwards and the EMT's put me on a stretcher and took me to the hospital. Once there, the doctors shot me up with some Demerol and took an MRI.

After looking at the results, the doctor told me I had a couple of herniated disks and that one was completely crushed. He gave me a bunch of pills and sent me home. I called Vince and told him what was going on.

"What are we going to do?" he asked.

"I can do *WrestleMania,* but I think it would be best if I could have the February Pay-Per-View off. This is very serious."

"I want you to come here. I have a doctor I want you to see. Let's get a couple of opinions on it. We'll get you better for *WrestleMania.* That's the important thing."

Vince wanted me to go to New York to see a doctor who had treated Dennis Byrd, the New York Jets lineman who had broken his neck during a game. So I flew to New York and went to see him. The doctor took another MRI and examined me. "You are through. You will never wrestle again," he said.

I started to well up. I asked him if he was sure. He told me that I had so much damage that if I took one more shot to my back, my legs might go out on me, and who knows what would happen then. He told me in no uncertain terms that I was finished.

For the second time in my life, I had to tell Vince that I was done. He asked me what we were going to do, and I said, "I don't care what the doctor said, I am going to *WrestleMania.* I'll have surgery afterwards." I was very adamant about putting Steve over.

I was so bummed. Things had really turned around for me, and I was having fun again. Vince had brought in Mike Tyson to work with DX at *Wrestle-*

Mania, Road Dogg and Billy Gunn were going to join Hunter and me. The company as a whole was on a roll. Now it was all over for me.

I didn't want to stay in New York to get treated. I wanted to be near my family, so I went back to San Antonio. My doctor, Pablo Vasquez-Seonne, also told me that it was too risky to wrestle. I told him I had to. I gave him the date for *WrestleMania XIV,* March 29, and said, "I am wrestling. Just get me there." I spent all of February rehabbing my back. I had a shiatsu message therapist come down to San Antonio, and he worked with me every day. He did his thing, but it didn't make a difference. I was in constant pain. It didn't matter whether I was lying down, standing up, or sitting. I just couldn't get comfortable. The pain would start in my back and shoot down my left leg. I doped myself up all day to deaden it as much as possible.

I flew in every week for TV to shoot interviews or vignettes, and I became a real bear to deal with. I'd snap at the smallest things and constantly make threats about not showing up at *WrestleMania.* Everyone in the company was looking to the future, and that meant they concentrated their time and efforts on Steve Austin. I was looking for a pat on the back, some acknowledgment that I was doing something courageous for the company, but none came. I felt neglected. It hadn't been that long ago when everything was about me, and I was resentful. My way of getting back at the situation was to make life as difficult as possible for everyone. It wasn't the right thing to do, but I was immature and that's how I handled it.

| | |

WrestleMania was in Boston that year, and the day before the show we had a big public appearance scheduled at Government Center. Hunter, Mike Tyson, and myself were going to do a public "workout" and humiliate Steve. Ten thousand people showed up for it, and security was not that good. People were grabbing and hitting us, and I got zinged in the head with a battery as I was leaving. I lost it and started cutting promos on everyone in sight. I threatened to not show up the next day unless they provided me with personal security guards. They took my threat seriously because they not only got me a security guard, they got one for my parents, who had come up to Boston to see that I made it through the weekend.

I came to the arena with my parents and found out that Vince set aside a personal dressing room for me. He knew how angry and depressed I was and wanted to give me something special. Vince also wanted to do everything possible to ensure that we got through the day according to plan. He couldn't afford to have me blow up and walk out at the last moment. Vince was in a difficult situation. I know he cared about me and wanted to take care of me, but the company's future was riding on Steve. He needed to put his focus there.

When he came into my dressing room, he said that he appreciated my doing this. "Shawn, on behalf of myself and the company, I want to thank you. I know this is a difficult time for you, but when it is over, you'll always have a job here."

My dad wasn't too impressed with Vince's speech. "You better hope my boy doesn't get hurt out there. If my son gets hurt, you are going to have a problem."

Vince was very respectful to my father. "We'll do everything we can for Shawn. Whatever you need today, just let us know." Vince understood that my dad was just trying to protect his son. When I came back at *SummerSlam* in 2002, my dad apologized to Vince for his outburst. "I was hard on you and I was wrong."

"You were doing what any father would do. I would have done the same thing. I've always had a great deal of respect for you, and I have more now." They shook hands and that was it.

Steve soon came in to discuss our match. "What do we have to do to get through it, kid?" He set it up. The match was very similar to one that he and Hunter had been working. Nothing stellar, but creatively I wasn't there. My back was killing me, and I had to deal with my career coming to an end. However, I was also upset for another reason: the night before I found out that Earl Hebner had a brain aneurysm.

Shortly after I began my singles career, Earl refereed one of my matches. I liked him so much I went to Vince and asked for Earl to ref all my matches. We had been through Montreal together and a whole lot more. I wanted him to be there for my last match. He was my friend. I visited him in the hospital before coming to the arena. He was not in good shape, and I didn't know if he was going to make it. You never know with something that serious. I wasn't going to let him know how worried I was, though. I told him he was going to get better and gave him a hug and kiss. Right before I entered the arena for my match, I turned to the TV camera that was following me and I said, "This one's for you, Earl."

I didn't leave my dressing room the whole day. After Steve and I talked about the match, we went over what I was going to do with Tyson, who was working as the "special enforcer." He had joined DX in the run-up to 'Mania, but was going to turn on me. The referee would get knocked out, Steve would hit me with his Stone Cold Stunner, and Tyson would come into the ring and count the cover. Afterwards, we would start arguing and Tyson would knock me out with one punch.

Mike was very into it, and as I was explaining that he would punch me, he started throwing some punches in the air real fast. I had to tell him to slow down and take it easy. I was trying to get him to hit me so he wouldn't knock me out. I said, "Don't worry, Mike, just get the punch somewhere around me, I'll go down." The last thing I needed was a broken jaw.

The creative team wanted Mike to drape an Austin 3:16 shirt over me after he had laid me out. I didn't want them doing that. I believed losing was enough and that covering me up with the shirt was overkill.

Pat pushed really hard for it, and I made a big stink. I told Pat, "If you are going to do that, I'll get up and leave." I made all sorts of threats about that, and they agreed not to do it. They did it anyways. I guess turnabout is fair play. It wasn't so long ago that I had been involved in a swerve of sorts. I was hot about it, but it never once occurred to me to rile up the whole business and make Austin and Vince out to be a bunch of no-good jerks. Somehow a rumor got out that Undertaker stood in the hallway taping his fists as I made my way to the curtain. The insinuation was that 'Taker was letting me know that I better do business and not try any funny stuff. Plain and simple, this never happened. It was "reported" as fact, but is nothing more than an urban legend that someone felt compelled to make up.

I threw down four pain pills and somehow made it through the match. I had wrestled hurt so many times that I could deal with the pain. The bigger problem was that my body wasn't moving like it normally did. Something simple

like shooting off the ropes took a tremendous effort. I felt like I was running in quicksand, and that made me fatigue much faster than I normally would have. My body had always done exactly what I wanted it to do when I wanted to do it. This night, it shut down. After it was over, I went straight to my dressing room, laid on the floor, and started icing my back. Vince came in.

"Are you okay?"

"Yeah."

"That was one of the most amazing things I've ever seen. You are a special person. Thank you."

I broke down and started weeping. Ever since the doctor had told me that I was finished I had been a very angry person. After Vince's words, all that anger momentarily disappeared. I was relieved it was over. Everything I had bottled up came pouring out of me. My folks came in to check on me as well. My mom was upset because she saw me lying there in pain. My dad, who always tries to be the pillar of strength, just wanted to know if I was okay. I said I was fine. They asked if I wanted them to stay and I said that wasn't necessary, and they went back to the hotel. Steve came in and said thanks. He didn't stay long because he and Vince had to do a press conference. Hunter was in my room as well. He told me I did a heck of a job, and then sat there. He'd often sit with me and not say anything. That was his way, and I liked having him there.

I laid on the floor for some time trying to gather my thoughts. It would have been nice if I could have walked up to my friends, shook their hands, said goodbye, and left on a nice note, but that wasn't who I was then. I started thinking about Tyson draping the Austin 3:16 shirt on me and my blood started boiling. Now, I just wanted to get out of the building. I packed up my things and headed out with Hunter. As we were walking, we passed the room where Vince, Steve, and Tyson were holding their press conference. I kicked open the door and walked in. Shane McMahon was standing nearby and he came over to me and asked what in the world I was doing. I didn't make a scene or anything, but I let him have it for a few minutes. I told him how the shirt thing was b.s. and how I deserved better after all I had done for the company

My career had ended on a very sour note.

| | |

I flew back to San Antonio pretty much a lost soul. I was angry, confused, scared, and ravaged by guilt. I didn't know what I was going to do with the rest of my life, but more importantly, I didn't know who I really was. The past three tumultuous years had broken me. Even though I hadn't always acted decently, I had always believed I was a good person. I couldn't be the sorry s.o.b. that so many claimed I was. Now, I wasn't so sure.

I had tied my self-worth to my job. I thought as long as I was the best, as long as I could steal the show every night, I would be happy and everything else would melt away. At times I was happy, but it never lasted. So I'd throw myself further and further into my work, but nothing changed. A day of happiness would be followed by a week of anger and confusion. To alleviate my pain, I took the pills. This only ended up confusing me more. Was I a bad person because I did drugs? Or did I do drugs because I was a bad person? It was a never-ending cycle that brought me further and further down.

Dr. Vasquez had watched me wrestle Steve and was in total disbelief. He couldn't believe what I had done, considering my condition. He wanted to avoid surgery if we could, and recommended that I try rehabbing my back. What I should have done is take a month of vacation on an island, come back recharged, and rehab hard. Instead, I went right into the rehab and gave it a half-baked effort. It didn't improve. I was in pain twenty-four hours a day, so I just gobbled down more and more pills.

I wallowed in my misery and took it out on the people close to me. Interestingly, I didn't miss performing at all. The company was really taking off, and I would occasionally be asked in interviews if I was frustrated that I couldn't be part of it. I honestly told them no. I was happy for Vince. He and the rest of the guys deserved their success. I actually came back late in 1998 for a brief stint as Commissioner, but I didn't stick around. I needed to be away.

I went hunting for the first time in my life that fall. I enjoyed it and was good at it. The peace of the outdoors was soothing, and I began hunting as much as my back would allow me to. I also bought San Antonio Spurs season tickets. I was a huge fan, but because I had been on the road for so many years, I never had the chance to see them play. I went to as many games as possible.

Towards the end of the year I went to see Dr. Vasquez. My back was not getting any better. He told me that surgery would probably alleviate the pain, but if I went through with it, my mobility would be gone. I don't think he had ever dealt with someone who had my problems and then went on to have a physical

Salmon fishing in Alaska.

lifestyle. The pain was so bad, I didn't care about future mobility. I didn't have any now, so I figured, what's the difference?

In January 1999, he fused my back at the L4 and L5 vertabrae as well as making more space between my L5 and S1. He cut a piece of my hip out and placed that between the L4 and L5 vertebrae. He then took a metal plate and screwed it all together. The surgery was supposed to take about three hours, but I had even more damage than what had showed up on the MRIs, and it took closer to four and half hours. It was worth it. The pain was gone. Within a few weeks, I could get around all right. My spirits had been lifted, but it wasn't only because my back felt better.

rebecca

One Monday night towards the end of 1998, I was
watching television, flipping back and forth between *Raw*
and *Nitro*. I liked watching *Nitro* because it gave me a
chance to see Scott Hall and Kevin Nash do their thing. This
Nitro Girl came out and started dancing. They called her
Whisper, and she was the most beautiful, sexiest woman I
had ever seen. Every Monday, I started turning in to *Nitro*
just to see her.

Shortly after I first saw her dance, I was talking on the
phone to my buddy Rich Minzer, who works at the Gold's Gym
in Venice, California. He is a great guy and always took care of

the boys when we were out there. We had become friends over the years, and I told him about this woman I had seen on *Nitro*. Two weeks later he called me. "Guess what? Guess who's out here?"

"I don't know."

"WCW."

"Good, tell Kevin I say hi."

"No, you don't understand. The *Nitro* Girls are here. Whisper is here. The TV doesn't do her justice, Shawn. She's twice as beautiful in person."

"No way!"

"Can I tell her you like her?"

"No, don't tell her I saw her on TV, she'll think I'm an idiot."

"I'll ask her if she'll give me her phone number for you."

"No, are you kidding me?"

"Well, wouldn't you like to try and meet her?"

"Yeah, but what are you going to do, tell her this guy saw her on TV? You'll freak her out. Don't say anything."

He ended up telling another *Nitro* Girl, Spice, about our conversation, and she thought it was cute. So she and Rich convinced Whisper, whose real name is Rebecca, by the way, to give Rich her number to give to me. Rebecca hadn't dated in a while and figured, why not? If it's meant to be, something will happen.

Rich called me the next day with her number. He also told me that Rebecca wasn't a wrestling fan and didn't know who I was. He said, "That's great, because if she likes you, it will be for who you are and not because you are a big celebrity."

I was thinking, if she doesn't know who I am, then I have nothing. So I didn't call her. He called me back a couple of days later and couldn't believe I hadn't called. I told him, I had no idea what to say to her. He was adamant that I call her and played me a message Rebecca had left for him on his phone. She had said, "Thanks for taking care of us out in LA, Rich. I just wanted to let you know Shawn didn't call. I appreciate you thinking about me in that respect. I guess it's not meant to be."

I knew I had to call her now, so I hung up with Rich and dialed her number. I was so nervous, and hoped she wasn't home. Much to my relief, the answering machine picked up.

"Hello, this is Rich's friend, Shawn Hickenbottom. I'd really love to talk to you.

If you want, give me a call back. My number is . . ." I let out a huge sigh of relief!

She returned my call that evening, and we talked for a couple of hours. We continued talking every night for the next two weeks. Neither of us slept much, and we would talk until four in the morning. Then we'd hop on the computer and e-mail each other back and forth. It was puppy love running amuck.

Valentine's Day was coming up, and Rebecca happened to be doing a personal appearance in Sacramento. I wanted to do something special for her. I asked her where she was staying and then called a local florist and told them I'm crazy about this woman. Do whatever it takes. I had three dozen roses sent to her room. She called later that night when she got back to the hotel. "You are very smooth," she said. "I think it's time we meet."

She lived in Atlanta, so I told her I would be more than happy to fly her to San Antonio.

"You don't have to do that," Rebecca replied. "I'll fly there myself."

That moved me. I had never been in a relationship where I didn't have to pay for everything. It wasn't the money, it was just the fact that she offered, and she was willing to spend her money to see me. She didn't care that I was a wrestler or celebrity. She wanted to meet Shawn Hickenbottom.

I met her as she came off her plane, and I was floored. The TV did not do her justice. She was beyond gorgeous. We smiled at each other and said hello, and then I gave her a peck on the cheek. I held her hand on the way to the car. She was like no one I had ever been with before. It was fairly early in the evening, so we decided to get something to eat. Being the classy guy that I am, I took her to Denny's. She loved it.

We spent a wonderful couple of days together, and as she was leaving I gave her a Shawn Michaels T-shirt and asked her to wear it at the next *Nitro.* I thought Kevin and Scott, who didn't yet know about us, would get a big kick out of it, thinking that she was a fan of mine.

Rebecca wore the shirt before the show and received her fair share of stares. At one point, she walked by the ring and Bret Hart happened to be in there working with a crew from *MADtv.* She didn't make a big production or anything, but he saw her and scowled.

A few weeks later, Rebecca was scheduled to do a series of photo shoots in Los Angeles. I figured I might as well go out there and spend some time with her. I flew to LA on a Monday. She was in Sacramento again, this time for *Nitro,* and planned on driving down after the show. It's about a four-hundred-mile drive, and she left Sacramento around eleven o'clock. I didn't think I'd see her until at least five the next morning. She arrived well before four. We went to one photo shoot, canceled the others, and only went as far as the balcony for the next two days. I just couldn't be with her enough.

As I was driving her to the airport so she could catch the red-eye back east, I was thinking to myself, "I am in love with this woman." I had only known her for a couple of weeks, but this was love. I was sure of it.

I dropped her off at the terminal and she started walking inside. Suddenly, I had this urge to tell her how I felt. Maybe it was because we were in LA and I had seen a lot of movies, but I just had to tell her. I jumped out of my car and ran inside the terminal. She was getting ready to take the escalator up to security.

"Rebecca," I yelled.

She turned around. "Yes."

"I hope it's okay, but I think I'm in love with you!"

She dropped her bags, ran to me, and said, "Really? I love you so much too. I thought it was just me!"

Three weeks later we flew to Las Vegas and got married at the Graceland Wedding Chapel. No Knobbs, no Sags, no Al Madril, not even Mom and Dad. Just Rebecca, myself, and Elvis. It was perfect.

I I I

If you ever wondered how the Monday Night Wars affected Eric Bischoff—the man who ran WCW—I'll let you judge for yourself.

Before Rebecca and I were married, I was going to do a press junket for an upcoming overseas tour, and I was flying through Atlanta. I figured I'd go a day early and spend that day with Rebecca. When it was time for me to catch my flight, she took me to the airport. We were waiting in line to check in, and by pure chance, Eric Bischoff was in line in front of us. He looked back, and we broke out laughing. He didn't even smile.

We didn't think too much of it. I checked in and flew across the pond. While I was there, Rebecca called and told me that Eric Bischoff had ordered her to be removed from the filming of a new *Nitro* opening. While Rebecca was at the shoot, Terri Byrne, one of the *Nitro* Girls, received a call on her cell phone and told Rebecca that Bischoff, having seen her at the airport with me, thought Rebecca was jumping ship. He said she couldn't be in the shoot and told her to go home.

"I'm dating the guy," Rebecca told the girls. "I'm not going to go up there. What am I going to do, wrestle? I'm in love with the man."

Bischoff was so paranoid he was worrying about a *Nitro* Girl leaving! Well, after I asked Rebecca to marry me, she went up to him and asked him if she could get out of her contract because she was moving to San Antonio to be with me. When he found out she was marrying me, he refused to let her out.

"I'm not going to the World Wrestling Federation," she told him. "I'm marrying Shawn. I want to be his wife and be a mother."

Bischoff still wouldn't let her go. I called Kevin to ask what was going on. He must have just watched an FBI movie that day because he told her to wear a wire and record all her conversations with Bischoff and then get a lawyer.

When she told me that, I said, "Don't do that! Let me call Skip." I called him and he got in touch with the legal folks down in Atlanta. They came to an agreement whereby Rebecca could leave and marry me, but she couldn't work for anyone else for the length of her three-year contract. I still have no idea what Bischoff could have been thinking.

26
showstopper productions

I had often thought about training aspiring wrestlers when my career was over. Now that I had to find something to do, I started bringing the subject up to friends. My lawyer, Skip McCormick, liked the idea. He understood that I could use my name as a brand and saw a lot of potential in a wrestling school with my name on it. I spoke with Jose as well, and he wanted to work with me.

If we were going to do this, it had to be a first-class operation. Most wrestling schools were just a ring in a building. I didn't want that. I wanted a real wrestling academy. I wanted to give my students all the tools they would need to succeed. I wanted them training, doing interviews, and learning everything about the business. I even wanted to lodge them if it made economic sense. (It didn't, but we worked out a deal with an apartment complex to get our students a reduced rate.)

Skip took care of the business end of things, and I came up with a training program. I hired Rudy Gonzales, a great worker who had wrestled in the area for some time, to be the lead trainer. Since I couldn't wrestle because of my back, I would coach from the outside and Rudy would work with them in the ring. Jose would coach from the outside as well. I also hired my old trainer, Ken Johnson, as well. I worked with a physical trainer too, and together with Jose, developed our training program.

When The Shawn Michaels Wrestling Academy opened for business, it was a first-rate operation with great facilities. I bought a ring and nearly $10,000 worth of training equipment. We solicited applications from all over the country and offered a full- and a part-time program. Full-time students trained three hours, three days a week, for three months, while the part-timers trained an hour and a half, for six months. I charged $3,500 for each program. My dad had paid three grand in 1984, so I figured our students were getting a heck of a deal. As part of our program, we guaranteed our students the opportunity to wrestle in front of live crowds. We could do this because I took over a small local promotion that I named the Texas Wrestling Alliance.

We enrolled twelve students in our first class. Two of our students ended up wrestling for WWE: Garrison Cade and Brian "Spanky" Kendrick. A third, Brian Danielson, has worked in Japan and may yet come to WWE. Those three were head and shoulders above the rest of the class, but there were about four more guys who, had they had the "nothing is going to stop me" attitude, might have made it as well.

I enjoyed running the academy. Teaching and being around enthusiastic young guys was a real blast. I had always loved wrestling. It was all the other junk that drove me crazy. So naturally, I became heavily involved in producing and promoting the Texas Wrestling Alliance and soon drove myself out of my little business.

At the same time that I was running the academy, I also began working as a sportscaster at KENS 5, the local CBS affiliate. Bob McGann, the station manager, bumped into me at a Spurs game and asked if I wanted to come aboard the local news and do the sports. I told him I had no experience, but he offered to train me. He had seen me on TV and thought I could be good. I liked sports and knew something about television, so I figured I might as well give it a try. The people at the station were very kind and patient with me. I did a fun segment covering the high school football game of the week and a few other things, but I certainly didn't take to it like I did wrestling; and, I was nowhere near as good. I had a name and was fairly entertaining, but I didn't have any journalistic training.

Because of my connections at the station, I was able to get the Texas Wrestling Alliance on the television. We produced a half-hour show that aired late on Saturday night. At first, it was really cool. I was like a mini Vince. I actually called him to tell him what I was doing and to apologize once again for being such a pain. I told him I didn't know how he managed to do what he did. I was overwhelmed with my tiny production. I couldn't imagine being in his shoes.

I asked him, "How did you ever deal with me and everyone else?"

A workout at my academy.

"It's just one of those things that you do, Shawn. But you were always a joy."

"Oh please."

"Are you giving yourself executive producer credit?"

"No."

"Why not?"

"I'm not the executive producer. One of the guys from KENS is doing all that stuff."

"Are you writing the show? Are you telling everyone what to do? Are you in charge of the guy in the truck and telling him what you are doing?"

"Yes."

"You are executive producing the show. That's one of the many things you learned here. Didn't you realize when you came to production meetings and you set up a lot of your matches, you were producing your matches?"

"I didn't know."

"You are the executive producer." How could I not love the guy?

I enjoyed being an executive producer, but it was costing me $5,000 a week to executive produce the show. I was making money on the academy, but the losses from television were starting to add up. Also, once we started on television, guys started complaining about how they were being "used." Mind you, we were wrestling in front of a few hundred people in bingo halls, but I kid you not. Rumors started swirling about. People wrote complaints on our website. Some of the guys started talking about the "organization." There was no organization. It was just me! I wanted to scream, "Shut up!" Running the promotion was not worth it financially or emotionally.

While the promotion turned into a bit of a headache, I liked working at the academy. The problem was, I knew that most of the kids didn't have a chance to make it. I didn't want to take their money, knowing this, and got out of the training business. We taught our students well and had no problem filling slots. The Shawn Michaels Wrestling Academy was profitable. I just couldn't look a young man in the eye and take his money, knowing full well that he didn't have it in him to make it in this business.

27
unearned love

Six weeks after Rebecca and I were married, we found out we were pregnant. Our first clue was that she started cleaning everything in sight. She joked she was nesting.

When she ate five jars of peanut butter one day, she stopped joking, and I went out and bought a pregnancy tester. Yep, we were pregnant.

Before we were married, we had talked about how we wanted to have kids right away. Once we were married, we realized how much we enjoyed being with each other, so we talked some more and decided maybe we would wait six months so we could spend some time together alone.

Of course we didn't do anything, we just talked about it, and apparently, talking about it isn't enough. When we found out, we were so excited. We were going to start our own family.

Not everything was perfect, however. I still hadn't kicked the pills. I had tried to quit when I first met Rebecca, but I couldn't. Between the painkillers and muscle relaxers, I was downing thirty to thirty-five pills a day. I'd take a handful when I first woke up, another batch in the afternoon, and then a final bunch at night.

Every evening, Rebecca would make me dinner, and I'd invariably pass out halfway through eating it. If I was eating on the couch, she would lay me down, and if I had passed out on the floor, she propped my feet up to relieve the pressure on my back. Once she took care of me, she walked into one of our large closets and prayed that I would stop taking those pills. After she prayed, she would go to bed alone. I usually woke up a couple of hours later and stumbled into bed beside her. We talked about my problem and she said, "I miss my husband. I go to sleep every night by myself."

Her words crushed me, but I just couldn't quit. One night after downing a bunch of pills, I tried to make it to bed and ended up falling and cutting my eye open. Another time, I passed out and spilled my dinner all over myself. Both times, she cleaned me up and made sure I made it to bed safely.

It was so unfair, what I did to Rebecca. I was failing her—and my unborn son—miserably. Yet she continued to love and pray for me. I tell people that she saw more in me in the first two weeks we knew each other than anyone else has seen in me my entire life. Even though I wasn't doing anything to deserve it, through her actions and words she was showing more love than anyone ever had. We talked about my problem, but she didn't nag me. That isn't her way. I had always been a man of my word, and I told her I would quit when our baby was born. She believed me and kept caring and praying for me.

| | |

Cameron Kade Hickenbottom was born at 7:09 P.M. on January 5, 2000. He was so beautiful. I remember thinking: I've always known there was a God, and I've screwed up in life, but please, Lord, don't let anything happen to my baby. I didn't sleep the first two weeks we brought him home because every half hour I would get up to make sure he was still breathing.

I loved Cameron and I loved Rebecca. But I still didn't stop taking those pain pills. My excuse now was, well, he's just an infant. I'll quit before he's old enough to notice. I didn't though. Cameron's first birthday came, and I was still downing them.

Soon after Cameron's first birthday, the office called and asked me to come to *Raw* in Cleveland. This was the night Vince and Shane McMahon were taking over WCW, and Shane was down in Panama City, Florida, at the very last *Nitro*. I don't know if they had a particular plan for me, or if they just wanted to discuss if I could play a part in the great changes that were happening with the takeover, but I went to Cleveland thinking I might be on television that night. When they decided they weren't going to use me, I went to watch the show in Vince's office. While I was watching, I took some pills.

I went to the *SmackDown!* taping in Detroit the next day, and Jerry Brisco came up to me and said that Vince wanted to see me. "Shawn, did you take something last night?"

I denied it for a while, but eventually admitted that I did.

He was real straight with me. "We are sending you home. We wanted to give you a chance, but we can't have that. Even Hunter said you were out of it."

"Hunter said I was out of it?"

"Yeah, it was obvious."

"I wasn't that bad."

"No, you weren't bad, but it was obvious that you were under the influence of something. I'm just telling you as your friend that you have to stop that stuff."

I went into one of my self-righteous tirades and told them they don't need to tell me what I need to do. So I said, "Fine, I'm leaving."

On the way out, I saw Hunter, and I really laid into him. "You no good, back-stabbing s.o.b. After everything I've done for you . . ." I went off for a few minutes and then stormed out of the arena. I didn't talk to Hunter for another year and nearly ruined a friendship with one of the most decent and caring individuals I've ever had the privilege to call my friend.

Hunter had stuck with me through thick and thin. When he first came to WWE, he knew he'd get a lot of heat by hanging out with Kevin, Scott, Kid, and me, but he didn't care. He ate all the heat from the "Curtain Call," yet he never wavered in his support for me. He took me to my room many nights and woke me up many mornings when I couldn't take care of myself. He was a great friend, and I treated him horribly.

| | |

Nine months after Cameron was born, Rebecca nearly left me over my problem with drugs. She was as patient as anyone could ever be, but she had had enough. "Shawn, I love you," she said, "but I have to protect this child, and if I have to leave, I will. It's not going to be long before he can notice what's going on with you." Rebecca might have been only twenty-three years old, but she grasped the seriousness of raising a child, even if I, at thirty-three, couldn't. She left that night and stayed at a hotel.

Rebecca came back the following day to discuss our situation. As Cameron was sleeping, we both looked at him, and I promised I would work on my problem. She told me she'd stay, but that she wanted to change the way she had been living. She said, "I am a Christian, and Jesus Christ has given me everything. I have a beautiful child, and a husband that loves me. You have your problems, but I know you do love me. Now I need to be who I am. I need to get back to my walk with the Lord and not be afraid or embarrassed to show you how I exercise my faith."

The first time I ever spoke with Rebecca, she asked me whether I believed in Jesus. I was raised Catholic, so I told her, "Yes, I do. I'm Catholic." We continued talking and I asked her what her religious background was. She said she was Christian. I said, "I know, but what denomination?"

"I'm just Christian. I grew up going to a Southern Baptist church, but I'm just a Christian." We didn't really talk about our religious beliefs after that.

I believed going to church would help me to kick my habit, and I had also been thinking that we should raise Cameron in a religious family. I happened to be taking a Kempo Karate class at the time and the instructor's wife, Dee Swann, completely out of the blue asked me, "Shawn, if you died, do you know if you'd go to heaven?"

"Yes."

"How do you know?"

"Well, for the most part, I've been a good person."

We talked for a little while longer, and then Dee gave me the Book of John to read. I read it at home not too long afterwards, and it moved me greatly. I now understood that Jesus Christ died for my, and all humanity's, sins. Jesus didn't know me, and didn't care how messed up I was. He still loved me. Just as Rebecca was showering me with unearned love, so too had Jesus Christ. I began feeling a change within me. I wasn't quite sure what it was, and I didn't stop taking pills completely, but I was now on my way towards becoming a different and better person.

Dee also invited Rebecca to her Bible study fellowship. Rebecca was already strong and beautiful, but after she started going to the Bible study fellowship, her face shone with the glory of the Lord and she was even more loving and beautiful.

| | |

We had been going to my Catholic church for a while, but Rebecca grew increasingly dissatisfied with it. She didn't think it was true to the Bible. There was plenty of ritual and ceremony, but it didn't teach us how to apply the Bible to our daily lives. She wanted to try another church called the Cornerstone Church that was run by John Hagee. She said she used to watch him on television when she lived in Atlanta and really liked him. I was thinking, "Great, it's one of those TV churches!" But since Rebecca had gone to mine, I agreed to go to this one.

We went on Father's Day, and Pastor Hagee wasn't there. Someone else led the service, and I wasn't too impressed. Meanwhile, a lady who was sitting in front of us was making a big deal about Cameron because he was moving around and making some noise. I told Rebecca I didn't think this was the place for me. We went back to my church the following week, but it only made Rebecca tense. So I offered to go back to Cornerstone one more time.

Towards the end of 2001, I mentioned to Rebecca that I thought something was happening with me. I told her, "I know I need to change, but I just can't read the Bible." I didn't like the language with all the *thy*'s and *thou*'s. Christmas was coming up, and she bought me a study Bible, *The New Living Translation,* which is worded in modern English. She also bought me some other books, including *Straight Talk to Men,* by James Dobson. She said she wasn't pushing it on me, but since I had expressed an interest in these things, she thought I would enjoy the books.

I started reading Dobson's book and couldn't put it down. Dobson explains how God and the Bible define what a husband and father are supposed to be. I heard him saying, "Shawn, you aren't being a real man, and you are a complete zero." He used much softer language, of course, but that was the message I was getting.

Dobson's words really hit me hard. I was what he called "a man of the world." I looked like I had the life everyone wanted. But from God's standard I was a zero. I was not leading my home. I was not leading my family. God had a plan and a purpose for my life and my family, but I alone was keeping it from coming to fruition. If I truly loved Rebecca and Cameron, I'd step up and be the man I was born to be instead of the man I selfishly wanted to be.

About this time, Vince called me. He said that the nWo, Kevin, Scott, and Hulk Hogan, were coming in and asked me to come up for a meeting to see if I wanted to come back. I told him, "I know this is going to sound strange, but I think something is going on with me. I think God is trying to tell me something. I can't come back right now. I don't know if I have the strength to come back now. There is something going on with me that I can't miss. My wife and son can't afford to have me miss what is going on."

"Okay."

Vince had kept me on contract the whole time I had been off, and I offered, "If you want to cancel my contract because I haven't done that much, I understand, but I just can't come back right now. This is really important."

"I understand. I'm glad to hear that. When you feel like you've found out what is going on, you call me. We'd love to have you back, and you've contributed so much to this business that you ought to be able to be a part of this again. You worked too hard not to."

"I appreciate that, and I'll call you when I know."

With each step of conviction that I was taking, I was cutting back on the pills. By this time it had become only a Friday night thing—still completely unnacceptable, but I was making progress.

| | |

A couple months earlier I decided I was going to resume an active lifestyle whether my back hurt or not, and it turned out, for the most part, that the more active I became, the better my back felt. One Friday, I had trained a bit hard and had taken a few pills. They hit me real hard. I was lying on the couch as I normally did after taking my pills, and I decided to call Kevin Nash. He could tell that I wasn't right, and he asked me if I had taken any pills. I told him just a few. We talked a little longer and then we hung up.

Later, I laid down on the couch after Cameron and I had eaten our dinner and some cookies. He crawled up around me, pretended to be asleep, and said, "Daddy's tired." It was just about Cameron's bedtime, and Rebecca offered to read his bedtime story. I was adamant that I could do it and slurred my way through the book. Afterwards, I came back to the couch and passed out. I awoke a few hours later and crawled into bed with Rebecca. We talked about what happened, and I couldn't even remember eating with Cameron. I don't know if I've ever felt so awful in my entire life, and I broke down crying.

Lying in bed, I called out to the Lord for the first time in my life. "I don't want to be like this anymore. Please, God, I've tried and I love my wife and my son so much."

I woke up the next morning and felt different. Kevin called me a little while later. He was concerned about me because I had sounded so bad the night before.

"Are you still doing that stuff?" he asked.

"Just every once in a while."

He told me I had a wife and son and I needed to stop. He was pretty firm about it. Then he asked me how long it had been since Hunter and I talked. I told him about a year. "That's b.s.," he said. "And when we were in San Antonio that was b.s. too when you guys didn't talk." He was referring to a time when

WWE came to San Antonio and I went to the show but didn't talk to Hunter. He went on this rant about how close we used to be and asked what happened.

I told him, and he said, "Shawn, it's your fault. Hunter put his head on the chopping block to bring you back and you cut it off. You were wrong."

"You're right," I said.

When I got off the phone with Kevin, I called Hunter and apologized to him. I told him there was some weird stuff going on with me, but I know we were friends and he did something kind for me. I was wrong to do what I did. He accepted my apology and told me he was hurt by the whole matter because we had always been such good friends. It was a great conversation and we were friends again.

That night I slept well for a change. When I woke up, I turned to Rebecca and I said, "It's over. I'm never going to take any more drugs. I don't think I'm ever drinking again either."

"That's great," Rebecca said. Even though she had heard me say this before, she was trying be encouraging.

"Yes. Something is different today. I know you've heard this before. I'm not asking you to believe me. I'm just telling you. It's over."

"Well, good, honey. I hope that it is. I believe the Lord has done all this."

"I think you are right."

"Just pray and ask and he will take you where you need to go."

I really felt like I could put the drugs behind me for good, but I also knew that my transformation was not complete. Later that day, I went out to run some errands with Cameron and all of a sudden I found myself in the Cornerstone Church parking lot. We had been back for some services, and I found Pastor Hagee very appealing.

"What are we doing, Daddy?" Cameron asked.

"I don't know."

We just sat in the parking lot for a while. When I came home, I told Rebecca what happened and said, "I think I am going to go in there and ask for a Bible study. Maybe that's what I need. Yours seems to have had a really positive effect on you. Something is still missing in me."

The next day I drove over to Cornerstone, went into the office, and told the lady sitting at the desk that I would like to go to a Bible study. She looked at me for a minute, and after she realized I wasn't going to rob the place, she said, "Okay."

Just then, a man poked his head out of an office. He had a big southern accent and he said, "You can come to mine."

"Thank you."

He introduced himself as Keith Parker and told me to be at his house at 7 P.M. the following day. I drove to Keith's and he invited me in. He then asked, "Do you wrestle?"

"Yes."

"I don't watch, but the gentleman I was showing around the church yesterday told me you were Shawn Michaels, but I didn't know." He told me they do a weekly Bible study here and to be a part of the Bible study I need to be born again. "Have you been born again?"

"No. Just the one time that I know of."

"Have you ever said the Sinner's Prayer?"

"No. I've said a lot of prayers, but I don't remember saying one that is called that."

"It's not really any particular prayer. Have you accepted Jesus Christ as your personal lord and savior?"

"No."

"Would you like to?"

"Yeah, I think I would. Something's been going on with me."

Keith led me in the Sinner's Prayer, and I wept like a baby. All of a sudden the gates of heaven opened up. I felt free and so alive.

The Sinner's Prayer is made up of three different verses: confessing that you are a sinner, professing that you believe in Jesus Christ, that He died on the cross for your sins and that He rose from the dead, and then accepting Him as your personal Lord and Savior. You ask Him to come into your heart to change you. Then you are born again.

I came home after the Bible study and I told Rebecca, this is it. It happened. I said the Sinner's Prayer, I am born again, I am saved. She hugged me, and I asked her if she knew what that was. Of course she did. Rebecca had known this was what I needed the whole time. I asked her why she didn't say something. She said that she learned from her Bible study fellowship: *The wife should win her husband over to the Lord by her actions and not her words* (1 Peter

3:1). When Rebecca would go into our walk-in closet and pray for me, all she heard back was "You change. You be the woman you are supposed to be and he will be the man he's supposed to be." Her love, her actions, touched me and allowed me to find it on my own and let the Holy Spirit lead me. It's still hard for me not to get emotional when I talk about how Rebecca loves me and what she did for me. That's why I say I will love that woman for all the days of my life.

That night I prayed, "Lord, don't ever let me forget how I feel right now. I don't want this feeling to stop." Almost four years later, I feel just as good as I did then.

Keith and his wife Priscilla taught me something else that night. They said, "Shawn, after this, it's important that you keep doing the things that keep you strong. That you continue praying to the Lord and talking to him, reading his word and letting him talk to you. You can't have a relationship with somebody once a week at church. It's an everyday thing. It's not about church."

What they said made perfect sense. My relationship with Rebecca wouldn't be much if I only gave her an hour every Sunday. From that day forward, I dove into Bible study, reading, and praying, and haven't stopped.

I don't practice a religion. I have a relationship. My family doesn't step in and out of the secular and the spiritual. We live the spiritual life. We have to live in the secular world, but we don't repress our spiritual life in it. That's our choice. I want to be good at this, so I feed the spiritual, not the secular. And, faith without works doesn't mean a thing. Rebecca and I volunteer our time and money to do as much as we can for our community. We do our best to serve the Lord through doing good works. I put my life into wrestling because I wanted to be a great wrestler. Now I want to live a good spiritual life, so I try and live it as much as I can. I enjoy working at it, just as I enjoyed training to be a wrestler. I don't find it to be a sacrifice. We have a joy in our life that is unspeakable.

28
redemption

After I had been saved, I called Vince up and let him

know what had happened to me. I asked him if he still

wanted me to come back. He told me that he was happy for

me, and then said since he wasn't sure what he was going to

do with the nWo, he didn't have anything for me. I under-

stood and told him to call me if anything changed. I also said

that if I did come back, I didn't want to compromise my

Christian values. He had no problems with that.

A month or so later, Vince called again, and we dis-

cussed the possibility of me coming back and being in the

nWo. We didn't talk about me wrestling, just being a

mouthpiece. He wanted me back and emphasized that I had contributed too much not to be a part of the company again.

That Sunday, I was in church and the pastor was giving a sermon explaining how the Lord talks to us, and we have to listen to him. "Pray, and the Lord will answer," he said. "If you don't hear anything, maybe he isn't saying anything. Maybe you should stay exactly where you are. But if he wants you to be somewhere or do something, he is going to make it happen."

Right then, my phone rang. It was Bruce Pritchard from the creative team. I picked it up and told him I was in church and had to call him back. After the service, I called Bruce and he said they wanted me at TV on Monday. After what the preacher had said, and the timing of Bruce's call, I knew the Lord was speaking to me. I told him I'd be there.

||

On June 3, 2002, in Dallas, I made my return. When I arrived at the American Airlines Arena, one of the first things I did was find Pat Patterson and apologize for everything I had put him through. He hugged me and told me how much it meant to him and how he had hoped that I would call him. I told him there were times when I wanted to write him a letter and I was sorry I didn't. Pat had always been so supportive of me. I needed to let him know how much I appreciated him.

When I saw Vince, he gave me a big hug. I also apologized to him for all I had put him through over the years. "I don't know where this is going, but I am going to try and do my best to make it up to you. I'm sorry."

"You know what I want, Shawn? Remember what I said when you first won the title? I want you to enjoy this. I remember you didn't enjoy that. I want you to enjoy this time."

"I will." And I have, every bit of it.

I saw Kevin from a distance. He had that big smile on his face, and as he approached me, he said, "You came out of that water a different man. I can tell. I can see it on you." I had been baptized again as part of my rebirth. Saying the Sinner's Prayer saves you. Being baptized is a symbolic gesture of dropping the old man and coming up a new one. It was almost as if I was circumcising my heart. When I came out of the water, I felt brand-new. Kevin was right. Kid was there and he noticed the change in me as well. Hunter and I had a nice little talk, and 'Taker and Steve were very cordial as well.

I think a lot of the folks that knew me were understandably skeptical about my purported changes. They had heard about my transformation, but given my past, they wanted to see me before they believed I had changed. I understood and was excited to show them who I had become because for the first time in my life, I was proud of who I was. Once they realized I had changed, all the tension went away, and I didn't feel any resentment from anyone.

That night Kevin introduced me as the newest member of the nWo. Again, there were no plans for me to wrestle. I explained to the fans that Kevin had always been there for me, and now I was going to be there for him.

On July 8, Kevin tore his quad during a match in Philadelphia. The next

morning I was driving to the airport to fly home, and the first creative idea that I had since I came back popped into my head. I was thinking about Kevin's injury, my injuries, Steve's injuries, and all the guys who had gotten hurt. I thought, what if I do a story line with Vince, who will play the role of the slave-driving boss. I'll say, "You [Vince] run everyone into the ground. You did it to me. Now you did it to my buddy Kevin, and you don't care. You use us and abuse us, but you are not doing that to me anymore. I'm back for one night only. You and I in a Street Fight!" I figured, with my back that was about the only kind of match I could do. I'd be in there with Vince, and the fans wouldn't expect a classic wrestling exhibition. Street Fights are easier for me because of their slower tempo. When I got to the airport, I called him and described my idea.

"Are you sure you can do this?"

"You will have to do all the work, I'm just going to beat you up."

"Let me put that in the old computer and get back to you."

After I hung up the phone, I realized that I had offered to come back and wrestle without talking about it with Rebecca. I didn't want to commit to this without discussing it with her. As I boarded the plane I began meditating and asking the Lord what he wanted me to do.

I happened to have just finished Deuteronomy and began reading the book of Joshua. It opens with the Children of Israel at the brink of the Promised Land and Joshua is really stressing over taking them in. Kevin had always been wise and a man I looked up to. In a very metaphorical way, and within in the context of our lives within the business, I sort of likened him to Moses, and now he was out. I had come back in a supporting role, and wasn't going to try and be a spotlight guy. But now, he was out and I'm in. I was thinking how Moses was out and now Joshua was in. I thought I have to do this. The Lord told Joshua to be strong and courageous. "I'll be with you as I was with Moses." The words "strong and courageous" kept running through my mind. I'm sure this sounds freaky, but I was asking the Lord if I should go back, if He wanted me to wrestle. All I heard was, "Be strong and courageous." When I returned home I told Rebecca all of this. She said, "Go do it." I asked, "Are you sure?" She said, "I am at complete peace with this."

Vince called back a couple of days later. "Are you sure about that idea?"

"Yeah." I told him about the book of Joshua, and I said, "I know I can do it."

"I'm a little unorthodox, I might hurt you. I'm not that good."

"It doesn't have to be that good. I'm just looking for a Street Fight."

"Well, Shawn, if you do it with me, could you do it with Triple H?"

"Yeah, but I didn't really see that as an option. He's the top guy. What does Hunter think?"

"He's all over it. He's the one that offered. He told me, 'If he's going to do it with you, why can't he do it with me? I'm better than you are.'"

"I just didn't really think I could be in the main event."

"Your coming back is going to be big. Let's get everything we can out of it. We'll change the story line, obviously. We'll go on with the DX story about you being the guy that brought Hunter up and now he's the ungrateful star."

"All right. Sounds good to me."

On July 22, in Grand Rapids, Michigan, Triple H tricked me into reforming DX and then nailed me with the Pedigree. Our angle was on, and we were off to *SummerSlam,* which was being held in the Nassau Coliseum on Long Island one month later.

Since I hadn't been in the ring for such a long time, Hunter suggested that we might want to practice on the Friday before our matchup at the company's head-quarters in Stamford. I was never a "practicer," but I figured I might as well try.

Four years is a long time not to be wrestling, and we really had no idea what would happen. This was a very big deal for our family, and Rebecca suggested that instead of going up to Stamford, the Friday before *SummerSlam* I should spend several days eating right, praying, and getting my confidence back. We were talking about a major match at a Pay-Per-View, and we didn't know how my back was going to hold up. So I went up to Stamford early in the week and prayed a lot. I even fasted for a day. Vince brought in a physical therapist who showed me a simple stretch where I lay on my back with my knees up and roll my hips. I did it first thing every morning and it made a huge difference.

On Friday, I went over to WWE's photo studio, which also happens to be where they house their practice ring. Hunter and I stretched a little and then he asked what I wanted to do. I didn't really know. I had never practiced a match before, so I hit the ropes a few times to see how I could move. I felt okay. Then I jumped off the top rope, to see how my knees were. I wasn't wearing my braces, but they felt fine. Tom Pritchard, one of the trainers, was there as well, and I hit the ropes one more time, jumped up, and did a sunset flip with him. That too felt normal. Then I stopped and told Hunter, "It's going to have to be there." I believed the Lord would take care of me. Practice just didn't feel right. Hunter and I left and went back to the hotel to discuss what we were going to do in our match.

| | |

Rebecca and Cameron, as well as my mom and dad, came up for *SummerSlam,* Kevin Nash flew up to watch our match too. Hunter reassured my mom that everything would be all right: "Don't worry, I'll take care of him. I'll do everything I can to make sure he's okay."

"Don't worry, he'll be fine," Rebecca said. She had faith.

I was a bit nervous as the match started, but after I executed the first tackle and drop down and threw Hunter over the top, it was as if I had never been away. We put on a great show.

Arn Anderson, who was working as an agent, told me that wrestling isn't like riding a bike. After four years off, I'd have to start slow and shake the rust off. He said, "It's not like riding a bike." When I reached the back after the match, he walked up to me and said, "I guess for you it is like riding a bike. You didn't miss a step. It was awesome."

The entire day turned out better than I could have ever hoped for. This was the first time I ever performed in front of Rebecca, and I loved her being there. There's just something about having your girl see you do what you love to do. After the match, Ric Flair came up to her and said, "He's still the best." She said, "I know he is."

Hunter deserves a lot of credit. He was unbelievable. Hunter is different from Kevin, Kid, and Scott, in that those moments of intimate transparency and bonding and friendship are there, but not as often with him as with the others. He's more reserved. The only way to get it from him is to look into his eyes. I saw it in his eyes after our match. Hunter told me, "You didn't need me to take care of you." I realized that Paul Levesque is one of the best men I've ever known.

I was a bit sore after the match and the next day as well. It was the normal

post-match soreness, though. My back was fine. Once I was off the pills, I learned the difference between stiffness and pain. I knew I wasn't hurt. Everything was wonderful.

| | |

SummerSlam was supposed to be a one-shot deal. We found out I could still wrestle, but I wanted to take a few months and see how everything responded. I thought maybe I could come back at *WrestleMania* for something. So I went home, cut most of my hair off, and sat around and ate cookies with Cameron.

Towards the end of October, the creative team asked me to come up to the company's restaurant in New York City and cut a promo during *Raw*, warning Triple H that I could attack him at any time. We didn't have anything planned. It was just something to do because maybe down the road something might happen.

Apparently my promo went over pretty well because later that week, Vince called me and told me that he was going to put me in the Elimination Chamber match at *Survivor Series* in Madison Square Garden and have me win the World Heavyweight Championship. I had no idea that this was in the works.

"It just feels so good," he said. "The old guy comes back, and he gets the title in the Garden. It just feels right."

"I'm out of shape, I cut my hair off. I'm not ready."

"Ah, you'll be fine. It just feels so good. They'll love you."

What was I supposed to do, say no to the championship? He told me I'd have the title for a month and then drop it back to Hunter at *Armageddon*.

So I went and told Rebecca they were going to put the belt back on me. "He is a God of Redemption!" she exclaimed.

"It's crazy," I agreed. "Can you imagine where the Lord has brought me in such a short time?"

We were only two weeks out from *Survivor Series,* and besides having a Dutch boy haircut, I was in terrible shape. I had been eating too many cookies with Cameron. I figured the only thing to do was train as hard as I could and get in the best shape possible. I hit the gym hard and ended up overdoing it. My left knee starting swelling up.

As soon as it happened, I called Vince and told him. "We can change plans. Don't feel like you have to give it to me." I was thinking what would happen if I won and then my knee went out and I couldn't wrestle again. We would have to deal with "Shawn won't drop the belt again" stuff. I mentioned this to him. I told him I'm not going through that again.

"I'm not changing anything, you'll be fine."

I don't believe Vince ever thought that I would try to pull anything on him. I think he admired my honesty. When I told him that I didn't do steroids and that I wasn't going to give him back the Intercontinental belt, I actually think he admired me for that. Folks can write and say whatever they want to, but I was honest with Vince all the time. He didn't get a lot of honesty back during the eighties and nineties. I believe that made the difference in our relationship.

At *SummerSlam,* I wore jeans because it was a Street Fight. They didn't want me in jeans for this match. Julie Youngberg, our seamstress, suggested some earth-tone tights. I figured, why not? She had always made great outfits for me in the past. Unfortunately, she didn't have time to finish them. They were puke brown, and as I readied myself to go out for the match, Hunter looked at me with that "I can't believe you are going out there in those" look on his face. I turned to Rebecca and said, "I feel stupid. Do I look like an idiot?" Stephanie and Hunter were trying not to laugh. Rebecca gave me a kiss and said, "You look great."

There were six Superstars in the match. Kane, Rob Van Dam, Booker T, Chris Jericho, Hunter, and myself. We never found time for all of us to get together during the day, so when it was time for the match, all we knew was the order we would enter and that I was going to win.

During the match, Kane was supposed to come out fourth, right before me. Well, the third light went on and his cage opened up, so he had to come out. At this point, I was out there with my Dutch boy haircut and my puke brown tights, the match was messing up, and we didn't have a finish. Then Van Dam jumped off the top rope and landed on Hunter's throat, hurting him badly. Everything was falling apart and falling apart fast. Years ago, I probably would have gone nuts and started screaming at everyone, but I had come a long way. I stood in my little cage and tried to make light of it, yelling, "This isn't good. This isn't good at all." I was actually having fun with the whole disaster.

When I entered the match, I asked Hunter how he was. He could barely make a sound. He was going to finish the match, though, because he is as tough as they come. I reversed a Pedigree attempt and Superkicked him for the win.

My fourth WWE championship was definitely different from the other three. "Nice" is the best way to describe it. There were so many different issues surrounding my previous three championships, and I was such a different person then. There wasn't anything deep or transforming going on here. This was simply pleasant.

At *Armageddon,* I dropped the title back to Hunter. We had a best Two-Out-of-Three Falls contest consisting of a Hardcore, a Steel Cage, and a Ladder match. I banged myself up pretty good and told Vince that I needed some time off. I said I can do promos and a little interference, but I didn't want to wrestle again until *WrestleMania XIX.* He was fine with that. The next day at *Raw,* he wanted me to do a little promo with Chris Jericho. Chris and I went out there, and the whole arena lit up. We went to the back and Chris said, "That was awesome!" I admitted it felt pretty good too.

Vince walked up to us. "There was something there. Did you guys feel that?"

"Yes, we were just talking about that, but I'm done until *WrestleMania.* "

"I know, but there is something there. This is something we may have to come back to."

On January 6, 2003, I flew to Phoenix for *Raw* and met with Chris and Michael Hayes, the onetime Freebird and longtime television writer, to figure out how we could get to *WrestleMania* without having me actually wrestling. We came up with the idea that Chris would start claiming that he could do everything better than I could. With the *Royal Rumble* coming up, he would claim that he was going to go wire-to-wire and be the first one since me to do that and win it. Then Chris would brag how his moves were better than mine and how he could actually execute my moves better than I could. Chris could demonstrate all this on other opponents, and I wouldn't have to get in the ring until *WrestleMania.* Vince loved the idea.

At the *Rumble,* I entered first and he entered second. He busted me open with a chair and got rid of me in no time. A little while later, I came out from the back, beat him up, and eliminated him. Everything worked as planned.

The last time I had been at *WrestleMania,* I was a complete disaster. My back was shot, I was hooked on pain pills, and my spirits were shattered. *WrestleMania XIX* was a completely different experience. I was excited to be a part of it and comfortable in my supporting role. I brought my family out, and we had a very nice time in Seattle. Chris and I had a great match. Some might say we stole the show. For me, it was redemption, and I was getting closer to feeling like I was the performer I had been before injuring my back. This match told me that I could still

Working with Chris Jericho helped me feel I could get it all back.

wrestle pretty darn well. I was not the Showstopper yet, but I was getting close.

I explained how I was feeling to Rebecca, and we decided that I could begin working on a more regular basis. This meant that I would have to train more and watch my diet. Rebecca was very supportive. She gave me a new diet and took an active role in my training routine. With her at my side, I knew I could do it.

Before I went and told Vince about my intentions, I wanted to pray about it. I went and saw Pastor Hagee, and I heard him say, "Sometimes you pray and you don't hear anything because sometimes the Lord doesn't have anything to tell you. You are right where you ought to be."

That's exactly where I was. I felt I was a wrestler and that I should wrestle. I told Vince that and have been wrestling a full-time schedule since.

29
a wonderful life

By *WrestleMania XX*, the Showstopper was back. I was

coming off a great match against Hunter in San Antonio and

felt I was as good as I had ever been. More importantly, I

was enjoying this ride. My peers liked me. They wanted to

work with me not only because I would bring out their best,

but also because I was a much better person to deal with. I

had always hoped that people would like and accept me for

who I really was, and now that I had changed, they did.

I can't tell you the number of wrestlers who asked me

to work a Ladder match with them at *WrestleMania XX*.

I guess everyone thought it would be a good idea since it was the tenth anniversary of the first one. I was flattered by the offers, but I didn't want to do it. I knew that no matter who I wrestled and how good our match might be, it would inevitably fall short of the original. I wanted to be part of a new "first." That's why I was so happy to be able to be in the main event at *WrestleMania XX*, a Triple Threat match for the World Heavyweight Championship with Hunter and Chris Benoit.

I was working the biggest match on the card, but I derived more pleasure from the fact that I was going to be able to play a part in Chris's moment of glory. Chris was going to win the World Heavyweight Championship, and after nearly twenty years of making other people look good, he was finally going to get his pat on the back.

Chris Benoit is a guy who really loves what he does and who wanted the title as badly as I did. Chris is also one of the most genuine human beings I've

met in this business. Chris deserved this moment, and Hunter and I were determined to do our best to let him enjoy his reward. The people were really behind Chris, and the match turned out really well. When Hunter tapped out to Chris's Crossface, the sold-out crowd at Madison Square Garden erupted with joy. I had been knocked out of the ring and was hurting, but I was smiling on the inside. I knew how Chris felt.

One constant in this business is that you never have too much time to celebrate what just happened, because the next show is always right around the corner. As soon as we were done with *WrestleMania,* we had to start planning for our next Pay-per-View, *Backlash.*

Backlash was going to be held in Chris's hometown of Edmonton, Alberta, Canada. We talked about a Triple Threat rematch and I suggested if we really wanted to get him over, he should make me tap out to the Sharpshooter. I said, "I know it's not Montreal or Calgary [Bret Hart's hometown], but everyone hates me in Canada, and Chris was trained by Bret's father. They'll go crazy for Chris."

A part of me thought it might be risky tapping out to Chris. When you are a babyface fighting another babyface, you run the risk of being turned heel. But I really thought this was the best way to go for the match. Chris won, and the Canadian crowd loved seeing me tap out.

I wrestled for another two months before I had to take some time off. Cameron was about to become a big brother.

| | |

On August 19, 2004, Rebecca gave birth to Cheyenne Michelle Hickenbottom. She was the most beautiful baby in the world. I know all parents say that, but she *really* was. Right after I had been saved, I told Rebecca that if I could go back and change anything, the first thing I would do would be to change how it was when she was pregnant with Cameron. Because of my drug problem, she had to go through that alone. I was determined that if we had another child, I would be there for her. It was something that I prayed I could make up to her. Now I had been given this second opportunity, and I made sure that I was there for her whenever she needed me. It was glorious.

Cheyenne's birth was also different from Cameron's in that we didn't know if it was going to be a boy or a girl. I was hoping for a girl and when she came out, we were overjoyed, and Cameron was excited as well. We were a little more confident the second time around. When we brought her home, we put her in her room right away. I still got up out of bed every night, though. I just wanted to look at her and watch her breathe and sleep.

| | |

I returned to work in the middle of September and was wrestling Ric Flair in Helsinki, Finland, on October 6, when I hurt my knee *again.* We were awfully close to the ropes (I call Ric the King of the Short Shoot), and he decided to shoot me in. At the last second, he must have decided not to shoot me in because he jerked me back in the opposite direction. As my weight shifted, my knee gave out, and I heard a crunching sound. I immediately felt a searing, stabbing pain. I called for my superkick and we ended it right there. We were over in Europe for a week, so for the rest of the tour they put me in tag matches so I wouldn't have to do as much in the ring.

When we returned to the States, we were only two days away from *Taboo Tuesday.* This was a new Pay-Per-View where fans, by voting on wwe.com, would decide who fought whom. Edge, Chris Benoit, and I were in the running to fight Triple H for his championship. The voting was going to take place right up until the show started, so we had no idea who was going to wrestle Hunter. They were going to announce the winner during the show.

Unlike our other Pay-Per-Views, which are all held on Sundays, this one was going to be on Tuesday, in Milwaukee. On Monday's *Raw,* in Chicago, the plan called for Chris, Edge, and me to wrestle in a three-way match.

On Monday night, I was in my match with Benoit and Edge, and I hurt my knee once again. The pain was horrible. Somehow I made it through the match, but afterwards I couldn't move. I had to be helped to the back, where Vince and Shane came over to see how I was doing. I blurted out, "I'm sorry."

"How is it?" Vince asked.

"It's gone."

"What about tomorrow?"

"It isn't going to happen. I can't walk on it. I'm sorry. I guess I'm getting too old. Maybe I am done. I hope I haven't put you guys in a bad position, but I can't move on it."

"That's all right. We'll figure out something tonight."

Chris Brannon, our trainer, gave me a set of crutches and Ric took me back to the hotel. By the next morning my knee had stiffened up and the pain was even worse. I could barely get dressed.

Ric and I drove to Milwaukee. I figured I'd go into the building and say hello to some folks and then see if they could get me a flight home that day. I stepped into the production meeting to apologize to Vince again and he said, "We are just discussing tonight."

"Mind if I sit in and see if I can help?"

"No, not at all."

We started going over the possible options, and I was sitting there thinking that I had put them in a really tough position. "Can I ask you a question?"

"Sure," Vince answered.

"Are you just looking to get through this tonight?"

"At this point, yeah. We are just trying to find out who would be a good substitute for you so the fans won't feel cheated."

"There's a chance that they won't even pick me."

"Yeah, but there's a good chance they will pick you. Unfortunately, last night a lot of people knew you were hurt. You gutted it out and finished it, and they are going to vote for you."

"If they pick me, what kind of match are you looking for? I can gimp out there and let Hunter beat me up. I don't know how pretty it will be, but the more I sit here and listen to this, the more it seems like there isn't any other option."

Someone brought up the idea of just working the vote and having Chris or Edge win. Vince was adamant that wasn't going to happen. "We said the fans would decide this and they will. To do otherwise would be ripping them off."

We weren't getting anywhere, so I again brought up the idea of me wrestling.

"Are you sure?"

"Yeah. There's nothing else to do."

"On behalf of the company, I want to say thank you."

Then Hunter looked me in the eye just like he did when I came back at *SummerSlam* and said, "I won't let anything happen to you out there."

"I know you won't."

I left the production room and went to see the trainer to have him try and perform some magic on me. On the way there, I bumped into Ric.

"You going home?"

"No, I'm working. There's nothing else to do. Plus, there's a chance they won't pick me."

"They're going to pick you."

"Well, if they do I'll just gimp on out there."

Then, just as if he was cutting a promo, he belted out, "That's why you are who you are!"

I ended up winning the vote and had to face Triple H. Chris Brannon wrapped my knee, and I put my brace on it as well. I tightened the brace so tightly that as I made my way on crutches to the gorilla position, I couldn't feel my foot. I hobbled over to an adjacent room and loosened the brace. My knee hurt a little more, but I could at least feel my foot.

The Lord must have been watching over me that night, because I went out and somehow made it through the match. It was nothing special for those who didn't know how serious my injury was, but for those who did know, I made an impact. Some of the boys had tears in their eyes after the match. Chris Benoit came up to me and said, "I thought last night was something, but that was the most amazing thing I've ever seen. Don't let anybody ever tell you that you aren't one tough s.o.b."

I went home and found out that I had torn my meniscus. The bad news was that I had to have surgery. The good news was that I was able to spend the next two months, including the holidays, at home with my family.

I was at home rehabbing my knee when Michael Hayes called and presented me with the idea of wrestling Kurt Angle at *WrestleMania XXI*. Given my physical condition, I wasn't sure it was a good idea. I knew how good Kurt was, and I didn't know if I could keep up with him.

"Shawn," Michael said, "to be honest with you, I think you are in better shape than Kurt is. He has a really bad neck. You will be just fine."

I wasn't aware of Kurt's injuries. I was on *Raw*. He was on *SmackDown!* and I didn't know him well. All I knew was that he was really good. I thought it over for a little while and really couldn't come up with a reason why I shouldn't wrestle Kurt. We went to work on figuring out what we could do for a program.

Kurt, Michael, Brian Gerwitz, a TV writer, and myself threw a lot of ideas out there and what we finally came up with was that I would claim to be the best professional wrestler of our generation, and Kurt, with his Olympic, World, and NCAA championships, would claim to be the best amateur wrestler of our generation. Our match at *WrestleMania* would determine who was the best wrestler, period.

Because we were working on separate shows and couldn't confront each other all the time, it was a little tricky to come up with a program. We decided to do something similar to what Chris Jericho and I did leading up to *WrestleMania XIX*. Kurt was going to go back through my career and do everything that I had done, but do it better and faster.

Since Marty Jannetty had been such a huge part of my career, we thought about having Kurt work a match with him. He could show Marty that he was better than I ever was, and then beat him down to generate some extra heat.

As we were discussing this, I said to Kurt, "I like where you work with Marty. But if you just do that out of the blue, it will seem sort of strange." I then turned to Brian and asked, "Is there any way you can do something on our show like give him a warm-up match? We can give him a plug, and then the fans will know Marty's going to be on *SmackDown!* If this is all out of the blue it will be too weird."

"What about a one-night Rockers reunion?" Brian asked. "You guys have a Tag Team match, and then we have Marty wrestle Kurt on the next *Smack-Down!*"

I hadn't tagged with Marty since 1991, and the thought of "getting the band back together" really appealed to me.

Over the years, I had lost touch with Marty. Then right before *Bad Blood* in 2004, I was working a show and one of the extras asked me if I had talked to Marty lately.

"I haven't talked to him in a long time. I'd love to talk to him, though."

"I saw him at an independent show. I have his number."

I had to run off to a meeting, so I asked, "Can you write it down for me and put it in my bag? Don't worry about going in my bag, please put it in there."

I called Marty a couple of days later at the airport on my way to *Bad Blood*. When I got off the plane, there was a message from him saying it was good to hear from me and that I should call him back. I called from the airport and this time he picked up.

"Marty, it's Shawn. How are you?"

"Not that good." He told me that he had just been caught driving with a suspended license and he was looking at doing some time. Obviously, he still had his troubles.

I wanted to help him. "Marty, why don't you just come out to this Christian Athletes Conference that I go out to every June? I'll fly you out there. Just promise me you'll go. I'll take care of everything. I'm not going to beat you over the head with a Bible. It will just be a chance for us to talk."

He agreed to come, and I met him at the conference. The first night there, they have an orientation and they give an altar call. Marty said the Sinner's Prayer.

"Did you say that prayer?" I asked.

"Yeah. Shawn, I've been saved lots of times. I grew up in a Pentecostal home."

So we began to talk, and he told me things I never knew about him in all the years we were together. His mom was a strict Pentecostal lady, and she had left a bad taste in his mouth about church and God. He believed everything that goes wrong is God's fault. I just listened to him.

The next morning we got up and went to a prayer meeting. Then I started talking to him about everything that happened with me. Because I was actually living a spiritual life and not saying one thing and doing another, he listened and was moved. Marty was very bothered by people who say they are Christians and then go out and drink and do drugs.

As we continued talking through the rest of the weekend, I could see a small change taking place within him, and we drew closer. I ended up baptizing him in a pool.

| | |

I called Marty and let him know about the one-night Rockers reunion. He was stoked to come back and mentioned that maybe this could lead to something long-term. I made it clear to him that it was a one-time thing. I was afraid of what might happen to him if he hung his hopes on this turning into something more.

On March 14, in Atlanta, Georgia, the Rockers wrestled for the first time in thirteen years. The crowd loved us, and most of the guys in the back marked out for us as well. A lot of them had watched us when they were kids, and they just thought it was the coolest thing to see two stars from their childhood wrestle. We battled Rob Conway & Sylvan Grenier, La Resistance, and we moved around the ring like it was 1989. About the only thing that didn't go perfect was that we messed up a little when we did our double nip-up. The crowd gave us a standing ovation on the way back to the dressing room, and I couldn't have been happier. I was wearing one of the biggest smiles you've ever seen. Marty should have been ecstatic. Instead, he was a little down. He was a bit bummed about the double nip-up. "You know how we were," he said. "I just wanted everything to be perfect."

"We're not that way now. You know why those people cheered for us and why we were so different than the rest of the tag teams we have? The people saw our love for this business. It didn't matter that we messed up. It was the joy and the passion that you bring to doing it out there. That's what's going to make the difference. Don't let people see you sulking. You were good. It was awesome. You should be thrilled by it."

"All right, you are right."

The next night Marty went out and tore it up with Angle on *SmackDown!* Stephanie McMahon called me and said, "Vince says Marty looked great. He's wondering if we should hire him. Do you think we need to give him a job?"

"I'll tell you this much. Put Marty Jannetty with every twenty-five-year-old that comes in, and you tell them if they can't match his passion and desire when they are out there with him, then they need to get in another line of work. He still loves to do this and he is still good at it."

After Stephanie called, Kurt called me and said that Marty was great to work with. John Laurinaitis, the head of Talent Relations, called not too long after that and said that he was going to offer Marty a job. I thought it was tremendous.

Marty and I. For one night the old Rocker magic lived.

| | |

Two days before *WrestleMania*, Kurt called me to confirm that we were going to meet the following day to go over our match. We had thrown a few ideas out to each other, but we really couldn't come up with anything concrete because we still didn't know who was going to win. That was a serious problem because it's darn near impossible to lay out a good match if you don't know who is going to win. We were discussing this when I said, "Kurt, let me tell you what. This is my feeling, and you relay this to whoever you think needs to know. Babyfaces are going over on the entire show. Batista is going to win the World Heavy-weight Championship and John Cena is going to win the WWE Championship. That means we are going to need heels to work with them. If you stay on *SmackDown!*, you will have to work with Cena. If you come to *Raw*, you are going to have to work with Batista. I'd be more than happy to put you over. I think at this point in my career, losing doesn't hurt me. All I want to do is tear down the house. That is how I get over."

"Well, Shawn, I appreciate that, and I'll see you tomorrow."

The day before *WrestleMania XXI*, Kurt and I met with Pat Patterson and began laying out our match. Pat had retired a few months earlier, but when he found out that Kurt and I were going to wrestle at 'Mania, he be-came all excited and "unretired" for this one match. I was glad to have him with us. There is nobody better than Pat when it comes to designing matches.

We came to working out the finish, and I suggested that I should tap out to Kurt's Ankle Lock. I figured if I was going to lose, I wanted to lose to his best move. Once again, Kurt said, "I appreciate that." Pat didn't say anything. He simply looked at me like "You have come such a long way, my boy!"

By now you've heard me say this a hundred times: we had a great match, we tore the roof off the building, we stole the show, we tore the house down. This time, I'm not going to say that. I recommend that you go out and get the DVD or video, watch our match, and judge for yourself how we did. I will tell you what some other people thought about it, though.

After it was over, we came to the back and received a standing ovation—

not from fans, but from our fellow Superstars as well as the agents and creative folks. Undertaker, whose opinion I value, pulled us aside and said, "Unbelievable, guys."

When I told him that I felt bad about going a little long in our match (this meant someone else's match had to be cut short a few minutes), he told me, "Seven minutes well spent." Hunter, too, told me not to worry about going long. "Who cares," he said. "You guys were great."

Bobby Heenan, the legendary manager and announcer, called me. "Shawn," he said. "I got no reason to blow smoke up your rear end unless you want to pay my mortgage, but I just had to call you. I love this business, and this business means everything to me. I've been in this business for forty-one years, and I've never seen a match like that. That's the best wrestling match I've ever seen."

Nearly twenty-one years ago I packed up my old Toyota Celica and headed off into the great unknown. I didn't have much back then, just a few meager belongings and a dream of becoming a good wrestler. I think I did all right.

l l l

I decided to skip the post–*WrestleMania* party that night. Instead, I went back to my hotel room to be with Rebecca and the kids. I ordered a pizza and settled in to watch *The Polar Express* with Cameron. Soon he fell asleep in my arms. Cheyenne was sleeping softly as well. I looked at my children and then Rebecca. I smiled and said, "I'm living the greatest life a man could ever live."

acknowledgments

There are so many people that have helped me along

the way. It is impossible to name them all here, but to each

and everyone of you from my earliest days until now, I am

truly grateful for everything you've done.

Mom and Dad—bottom line folks, they were parents—

unfailing nonstop love and support.

Randy, Scott, Shari, and the rest of the clan—the family

unit works and is alive and well in San Antonio, Texas.

Cliff and Gloria Curci—it couldn't have been me, so

thanks for trusting your daughter's judgment.

Vince McMahon—thanks for not killing me, for your

unbelievable patience. Someday I hope you will let the rest of the world see the man I've seen for the last seventeen years.

Linda, Shane, and Stephanie McMahon—thank you for sharing Vince with us and making me a part of something special.

Pat Patterson—the only one who thought I could ever be a "top guy" before I actually was one. You never ever gave up, even when it was extremely unpopular to be on my side.

The Kliq—Kevin, Hunter, Scott, and Kid—I wouldn't have made it through without your friendship.

Kevin and Hunter—you two had to deal with "It" the most. FRIENDS, 'nuff said.

Kevin, Kerwin and the entire WWE production staff—the road crew, the stage crew, and the whole wacked-out bunch. There's nobody better, it's that simple. I'm simply not that good. A twelve-year-old boy can dream pretty big. You have created something that not only eclipsed even my wildest dreams, but something I am extremely proud of . . . that's right, I'm a wrestler for WWE.

Ann Russo Gordon—"who's that." In those dark years, you were the only lifeline of hope, both for me and the company. "Shawn, come off the ledge and get on the plane. We can take care of it." Ann, you really care about the talent. Thanks.

Jim Ross—no matter how hard I was on you, you never stopped trying.

Skip McCormick—you don't get as much work from me now. That has to be a good sign, right?

Aaron—thanks for taking the time and caring enough to get it right.

WWE fans—where to start? You saw "it" before anybody and you demanded they use it. There has always been one place where life and all its ups and downs could never get to me—out there in front of you. I've genuinely loved performing for you. Thank you for allowing me that honor.

I'd like to thank Shawn and Rebecca for their kindness, hospitality, trust, and sense of humor. It was a real pleasure to work with you.

To the entire McMahon family: Thank you for all the opportunities you have provided over the years. Thanks also to the following people at WWE:

Jim Ross, Joel Satin, Dean Miller, Katherine Kramer, Marco Turelli, Michael Chiappetta, Brian Solomon, Frank Vitucci, and Eli Zigdon.

To Margaret Clark at Pocket Books: Thank you for all your help and patience.

And thanks to Keith, Larry, Joy, Annette, Al, and Mom and Dad. Your help, not to mention all the meals, is greatly appreciated.

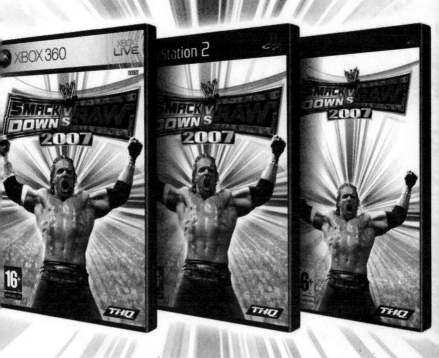

THESE ARE THE GAMES AND THEY'RE THAT DAMN GOOD!

AVAILABLE FROM ALL GOOD RETAILERS

THQ

www.wwe.com

www.thq.co.uk

e names of all World Wrestling Entertainment televised and live programming, talent names, images, likenesses, slogans and wrestling moves and all orld Wrestling Entertainment logos are trademarks which are the exclusive property of World Wrestling Entertainment, Inc. © 2005 World Wrestling ntertainment, Inc. All Rights Reserved.